DEFIANCE

DEFIANCE

DEFIANCE

A MEMOIR OF AWAKENING, REBELLION, AND SURVIVAL IN SYRIA

LOUBNA MRIE

Virago

VIRAGO

First published in the United States in 2026 by Viking,
an imprint of Penguin Random House LLC
First published in Great Britain in 2026 by Virago Press

1 3 5 7 9 10 8 6 4 2

Copyright © 2026 by Loubna Mrie

The moral right of the author has been asserted.

*All characters and events in this publication, other than those
clearly in the public domain, are fictitious and any resemblance
to real persons, living or dead, is purely coincidental.*

All rights reserved.
Penguin Random House values and supports copyright. Copyright fuels creativity, encourages diverse voices, promotes free speech, and creates a vibrant culture. Thank you for buying an authorized edition of this book and for complying with copyright laws by not reproducing, scanning, or distributing any part of it in any form without permission. You are supporting writers and allowing Penguin Random House to continue to publish books for every reader. Please note that no part of this book may be used or reproduced in any manner for the purpose of training artificial intelligence technologies or systems.

A CIP catalogue record for this book
is available from the British Library.

Hardback ISBN 978-0-349-01336-7
Trade paperback ISBN 978-0-349-01335-0

Designed by Meighan Cavanaugh
Printed and bound in Great Britain by Clays Ltd, Elcograf S.p.A

Papers used by Virago Press are from well-managed forests
and other responsible sources.

Virago Press
An imprint of
Little, Brown Book Group
Carmelite House
50 Victoria Embankment
London EC4Y 0DZ

The authorised representative
in the EEA is
Hachette Ireland
8 Castlecourt Centre,
Dublin 15, D15 XTP3, Ireland
(email: info@hbgi.ie)

An Hachette UK Company
www.hachette.co.uk

www.virago.co.uk

To my mother

Everything I am began with you.

TIMELINE

1918	End of Ottoman rule over Syria
1920	Syria becomes a French mandate
1946	Syria recognized as an independent republic
1947	The first Ba'ath Party congress is held in Damascus
1949	A series of military coups overthrow the civilian government
1963	The Ba'ath Party seizes power, establishing a new government
1970	Hafez al-Assad takes power in a military coup and becomes President
2000	Hafez al-Assad dies and is succeeded by his son, Bashar al-Assad
2011	Protests inspired by the Arab Spring escalate into the Syrian Civil War
2024	Opposition forces capture Damascus, and Bashar al-Assad flees, marking the end of Ba'athist rule

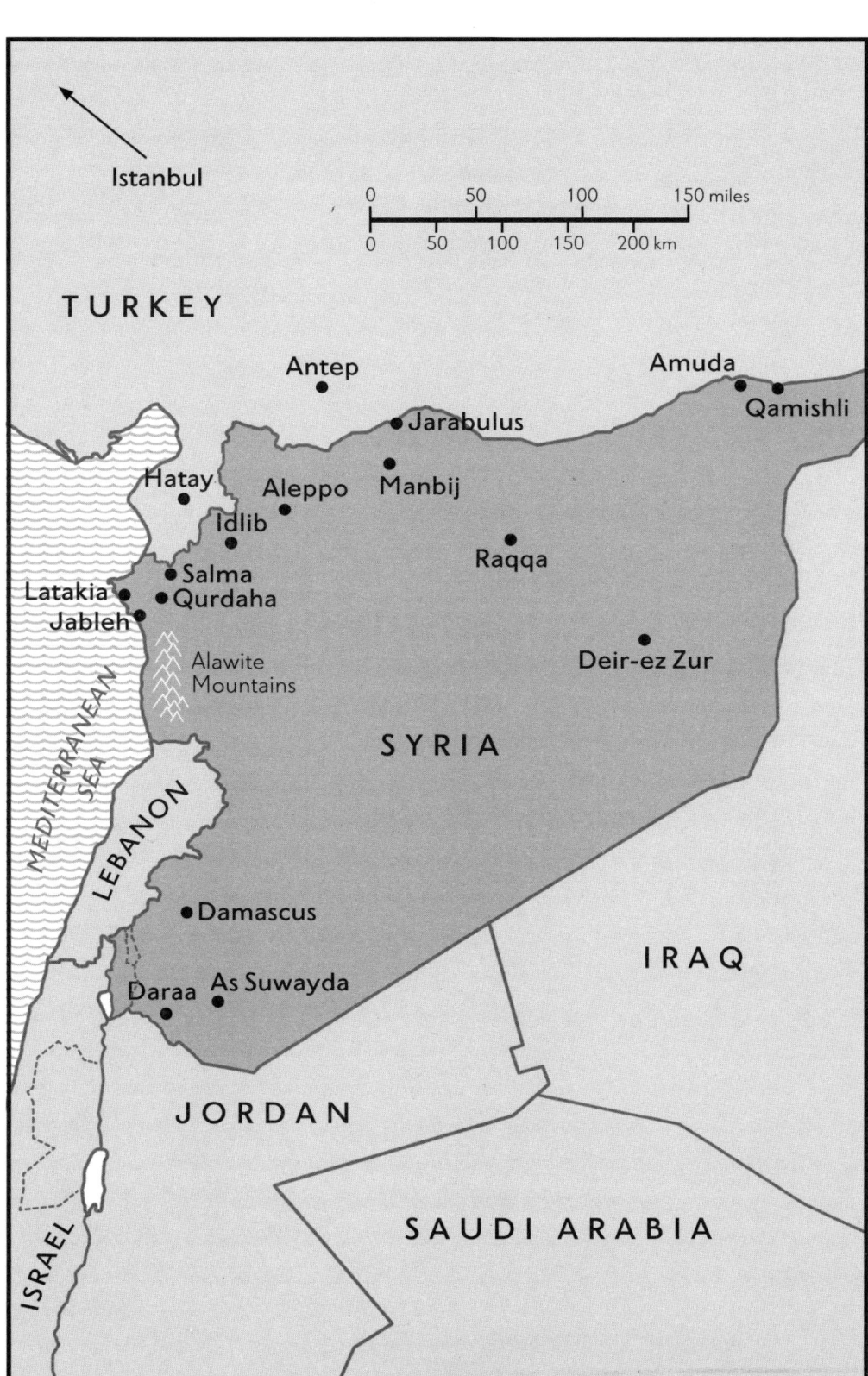

CONTENTS

PART I
1

PART II
135

PART III
233

PART IV
375

Acknowledgments
419

PART I

ONE

I slip off my shoes and leave them on the cement as my grandmother Wadia, my mother's mother, leans into a rough wooden door with all her weight until it opens. She leads me into a dim room, the only source of light a tiny window, a brass plate of frankincense burning on its sill. It takes time for my eyes to adjust. The walls are cracked, and their whitewash has faded to gray. A dark wooden bookcase occupies one corner. A dozen people sit cross-legged on a frayed rug, humming and whispering indecipherable prayers. Some are leaning back against the wall, their eyes closed. Others sway back and forth as they read texts from the pages of books cradled in their laps.

Grandmother's eyes draw close to mine. "This," she whispers, "is the sheikh's tomb." She nods toward the center of the room. There, layers of light green cloth cover a stone sarcophagus. She's brought me to dozens of tombs like this—tombs of sheikhs, God's messengers, who know the secrets of the Alawite religion, and whose burial chambers are sacred. She takes me toward the sarcophagus and drops to her knees. Eyes tightly shut, she bows over the cloth, touches her lips to it. Then she rests her forehead on the spot she's just kissed. The palms of her hands pressed against the sides of her head, she starts to whisper. I move closer and struggle to hear what she is saying. I go down on my knees. I lean my body against hers. She is silent.

I bow my head close to the fabric, imitating her gesture, and catch a sharp, terrible odor, the smell of old socks soaking in water. All those lips. All that human saliva and mucus, absorbed and dried into a rough crust. My fingers pinch the edge of the cloth and I draw it away to kiss the stone.

Grandmother grabs my hand and squeezes until it hurts. "It is forbidden even to lay eyes upon the bare stone," she warns. "It will blind you." I freeze. The thought of kissing the cloth is revolting. I close my eyes, hold my breath, and barely touch the harsh fabric with my lips. Then I place my forehead against it, cool from the stone beneath. Shivers pass through my body. I keep my eyes closed. I draw a deep breath and try to think of something to ask of the sheikh, lying there, cold under the hard stone. I cannot ignore the smell. I feel nauseous. I fear my grandmother will notice, and that I will suffer punishment—both from her and from God—for getting grossed out in a place of worship.

Grandmother takes a small pair of scissors from her bag and snips a swatch from the green cloth, then slips it into her pocket. Before I have a chance to wonder why she'd steal a piece of the stinky fabric, she commands: "Stay here. I'll be back."

She rises from her knees and walks toward the exit. I follow her with my eyes and spot a picture hanging above the wooden door. It's a printed portrait of Imam Ali. Ali is the son-in-law of the Prophet Muhammad and a martyr to Shi'ite Muslims.

The low sound of a woman weeping flows through the heavy silence that otherwise fills the room. I try to find its source. The sheikh's tomb blocks my vision. The weeping grows louder. I stand and move toward the bookcase. On its shelves are various editions of the Quran and other books. I take one about the size of my hand, open it, and scan the room. I see a woman dressed in black, a white funeral scarf covering most of her head, her back against the wall. An open Quran rests on her lap. But she isn't reading. Her eyes are closed. She is sobbing.

I sit down on the floor in the opposite corner of the room and try without success to focus on my Quran. I stare at the woman. My heart aches. She opens her eyes and speaks toward the tomb in whispers. Minutes later, she wipes her face with her scarf, puts the Quran aside, stumbles to the sarcophagus, kneels down, and places her hands upon it. She speaks to the tomb, as Grandmother did. I can't make out her words. She kisses the tomb, takes something from her coat pocket, and pins it to the bottom of the green cloth. Then she kisses the fabric again, stands, and walks away.

When she's gone, I put the Quran aside and go to where she knelt in front of the sarcophagus. Steeling myself against the smell, I, too, kiss the cloth. Pressing my forehead to the spot I kissed, I lift one layer of the cloth to see what she has pinned to it—a small picture. A girl with two braids, no older than ten. Keeping my forehead against the tomb so no one can see what I'm doing, I lift the second layer and discover more pictures. Women and men. Young and old, and everything in between. I lift layer after layer, looking for more. Until suddenly I see the dark, bare stone. I close my eyes. My heart drops. "Please don't make me blind," I whisper, and run out of the shrine.

I search for my grandmother, but the courtyard outside the shrine is empty. I start to cry. I wish I'd never come.

"What's wrong? What happened?" It's Grandmother's voice. Whimpering, I hug her and tell her about the child in the picture. "She is my age," I say. "She is dead," I say. "There were so many pictures."

"Not all the photographs are of the dead. Next time remind me to bring yours. People also bring photos of their loved ones so that they can be watched over and blessed by Ali. But for now, you can wear this."

She takes the green swatch of cloth from her pocket and rolls it into a cylinder. "Give me your hand." I watch as she ties it around my wrist.

"Don't take it off. It will fall off when it's worn out."

As we make our way home, our driver navigates sharp turns that tempt me to reach out and brush against the bushes lining the roadside; the landscape shifts from the olive groves and pine-scented coolness of the mountains to the flat expanse of Jableh. Here, mismatched buildings sprawl under the heavy stench of diesel and rising humidity. I can't stop thinking of the bare stone I dared to lay my eyes upon—twice—and whether I will be struck blind. Suppressing the urge to ask my grandmother if anyone suffered blindness from it, I remain silent. I know she will caution me to "shorten my tongue"—a polite way of saying "shut up" in Arabic—and discourage questions about our faith. "A good Alawite must obey," she often says. "No questions."

The Alawi faith is a branch of Shi'a Islam that traces its origins to the early Islamic period and the teachings of Ibn Nusayr, a Shi'a scholar who lived and worked in what is now northern Iraq during the late eighth and early ninth centuries. The term "Alawi" means "those who adhere to the teachings of Ali."

Alawite theology is syncretic, incorporating elements from Islamic, Christian, and Jewish traditions, as well as influences from Persian, Indian, and Greek (Neoplatonic) philosophies. Alawism emphasizes the importance of esoteric or hidden knowledge, which the faith holds was revealed by God to the imams, the Prophet Muhammad's successors.

This manifests in the form of rituals that are often more private and secretive than those of mainstream Shi'a Islam, scriptures in addition to the Quran, and the belief in tajyeel—reincarnation. Our deeds in one life determine how we are reborn in the next, allowing us to rise upward until we reach the highest levels of heaven. We can be reborn as holy figures, our dead bodies enshrined, our mausoleums sites of pilgrimage and worship, where we come for prayer and spiritual blessings. Local cultural practices and historical contexts also influence dress, another sign of the sect's broader divergence from mainstream Islamic practices: Unlike many Shi'a and Sunni Muslim women, Alawite women do not cover themselves with the hijab.

A religious minority in Syria, Alawites faced persecution for centuries under various ruling powers. Growing up, I felt proud listening to my grandmother as she explained how Zaman Awal, our ancestors, survived under the Ottomans—Osmanli—who ruled Syria from 1516 to 1918. Every time she cooked rice, she would tell me and my older sister, Alia, that we should be grateful; most of Zaman Awal lived and died without ever tasting it. "Why, Grandma?" I would ask, though I knew the answer.

She would pause over the steaming pot. "Burghul—bulgur—was all they had. Rice, in Ottoman Syria, was for city dwellers only: Christians and Sunnis. You and I, we were not allowed in cities. The Ottomans hated us."

The Ottoman Empire was the seat of the Sunni caliphate, and viewed Alawites as mysterious and suspicious because of their distinct religious beliefs and practices. Unlike Sunni Muslims, Alawites do not pray in mosques but instead have their own places of worship; in addition to not requiring women to wear the hijab, the Alawite sect also does not have any dietary restrictions and does not prohibit alcohol. These differences contributed to the distrust and disdain the Ottomans held toward the Alawite community, highlighting broader sectarian tensions between Sunni and Shi'a groups within the Ottoman Empire.

Grandmother would tell us that rumors had swirled around the Alawites for centuries. Some Ottomans believed that Alawites were possessed by devils. Sunni imams issued fatwas, legal condemnations by Islamic religious leaders, against us infidels. The most famous fatwa was issued by Ibn Taymiyyah, a fierce Sunni jurist of the fourteenth century, who preached a rigid interpretation of the Quran and strict adherence to the cultural habits of the great deserts of the Arabian Peninsula. Though Alawites considered themselves a subset of the Shi'a branch of Islam, their beliefs and practices have long been viewed with suspicion by Sunni orthodoxy. Ibn Taymiyyah denounced them as "greater disbelievers than the Jews, Christians, and Indian idol-worshipping Brahmans"—a fatwa that laid the foundation for centuries of marginalization and sectarian hostility.

All Alawite children have had the experience of going to bed afraid after hearing horror stories of the violence under Ottoman rule. Of all the stories my grandmother shared, one especially struck fear into my heart: an episode called the Piles. In the late fifteenth or early sixteenth century, the Ottomans raided Alawite houses in Aleppo and killed everyone they found. More than ten thousand Alawites were slaughtered with knives and swords, their severed heads stacked in pile after pile near the Aleppo citadel. Flies swarmed on blood as it was drying in the alleys around the citadel for days afterward. The few Alawite religious leaders who dared to remain in Aleppo and resist were captured, impaled on metal spikes, and displayed in public squares. Some Alawites hid among the Christians in their quarters of the city, but most fled into the coastal mountains overlooking the Mediterranean Sea.

This region, which became known as the Alawite mountains, is where the Alawites would live for the next three hundred years, and it is where my own ancestors took refuge, surviving off whatever the soil would yield. Whole wheat was the only grain available to plant, Grandmother told us, and they would harvest it, winnow it, and crack it using two rounded stones to make burghul. Then they would boil it with tomatoes and white onions from their vegetable patches and eat it with the oil of the olives they collected in their groves. Sometimes, they would soak the burghul with lemon, olive oil, and tomato juice and consume it that way. To this day, Alawites eat burghul on the first day of Eid and consider it a gift from God. Salt was another luxury for the impoverished migrants. Alawites trekked for miles to the seashore, bringing home jugs of seawater to fashion salty dough for bread.

In the aftermath of the First World War and the collapse of the Ottoman Empire, France established a mandate over Syria and Lebanon under the League of Nations mandate system, which, on paper, installed France as a trustee until the countries' inhabitants were considered eligible for self-government. The French administration restructured the region, creating administrative divisions, which included an Alawite-dominated enclave along the coast. As a result, Alawites experienced relative stability for the first time in generations and began to gain political prominence. During the 1930s and 1940s, Syrian nationalist movements grew stronger, pushing for independence from French rule, which was achieved in 1946.

The early years of independence were tumultuous and marked by political instability, as Syria underwent several military coups and changes in leadership. In 1963, the socialist and pan-Arab Ba'ath Party seized power and established a new government. But another revolution was on the horizon: In 1970, a prominent Ba'athist military leader staged a coup known as the Corrective Movement, consolidated power, and became the president of Syria. His name was Hafez al-Assad, and he was Alawite—the first Alawite president in Syrian history.

I always felt a strong link to my ancestors, and proud to belong to a community that had survived despite centuries of adversity. But as I grew older, I realized that my grandmother's admonishments to "shorten my tongue" weren't just a consequence of my youth: As a woman, there were limits to the questions I was allowed to ask about our faith. In Alawi tradition, women are considered spiritually subordinate to men. Alawites maintain that women cannot be entrusted with the core beliefs of the religion, which are passed down from one generation of men to the next. When a boy turns sixteen, he is assigned a sheikh from his hometown and studies with him in a local prayer room at the shrine every weekend. After two years, on his eighteenth birthday, if he completes his course of study, he is accepted as a fully matured, devout Alawite man. Even in my youth, this struck me as unfair: I never felt less Alawite than any man despite being forbidden to ask about the mysteries of our faith, let alone instructed in them.

Regardless of these frustrations, I grew up steeped in reverence for my faith and the president, the great man who had delivered us from the fringes of Syrian society to the very center of the nation's politics. He deserved our gratitude and devotion; I'd known this since I was small. What I did not know, as we drove home from the shrine that day, my hands tingling from brushing against the bushes out the car window, was that when his family's power would come to be challenged, my life would be changed forever.

TWO

According to my mother, when I was born, my father brought me to his chest and kissed me. "You will be called Lena," he said. Lena was the name of his mistress.

"Over my dead body!" my mother shouted from her hospital bed. My father insisted, but my mother held firm. Eventually, a family friend suggested Loubna. In Arabic, Loubna is the name of a beautiful tree that blooms with little white flowers, whose aromatic nectar is used in incense. It was also the name of a famous Egyptian actress. Begrudgingly, my father agreed.

Not many people from my father's side of the family drove the three hours from Jableh, a town on the Syrian coast near Latakia, to Damascus to meet me, as they had for Alia, who'd arrived a year and a half prior. There was a general sense of disappointment surrounding my birth. My father's family had hoped that the second child would be a son. My father was the eldest and the only one among his brothers who had yet to have a boy to pass down the family name. In any case, one daughter was enough; as the Arabic saying goes, "The burden of girls is with you until death." As for my mother's family, they'd never approved of my father to begin with.

Though both sides originated as poor farmers from the mountains around Jableh, my mother's father, Ali, was the first of his family to go to school. Like Hafez, he later joined the military, where he ascended the ranks. There were stories of my grandmother, Wadia, hanging blankets over the living room windows while her husband and other officers plotted the 1966 coup, prompted by divisions between the Ba'ath Party's two main factions, that would set the stage for Hafez's own coup in 1970 and further consolidate Ba'athist control. After the coup, Ali was appointed as a diplomat, raising my mother and her three siblings in cities around the world.

Ali and Wadia were a handsome couple, he with his wide forehead and large mustache, she with her big black eyes, short skirts, and diamond necklaces. My grandmother's earlobes eventually grew long from the weight of the heavy earrings she wore to embassy cocktail parties. Though the parties bored her—she didn't drink, hated the cold meats they served, and didn't speak their languages—she loved the glamorous lifestyle her husband's work conferred them.

THEY RETURNED TO Damascus in early 1980, when my mother was sixteen. Ali bought an elegant ground-floor apartment surrounded by a large garden, filled it with furniture from Turkey and India, and adorned it with Persian rugs that, according to my grandmother, were so beautiful and unique that people would travel just to see them.

Growing up, my mother had a French education, attending school in Tunisia and Turkey. Returning to Syria as a high school student, she struggled with the Syrian education system. After high school, she was admitted to Damascus University to study the subject for which her mediocre grades granted her entry: environmental engineering. In college, she got engaged, but her fiancé soon called it off; his mother looked down on my mother because she was Alawite. My mother was heartbroken, but my grandfather assured her that her education, her degree, was what she should keep her eyes on, not marriage.

Ultimately, she was the third of her siblings to become an engineer. Education had lifted my grandfather out of poverty, and he valued it greatly. Even when my mother's sister, my aunt Khuzama, eloped with a man my grandfather did not approve of and he refused to speak to her, he still ensured that she graduated with a degree in French literature and, later, sent word through my mother, asking her to apply to the Ministry of Foreign Affairs. With his influential recommendation, she secured a job and later became a diplomat herself.

One night in 1987, Grandfather Ali took a glass jar out to the garden to collect jasmine to dry for tea. He became tired and returned to his room, placed the jar on the nightstand, closed his eyes, and never woke up. It was a heart attack. He was only fifty years old.

When my grandmother found him, she hit herself so hard in disbelief that her body carried blue marks long afterward. My mother never remembered this day without crying. His death was her first and biggest loss.

For a week after Grandfather Ali's funeral, the house was packed with visitors. People from his village who had never been to the capital came to commemorate his legacy, as did ambassadors and high officials in the Syrian government. But the greatest honor for my family was that President Assad, whose palace was in the neighborhood, came to pay his respects.

AS FATE WOULD HAVE IT, the most consequential visitor to my grandparents' house that day was not the president, but a mysterious man named

Jawdat Mrie—or Doctor Jawdat, as people referred to him—though it would be a long time before anyone would understand why. Rumor held that Jawdat had amassed his wealth by traveling to other countries to assassinate fellow Alawites who opposed the government. My grandfather hadn't liked him; when he was alive, he wouldn't even let him in the house. But on the day of the funeral, Jawdat strode in, leaving his two bodyguards at the door. Inside, my twenty-three-year-old mother, who was fifteen years his junior, caught his eye. He tried to speak to her, but she refused.

For weeks afterward, he persisted, sending her flowers and gifts until, eventually, my mother responded. My grandmother opposed the relationship. Not only would my grandfather have disapproved, but my mother was still grieving my grandfather and her failed engagement. Wadia suspected that Jawdat was trying to take advantage of this vulnerable moment, to fill the void my grandfather and my mother's ex-fiancé had left. She begged my mother to buy time and consider her options.

But with the family shattered and consumed by grief and her personal life in turmoil, my mother didn't heed her mother's warning. A few months after they had met, my mother decided to marry Jawdat and demanded her werteh, her inheritance, to make it so.

After they were married, Alia and I were born in quick succession: she in 1989, I in January 1991. For the first three years of my life, my mother, father, sister, and I resided in Mazzeh, an upscale neighborhood of high buildings in a hilly quarter of Damascus. Mazzeh was surrounded by fields of prickly pear then, and during the summer months, sellers would roam the wide streets pushing carts loaded with the red fruit on ice. We lived in an apartment on the top floor, where my mother would sit on the balcony, sip her morning coffee, and watch the drying clothes hung out on nearby rooftops as the daily calls to prayer resounded from minarets across the city, like a chorus singing the same word of God in a strange echoing round.

During this period, our family had a maid, bodyguards, a driver, and plenty of disposable income. But despite all of these privileges, ours was not a happy home. My father had become intolerably abusive to my mother when she was pregnant with me, but she held on, hoping he would stop mistreating her. She desperately wanted their marriage to work. My grandmother had warned my mother that if she married against her will, she would have to deal with the consequences by herself, so she had no safety net to rely on. My mother also wanted to keep the family together so my sister and I would grow up with our father in the home, as her father had played such a large role in her own life.

Beyond her individual circumstances, there was also significant societal pressure confining her to this union and making a separation almost inconceivable. Divorced women often face severe stigmatization in Arab societies: They are blamed for the marriage's failure and considered selfish and incapable of managing their home and husband. No longer virgins, they are also seen as prone to casual sexual relationships and thus immoral. This stigma extends to their children; girls without fathers at home face difficulties in finding suitable partners. So, my mother put up with Jawdat's abuse and infidelity, which had begun nearly as soon as they were married, hoping that one day he would return to his senses.

My father took one mistress after the next, disappearing for days at a time. After Lena, for whom he'd tried to name me, my father started a relationship with a woman nearly twenty years younger than him. She was the sister of Adnan Kassar, a friend of Bassel al-Assad—the president's eldest son and heir apparent, a square-jawed, sharp-eyed engineer, army officer, and commander of the Presidential Guard who liked to race through Damascus in his sports car. Adnan eventually asked Bassel to do something about the married man and father of two who was harassing his twenty-one-year-old sister. Bassel sent my father a warning by seizing a valuable plot of land in Jableh that overlooked the sea, where Jawdat had been planning to build a beach resort.

My mother was terrified that the situation would escalate. She begged my father to stay away from the girl, but he wouldn't listen.

Not long afterward, Jawdat was placed under house arrest and his income cut out. My mother acted as any devoted wife would: Not wanting him to feel that this would impact his lifestyle or our family's, and to prove her loyalty and worth, she gave my father everything she had inherited from her own father. Through these gestures of devotion, she hoped that he would come to appreciate her efforts and perhaps change his behavior.

After a year, my father was freed—on the condition that he leave the country immediately. In 1994, when I was three years old, he moved to Sofia, Bulgaria. A few weeks later, my mother, sister, and I joined him there.

I don't remember much from that period, except for the white stairs leading up to our flat and the smell of burnt sugar and vanilla from a bakery across the street. My mother enrolled us in a school where we ate sour yogurt with every lunch and were forced to take naps on beds covered with thick brown blankets of itchy wool. The photos that remain show Alia and me in a park with nude statues, posing at their feet, looking up, pointing at the private parts with our hands covering our mouths.

My father didn't spend much time with us. When I asked my mother why, she'd say he was working. I remember being woken up in the middle of the night to the sound of them shouting at each other in French. The streetlamp backlit a big tree that cast scary shadows on my bedroom wall, and I'd cry for my mother. She would come in and hug and kiss me, and the familiar feel and sound and scent of her would settle me back down to sleep.

DEFIANCE

While we were in Bulgaria, Bassel al-Assad crashed his car speeding to the Damascus airport in a morning fog and died. On television, I watched the funeral cortege pass through streets packed with men and women in the throes of grief: screaming and crying hysterically, slapping their faces, pulling their hair. Syrian TV crews roamed the streets, capturing such scenes, and the footage was broadcast for the rest of the country to see on the only channel available, the Syrian state channel. Public schools, universities, and restaurants were closed for days thereafter.

High-end hotels stopped serving alcohol. Bab Touma and Kasa'a—the squares in Damascus where young people would usually congregate and blast music from their cars—were empty. State TV showed images of Bassel galloping gracefully on his horse and scenes of the funeral over-dubbed with recitations of the Quran. The Presidential Palace was grieving, and so did the rest of the country.

First among the mourners was the new heir apparent, Bashar al-Assad, Hafez's second son. Unlike his older brother, Bashar was not a well-known figure in Syria then.

At the time of his brother's death, Bashar was in the United Kingdom studying to become an ophthalmologist, far from the president's inner circle and seemingly disinclined to politics.

A FEW MONTHS after Bassel's death, my father asked my mother to take Alia and me back to Syria. I never learned what prompted his decision; my mother had no choice but to obey. Though she had vowed not to help my mother if the marriage failed, my grandmother allowed us to move into her grand house in Damascus, on the condition that we share a single room—the same room that my mother had left six years earlier.

Although I was very young, I could sense my grandmother's anger at my mother through the many restrictions she imposed on us. Alia and I were never allowed to enter my grandmother's room. When she was home, we could only leave my mother's bedroom to use the bathroom. My mother bought a small TV and a small fridge—presumably because we were not allowed to use the main fridge in the kitchen—and we ate our meals in our room.

Despite all of this, my mother tried her best to widen our world by taking us out almost every evening. She enrolled Alia in piano lessons. In photos of our small room, the floor is covered with coloring books and crayons. Not one of our birthdays wasn't celebrated; our grandmother made an exception to her rule that we be confined to one area of the house. My mother would make our favorite food, bake a cake, and invite her friends' daughters and a few of our school friends over.

My grandfather's presence was still felt in the house. His photos and many dust-covered volumes of books filled a full wall in the large living room. My grandmother forbade anyone to touch his belongings. Even his alcohol cabinet remained untouched. But not everything was kept away from us. Sometimes, when my grandmother was in a good mood, she would sit me down on her bed amid the smell of rosewater and flip through big leather photo albums, showing me pictures of Grandfather Ali and her in Brazil or Istanbul, posing in plazas full of birds. There were white marbled mansions, and so many photos of my mother as a young girl—with my grandfather, in a swimsuit on a swing in Istanbul, reading books. My mother had inherited her mother's green eyes and the round shape of her father's face.

My grandmother told me my mother was my grandfather's favorite. If my grandfather were alive, she said, he would never have allowed this mistake—this marriage between my mother and Jawdat. And although she never said it, I knew that my sister and I were part of this mistake; we were its consequences.

"When we have our own house" became a mantra my mother would repeat whenever we got upset about my grandmother's restrictions, but she didn't have the means to realize this. Though she worked for the Ministry of Agriculture, she did not earn enough to cover rent, hire someone to watch us after school until she came home, and support us on her own. My father wasn't sending any money.

I recall speaking on the phone with him during this period when he was still in Bulgaria. My mother would dial his number on a white phone that she would set on the carpet and hand me the receiver. I would play with the phone cord, wrapping the tiny spirals around my thumb. I don't remember what was said, only his sharp voice. Sometimes, he would simply hang up, and my mother would dial again. She knew he might never love us as her father loved her, but she wanted him to remain in our lives, even if he was not helping us financially.

I was aware we needed money, but I didn't want my mother to work. In the summer, when we didn't have school and my grandmother would travel to Jableh to visit her relatives, Alia and I resented being left alone in the house. In the mornings, we'd wake up to a plate of stale cheese sandwiches our mother had left; we would watch cartoons in the living room, a forbidden space when my grandmother was home, until my mother returned.

One of those days, while Alia and I were playing in the house—I must have been six or seven—I knocked over my grandmother's antique divider in her living room, shattering the white mosaic around its edges. I was hiding under my bed when my mother came home. She screamed in anger, and I heard the clatter of the silverware drawer as she grabbed her favorite weapon, a large wooden spoon. It wasn't the first time my mother hit me so hard it left my skin bruised. She would often shout that she had given up everything to raise us properly. But when she wasn't angry, she reminded us that she loved us more than anything. We were all she had.

Sometimes, we would visit a friend she had known before marrying Jawdat, and my mother would weep as they sat together. We never understood exactly what they were talking about, but I would run to her and hug her, begging her not to cry. At home, I would pick jasmine flowers from the garden, threading them together to make her a necklace.

Right after I finished second grade, I remember my mother calling family friends to tell them that Grandmother Wadia wanted us out by the end of the summer. It seemed like a desperate attempt to shame my grandmother for evicting us, or perhaps she was just seeking advice. Around this time, I remember her sobbing on the phone, speaking to my father in French. He promised to send money on one condition: We would have to leave Damascus for his hometown of Jableh, and indeed, one day, my mother announced that we were moving into a newly renovated apartment in Jableh, in the same building as my uncles, my father's brothers. In our new home, we would be surrounded by Jawdat's large family: His mother, my grandmother Tamra, lived across the street and owned several of the neighboring buildings, including the one next door where one of his sisters, my aunt Fadia, lived. Aunt Fadia's daughters, Leen and Lama, were the same age as Alia and me, and we would become instant friends. Other aunts, uncles, and cousins, like my father's other sister, Aunt Samia, were just a few neighborhoods away.

I don't recall much about leaving Damascus or even saying goodbye to Grandmother Wadia. I just remember how thrilled I was with the size of our new apartment. Although Alia and I would still share a bedroom, our living room was spacious, and we could move about it freely, which was wonderful. I remember riding my scooter through our bedroom with its large windows and down the hallway into the massive living room. I stood on the beautiful marble counters in the kitchen and smelled the fresh paint on the cabinets.

My first mornings in our new home, I would lie in bed with eyes closed, listening to the sounds from the street—sellers pushing carts of vegetables freshly picked from nearby fields, promising their corn was honey-sweet. In Damascus, the only noises we heard were occasional ambulances, car horns, and music blasting from cars, especially after nightfall. There were no street sellers in Grandmother Wadia's neighborhood, just a few upscale supermarkets.

Sometimes, when I heard the fish sellers, I would leap from my bed, rush to the balcony, and watch the silvery scales of large fish shimmer in the sunlight. Housewives across the street bargained from their windows, and the fish seller left his cart unattended during deliveries because everyone in the neighborhood knew each other, and no one dared steal from the guy we all depended on. In Damascus, I only knew the neighbors in my grandmother's building, but in Jableh, the balconies were so close together that women would shout good morning to each other. Conversations would erupt spontaneously—one woman on one floor with another on another floor—until others joined in, eventually leading to morning coffee invitations.

THE TRANSITION WAS HARD on my mother. For the first few days, she was on the phone with her friends in Damascus, sobbing constantly. She didn't know anyone in Jableh except my father's relatives. She had uprooted herself from everything and everyone she knew so Alia and I could grow up in the comfort of our own home, with our large family—my father's, the one that mattered.

My father had nine siblings, and those nine families produced thirty-five children. Everyone would gather at Grandmother Tamra's, a repulsive house whose living room with its bulky, unmatched couches had a large window overlooking a dusty loquat tree. All of the windows were always open, and flies meandered in and out, perhaps attracted by the smell of olive oil and fried eggs—my grandmother's favorite meal.

My mother had a few blurry photos of my father from our days in Damascus and Bulgaria, but nothing could match the portrait permanently displayed on Grandmother Tamra's living room wall. In it, he was wearing a white shirt with a collar that nearly reached his earlobes. My grandmother proudly told me that she had pressed it with cornstarch specifically for this day, the one where his photo was going to be taken at the studio. In his mid-twenties in the photo, Jawdat was admittedly handsome, with thick eyebrows and big brown eyes. Of my grandmother's nine children, my father was the only one whose picture hung in her room.

Whenever Tamra heard my voice in the house, she called me to come and sit by her bed because she said I was blessed with the scent of her eldest and favorite. He was the one who defined her identity: "Oum Jawdat," mother of Jawdat, as she proudly called herself. We were told that Jawdat had made the careers of his brothers and had sent her the money she used to buy the buildings she owned in Jableh. Her favoritism was legendary: My aunts often joked that it was better to curse God than Jawdat. I later heard that my grandmother didn't speak to her sister for nine years after an argument during which my great aunt had said she hoped Jawdat would never return from his travels.

I didn't like Grandmother Tamra. Whenever she kissed me, I felt the saliva on my cheek, wet and sticky, as if she had licked my cheek with her tongue. When she wasn't looking, I would try to bring my shoulder to my cheek to wipe her spittle off. She smelled of rubbing alcohol and had a hairy black mole right on the tip of her chin. Her hands shook, and she often drifted into sleep and murmured as if she were conversing with someone. Sometimes, she stretched out her leg, took a long needle, and injected something into her thigh. When I looked away, she would laugh and tell me I should look and learn because I might get diabetes like everyone in our family someday.

My aunt Samia was Tamra's main caregiver. She was loud, always shouting on the phone at her husband or her son, Hamada, for not studying.

DEFIANCE

Though she lived a few neighborhoods away, she came to Grandmother Tamra's most days to make sure she was taking her medicine, help her with her business, and ensure her renters were paying on time.

I LOVED THE SUMMER in Jableh for the freedom I enjoyed there. During summers in Damascus, when my mother didn't take us to the park, Alia and I were only allowed to play in front of Grandmother Wadia's building. We could not go beyond the gate because my mother worried that we would get hit by a speeding car. In Jableh, the streets were narrow, and cars drove more slowly. Children played outside, their mothers shouting from the balconies for them to come home for meals. My mother bought me a bike that I would lock under Grandmother Tamra's stairs.

When I wasn't playing with my cousins and Alia, I would go to a nearby store and buy bags of bright pink cotton candy. I never had to carry cash; the cashier knew me and kept a running tab of what I got for my mother to pay later. Sometimes, a small truck came and fumigated the neighborhood, leaving it stinking of something like diesel fuel. It was supposed to leave a film on stagnant water and kill mosquito larvae. We would run behind the truck and try to lose each other in the white cloud of spray. We rubbed each other's arms afterward to sniff and see who smelled the worst.

On most summer evenings, right before sunset, my mother and my aunts would take all of us kids to the corniche, Jableh's seaside promenade, which the French had built and lined with a marble wall half a century before. The corniche smelled of flavored hookah smoke, nuts toasting on carts, and boiled sweet corn. My mother would buy us whatever we wanted before we mobbed the patio of one of the many coffee shops along the water. There, we watched the sun sinking into the sea, as children and mothers had done for thousands of years. Young men jumped from big rocks into the water, as they had done for just as long, each one trying to impress the girls who acted as though the boys were not putting on a show for them.

I was mesmerized by the sea. Although I had seen it before on our short trips to Jableh to visit my grandmother, living near it was entirely different. The scent of the sea permeated my home, a constant soothing presence in the air. When we strolled along the shore at various times of the day, I noticed how the water seamlessly merged with the sky, both sharing the same hue. During sunset, the shimmering glow—white, yellow, and finally red—would vanish when the sun disappeared and all went black. Fishing boats chugged out from Jableh's marina to net fish that schooled just beneath the surface after dark. I saw their little lights out there in the darkness, away from the shore and the roaring cars, honking horns, and blaring music. It must have been quiet there, with only the sound of water lapping against the sides of the boats, the thud of feet, the splashes of the nets being tossed out and pulled in, and the flopping of the fish against the dock.

IN THE WEEKS THAT FOLLOWED, my mother had to make a few trips back to Damascus to retrieve what remained of our belongings at Grandmother Wadia's. On the first of these trips, Alia and I stayed at Aunt Fadia's with Leen and Lama. Because we were Jawdat's daughters, Aunt Fadia knew she couldn't hit us when we did something she didn't like; instead, she would hit her own daughters. Sometimes, she would punish them by putting their heads in the toilet for reasons I can't recall, and later, we could hear them sobbing as they washed their hair. When my mother returned, we begged her not to leave us there again.

The next time my mother left, Grandmother Wadia came to stay with us. During that short visit, I discovered a side of my grandmother I hadn't seen before. She was loving and cooked us delicious meals, braiding my hair every night before bed. When she learned that Alia and I had never been to the shrine in the nearby hills, she immediately took us. Visiting the shrine became a tradition every time she visited us in Jableh.

"You only have one mother," my mother replied when I asked if she was still angry with Grandmother Wadia for forcing us to move to Jableh. I didn't understand why I should forgive people just because there was only one of them. It was a phrase I hated, probably because my mother often used a similar one when she insisted that I speak with my father, though he was mostly silent on the other end of the line. I would often pretend he was talking to me because I knew my mother would be upset if she realized he wasn't—or that he had already hung up.

Sometimes, when we were running low on cash, she would have me or Alia read to him on the phone from a piece of paper that said things like "Our fridge is empty. We are hungry." He would call our mother a whore and hang up, or he'd yell and accuse us of only calling him for his money, which was true. I dreaded these conversations so much that when I sensed my mother was about to ask one of us to get on the phone, I would drop what I was doing, run to my room, and hide in our closet. But inevitably, when I heard Alia's cheerful voice greeting our father on the other end of the line, I would feel jealous. Other than money and his portrait on my grandmother's wall, his voice was the only thing that made me feel like he was real. That I, too, had a father. Something every girl needed.

During this time, my father was synonymous with the smell of gray 500-lira bills, with knocks on our door and men in black leather jackets, their faces grim and guns often on their hips, showing up to hand my mother envelopes of cash. I remember my mother laying the bills out on the dining table, budgeting so they would last us until the next time he sent money—a tall order, since she never knew exactly when that would be.

THREE

In September, every house in Syria, rich or poor, makes Makdoos, small eggplants stuffed with red pepper paste, walnuts, and garlic pickled in olive oil. They are a staple of Syrian cuisine. The eggplant harvest season is short, spanning just the first two weeks of September, and families usually make enough Makdoos to stock up their pantries for the coming year. This means days of constant labor: cracking walnuts with a wooden mallet, peeling and mincing hundreds of garlic cloves, boiling the eggplants, then salting and pressing them with the heaviest items in the house to squeeze the water out, and grinding pounds of sweet red peppers into a paste, which is spread on silver trays and left to dry in the sun on a balcony or rooftop.

Our first fall in Jableh, my mother dried her peppers on the balcony outside my bedroom window. For days, the room and the entire neighborhood were bathed in the aroma of red pepper. Once the pepper paste had dried, my mom mixed it into a large bowl with the other ingredients, pressed the stuffing into the eggplants, placed them into large glass jars, and smothered them with olive oil that had been squeezed earlier in the month in my family's village. Grandmother Tamra had sent us enough oil to last the whole year.

Once the jars of Makdoos were sealed and put away, it was time to bring out the wool floor rugs that had been tucked away in the summer, unroll them, and hang them in the sun to air out the mothball smell. Many families would show off their best-looking rugs, a measure of wealth, on their front balconies and hang the ugly ones in the back.

As the rugs were brought back inside, the school year would begin. Our new primary school was a few minutes' walk from the apartment. I remember our mother standing on the balcony when we set off, watching us until we disappeared. Alia and I would hold hands the entire way, and if we heard the class bell ring, we would separate and run.

In Jableh, the school day started with a mandatory ritual called the slogans assembly. Everyone from first to sixth grade would line up in rows in our uniforms: the folar, a three-cornered neckerchief that was a different color for each grade; a knee-length brown apron; and a side cap with the Ba'ath pioneer logo. The caps were only worn during the slogans assembly. They were thin and always slipped from our heads, and when the assembly was over, we'd jam them into our pockets or use them to smuggle sunflower seeds, gum, or cookies into class.

As we stood facing the boxy, orangish building, our principal, Jameela, would appear holding a thick wooden stick in one hand and a bell in the other. She would shake the bell, and the pitch of the sound often signaled her mood that day. When angry, she shook it so hard and fast that it produced a sharp, crisp chime that seemed to pierce the back of our heads. She would give one of the students from the front row the honor of holding up the Syrian flag. Then she would firmly remind us to stand up straight, like proper human beings. Once she deemed us ready, the call-and-response would begin.

"One Arab nation!" Jameela would shout.

"One eternal message!" we'd reply.
"Our goals!"
"Unity, freedom, socialism!"
"Our leader forever!"
"The entrusted Hafez al-Assad!"

We would extend our right arms straight in front of us and reach slightly upward, with palms facing down and fingers pressed tightly together. While this salute might be associated with the Nazi Party in other countries, in Syria, at public schools and events, it was our physical expression of unity and loyalty. It served as a gesture of allegiance, a promise from us to the country.

"Be ready to build and defend the unified Arab socialist community."
"Always ready!"

At the end of each response, we'd stomp our feet. Sometimes, still half asleep, we lacked the energy to give Jameela the resounding stomping she wanted. If she did not feel the earth shake under her feet, she would ask us to repeat the response until she was satisfied with our conviction.

Faded pages of *Al-Ba'ath* and *Tishreen*, the government-issued newspapers, patched up the broken panes of glass behind the rusted-wire-covered windows of our classrooms. The newsprint sheltered us from the wind and sun but never from the cold. We did not have electricity or heaters, and in winter, I kept my jacket on during class.

My private school in Damascus was cleaner. We had a pool filled with little balls where kids would pee, and as far as I knew, it had only one framed picture of President Hafez al-Assad, which hung in the principal's office. But in my new elementary school, his photos, words, and even stories about his childhood were a constant presence. Above the wide green chalkboard hung a large portrait of President Assad. On the opposite wall was a slogan in faded green Arabic calligraphy: "We are pioneers of the Ba'ath. We are the cubs of our lion." In Arabic, "Assad" means lion, so we, the children of Assad, were referred to as cubs.

DEFIANCE

. . .

WE WERE TOLD THAT, even in the winter, when he was our age, Baba Assad—Our Father Assad—used to walk miles and miles to school. Often, he would arrive with mud on his pants up to his knees. In other versions of the story, the mud reached as far as Assad's hips. It would take me years to learn that these tales were not true. Baba Assad attended school in the city of Latakia, not in the mountains. But at that point in my life, I believed that Assad had built these schools for us so we wouldn't suffer in the way he did.

As a third grader, I enjoyed the stories of young Baba Assad and his struggles to secure an education. They made me admire the president and how much he struggled for us. I saw not just the school but everything around me as his gift: the hospitals, the corniche, the park near my house, the streets, the sea, the immense blue sky arching over Jableh. I loved him so much that I would sometimes tear up when I saw him on television. My favorite clip was one of his visits to a school in a village near Jableh. He strode into the schoolyard wearing his military uniform. The children were lined up in rows as we were each morning, holding his picture, chanting and crying, "With blood and soul, we sacrifice ourselves for you, Hafez." The teachers were chanting, too. I loved this video and would fantasize about the president visiting our school one day.

However, we disliked these stories when they were used to admonish us for being late to class, missing homework assignments, or failing to memorize the lessons as well as our primary teacher, Nada, demanded of us. "You are ingrates! You have no excuse to not work as hard as he did," she would say. Most of the time, the shaming was directed toward the kids in the back rows.

Seating in Damascus was based on our height; because I was short, I sat at the front. In Jableh, I initially chose an empty seat in the back of the classroom because I was new. But when Nada found out I was Jawdat's daughter, I was enthroned in the front row, where I would continue to sit for the next four years of elementary school.

As the school year progressed, I realized that our seating followed one simple pattern: The smart, well-groomed kids were at the front, and the unkempt kids who kept their heads down, either sleeping or trying not to be noticed, were always in the back. Nada would say that the sight of these children right there in front of her would ruin her mornings. It didn't matter how often Nada slapped them, yelled at them, or reminded them of how thankless they were—they never changed. At that young age, it didn't occur to me that children whose parents worked long hours to make ends meet might not have the support they needed at home to keep up with homework and studying. In Syria's educational system, where a significant portion of learning occurred at home, those lacking parental involvement often fell behind.

And yet we benefited from this. Whenever someone shouted while Nada had her back turned, or one of us hid the chalk, the blame would unavoidably fall on one of the students in the back, and we would watch them be punished for our transgressions.

REGARDLESS OF WHERE WE SAT, we were all forced to suffer through the *Nationalist Socialist Education* textbook, which was mandatory in all Syrian public schools. When we were handed our copies at the beginning of each school year, the words "Nationalist Socialist Education" stood out in a pitiless black font against a gray background. Two flags appeared beneath the words: that of the Ba'ath Party and that of the Syrian Arab Republic, bound by an olive branch casting a shadow over a map of the Arab world.

A black-and-white smiling portrait of the president covered the first page. Inside, the book was divided into lessons, each representing the principles of the Ba'ath Party and its achievements. These lessons were structured around speeches the president had delivered, filled with quotations that would spill over from one page to the next, which we were required to learn word for word. We had to memorize definitions of democracy and instructions on how to build a strong and faithful population. We had to memorize what it meant to be a loyal citizen: Protecting the country, the Ba'ath Party, and our leader with our body and soul was an honorable duty. The lessons also covered Syria's constitution and the structure of our parliament, and listed the names of health facilities, schools, and dams built for us by the Ba'ath Party and our president.

One of the pictures included in the book was a snapshot of the president standing in a military uniform and sunglasses on the border of the Israeli-occupied Syrian Golan Heights, pointing at the Israelis—our enemies. When we reached this section of the book, Nada would explain to us that accounts of the killing of Jews in Europe were lies and these events had been fabricated by the United States to send Jews to Palestine.

She would tell us that Syria, under the leadership of Hafez al-Assad, was the last standing bastion against such lies in the Arab world. Later, we would read and memorize a poem about a teenage girl named Sana'a Mehaidli, known as "the bride of the South," a member of the Syrian Social Nationalist Party who, at the age of seventeen, blew herself up in a Peugeot filled with explosives as it passed an Israeli convoy in Jezzine, Lebanon. She was presented as a hero, an example to be followed. The fragments of her body lit our path to resistance.

At that age, I didn't understand the implications of any of this; I was more concerned with the daunting task of memorization. Missing a single word from one of the president's speeches would cost you the mark for the whole question. Mercifully, some quotations were only two lines, and we already knew them by heart because they were painted on the school's walls. Others were seemingly endless. I may have loved the president, but memorizing his words was torture.

I took my revenge by flipping back to the president's portrait on the first page. I would draw glasses around his eyes or doodle horns coming out from behind his bald head. When a kid from the year above me was caught doing the same thing, they sat him on a chair in the schoolyard and beat his bare feet with a thick wooden stick in front of the entire school.

"How dare you mock the man who built this school for you?" the teacher shouted. I held my breath, watching as the stick hit his feet.

Physical punishment was another thing that I had not encountered in my school in Damascus. But in Jableh, the threat of the stick was constant. "The stick is for those who disobey." These words were scrawled atop our blackboard, right under Baba Assad's portrait. There were two sticks for our twelve classrooms. Not knowing where the sticks were, the guilty students were forced to expose their upcoming punishment to all their peers by going from one classroom to the next, searching for the stick to bring back to the teacher. When the guilty student returned, the teacher would order them to step up to the podium and face the class so the rest of us could see what awaited if we misbehaved. The student would be asked to hold out their less-dominant hand, palm up, to receive the blows; striking the dominant hand would prevent the student from writing.

I felt the pain and shame of that stick throughout my elementary education, more times than I can remember. Fear pulsed through my nervous system as I waited alone, in front of my friends, my arm outstretched, hand trembling, defenseless. Waiting. Eyes shut tight. The rod hissing as it quickly cracked across my skin. I would squeeze my hand under my armpit in a vain attempt to numb the pain before the next round of blows—two, three, maybe even four or five, depending on the severity of the offense, ranging from drawing with colored chalk stolen from Principal Jameela's office to eating chips from a bag I'd hidden in my jacket. The sting would linger as I walked back to my desk and placed the bruised, puffed-up palm of my hand on the cold iron legs of my desk to ease the pain.

Sometimes, when the teacher didn't have time to fetch the stick, slapping was the quick alternative. It always followed the same ritual: Nada would remove the napkin she often kept in her fist to wipe away the chalk residue from her fingers. Then she would pull our ears a few times, swinging our heads left and right until we felt dizzy. This was followed by the sharp, stinging slap that sent pain radiating across the cheek as blood rushed to the surface. Occasionally, the imprint of her five fingers would remain visible for minutes afterward.

No one was above punishment. Nada, who was to be my main teacher through elementary school, slapped even her own daughter, who was in the same class, for forgetting her homework. When I pleaded with my mother to ask Nada to stop slapping me, she said I was not special; I was going to be treated like everyone else. Being Jawdat's daughter couldn't protect me in this instance. If anything, Nada doubled the punishment of those of us who sat in the front when we were caught red-handed. As Nada would explain: One misdeed by a clever person is graver than a thousand by those who wasted oxygen in the back of the room. So, when I saw the other child who doodled on the president's photo get punished, I ripped the graffitied page from my book and stuffed it into the bottom of my backpack. Once I got home, I tore it into tiny pieces and flushed it down the toilet.

LATER THAT WINTER, I witnessed my first "pledge of allegiance," the process by which, every seven years, all men and women over the age of eighteen voted on whether they wanted Hafez to remain in power for another term. There were never other candidates to choose from; ballots simply asked voters to check "yes" or "no." Our school was a designated election center.

On the appointed day, the school's halls were decorated with flags, portraits, and colorful ribbons hanging from the ceiling. Even though we had no classes that day, attendance was mandatory. We wore our full uniforms, including the little side caps with the Ba'ath Party logo. We lined up on each side of the schoolyard's rusty front gate to greet people as they came to vote, waving flags and portraits of the president. When a voter approached the gate, we opened our arms to welcome them, then clapped the Ba'ath clap: five claps in quick succession, then another five, then three more, and chanted, "We will sacrifice our blood and souls for you, Hafez!"

Inside the school building, Jameela encouraged us to observe the voting process in her office. Voters were gathered around two blue cardboard boxes, while others were standing by a white plastic table. The people at the table would record the voters' ID numbers on their ballots before sliding them into the blue boxes. I saw one voter write his name, then prick his thumb with a silver needle, marking his "yes" vote in blood. Another voter repeated the act, then a third and a fourth. The cheering coming from the office drew more kids in to see what was happening.

Days later, the election results were announced: 100 percent of Syrians had voted "yes." Hafez gave a speech congratulating the population for choosing what was best for the country. Our president, who had been in power for twenty-nine years already, would remain in the palace for another seven years.

IN THE WINTER, our apartment smelled of citrus and laundry detergent. My mother believed that oranges would strengthen our focus. She would set the peels on the heater until they wrinkled and turned black, saturating the air with their burnt sweetness.

But vitamin C never seemed to help me, though I am not sure what would have. I was always distracted. I would sit on my bed trying to study and forget about my homework as I gazed out the window. The sky would often be dense with clouds, giving way to downpours and thunderstorms. Sometimes, hail would hit the balcony like a drumroll, hammering away at the concrete. The electricity would often cut out, the lightning would flash through the window, and sheets of rain would blur my view of the building Grandmother Tamra owned across the street. Meanwhile, our clothes hung on a drying rack near the big heater, the rising steam filling the apartment with the sweet, floral scent of detergent.

Alia and I worked in separate rooms, one of us in the living room and the other in the bedroom, trying to memorize our lessons. Alia had always been a better student than me and incredibly fast at memorization. She would get angry when my mother wouldn't allow her to watch TV until I had finished my lessons. Sometimes, if my mother was napping, and we had written homework, Alia would do mine for me so we could be done and the three of us could watch TV together.

As in Damascus, the spirit of my grandfather Ali loomed over us. An enlarged photo of him and my mother hung in the living room. My grandfather was seated in a leather armchair, my mother leaning against him, smiling at the camera. The flash reflected off a small glass of some drink on the side table. I later learned that the photo was taken during one of the many parties my grandfather threw at their house in Damascus, where poets, politicians, and family friends would gather and talk until dawn.

Physically, my mother hadn't changed much since the photo was taken. She still had the same large eyes, short, light brown hair, and wide smile. I didn't inherit much of her appearance: My curly hair and round eyes and jaw often led people to liken me to my father.

On another wall of the room hung a beautiful oil painting of Istanbul, with the Bosporus and its small fishing boats presided over by a mosque, which had belonged to my grandfather Ali. My mother had promised Alia and me that she would take us to Istanbul when we were old enough and show us where her family had lived when Grandfather Ali was working at the Syrian consulate. She would take us to the places we heard about in the stories she had told us growing up.

My mother was a great storyteller. She talked nonstop about her life before my father, about her trips with Grandfather Ali, his warmth and intelligence, the food and the friends they enjoyed, and how happy she was then. At that time, I didn't appreciate how difficult it was for my mother to live in Jableh. She was almost always home—to the point that, throughout my childhood there, I never had to carry my own key. Besides Alia and me, she had no one. This isolation forged a deep, unhealthy, and unrealistic attachment between us. Whenever she visited my aunts, even though I knew she was just a building or two away, the separation anxiety felt unbearable. I would beg her not to go. Once she left, her absence felt like a knife slicing through my rib cage, making it nearly impossible to breathe. Alia would try to comfort me by pushing our living room sofas aside to create a large, open play area. "I am not going to be around forever," my mother would say after she came back, reminding me that I had to learn to cope with her absence.

One afternoon, in December of my fourth-grade year, once we'd had our after-school snack and given my mother the daily report of what had happened in school, she surprised us: For our winter break, the three of us were going to visit our father. It had been six years since we'd last seen him.

Jawdat had moved from Bulgaria to Ukraine, a country my mother described as blanketed in snow piles taller than me. In the days leading up to our trip, I was electrified with anticipation, barely sleeping. Besides the excitement of playing in the snow, which I had only seen on TV, I looked forward to seeing my father again and spending my tenth birthday with him. The blurry mental image I held of him would finally come into focus.

A week before our departure, the smell of grilling chicken filled the streets of Jableh. It was New Year's Eve. In Damascus, there was an official fireworks display, shot from the top of Mount Qasioun. In Jableh, people shot their own fireworks and lit sparklers on their balconies. I remember standing on ours, watching the air fill with gray smoke. In the distance, toward the mountains, we could see tracer bullets streaking across the darkness. My mother told us that people who couldn't afford fireworks smuggled from Lebanon discharged their guns instead.

That night, we went to Aunt Samia's house for dinner. For the first time, I saw my aunt wearing a dress—before that, I had only seen her either in a mismatched tracksuit or her house robe. Our upcoming trip to Ukraine was the main topic of conversation.

"You have to tell your father that I am your favorite!" Aunt Samia repeated over and over, pulling me close to her chest. Her hair spray was so strong I thought its fumes would suffocate me, and the glittery sequins on her collar scratched against my face.

She told Alia and me that this was our chance to reconnect with our father after so many years apart, and instructed us to hug him incessantly and kiss his hands and feet. "Think of your future," she said. We needed to remember that a girl's main asset was her reputation, and a girl with no father would never find a good husband. What Aunt Samia did not say, but surely very well knew, was that everything our father possessed would be divided at his death between Alia, me, and the men on my father's side of the family—his five brothers and their sons. To guarantee our inheritance, our father would need to explicitly state in writing how much he intended to leave us. Without these measures, the law would decide on his behalf, leaving our uncles and their sons with a claim to a significant portion.

Aunt Samia showed my mother magazine clippings of beauty products she wanted us to bring back from Ukraine. The most important item was something Samia had seen on television: soap that melts away body fat. "Just one wash, and the fat is gone!" Aunt Samia said. Then she handed my mother a small white triangle of densely packed paper and cloth: a charm she'd brought back from a recent trip to the Sheikh Ahmad shrine in Qurfays.

Of my father's four sisters, Aunt Samia was the most religious. When she wasn't swearing on the lives of her four children, Samia was swearing on the imams and sheikhs of the shrines. Whenever someone in the family found themselves in need or got sick, she would diagnose the problem as the result of an evil spell, and she always knew exactly the right sheikh in the right shrine to approach for help. If she wanted to lose weight, she would put her hand on a Quran and swear on the name of Imam Ali that she would refrain from eating bread.

When she broke her promise, succumbing to the aroma of the fresh loaves her husband brought home every morning from the bakery, she would go to the shrine to pay a kafara—a sacrifice of either cash or a sheep to be slaughtered by the shrine's caretaker in compensation for her sins.

I often went with Aunt Samia to the shrine—not to visit the sheikh's grave as I would with Grandmother Wadia, but to play in the shaded backyards connected to the shrine, where families would gather for generations. Thanks to its high elevation, it was always cooler there than in Jableh, and ideal for picnics. I was always fascinated by how the atmosphere outside the shrine remained lively and joyful, no matter how many people were weeping, pleading, and revealing secrets behind the shrine's doors. Tables were covered with grilled meat from freshly slaughtered animals, drink glasses were sweating, and music was blasting. Even class divisions seemed to melt away. Every Alawite, regardless of their family background, has memories of those childhood afternoons when the meat tasted better than any we would ever have later in life.

"If you manage to get your father to step over this charm three times,"

Aunt Samia said, now looking me in the eyes, "everything will change. This is your chance to reclaim your father." It was as if his absence from our lives was somehow our fault, not his, and it was up to us to correct it.

I REMEMBER BEING SHOCKED by how short the flight to Ukraine was. I had always thought the reason we didn't see my father was that he was very far away, but the trip only took three hours—shorter than the trip from Damascus to Jableh.

At baggage claim, a driver held up a piece of paper with our names. The car ride is a blur, but I recall that the snow along the road looked nothing like what I had imagined. It was dirty, almost black.

After an hour, we pulled up in front of a massive house on the outskirts of Odesa. The silhouette of a man, a lit cigarette in his hand, appeared in the orange glow of the open front door. My heart pounded, and I held my breath as the car slowed to a stop. As he stepped outside, the silhouette metamorphosed into an old, bald, three-dimensional man wearing brown slippers and a robe. He looked nothing like the portrait on my grandmother's wall.

My father dropped his cigarette on the stoop, crushed it, and extended his hand toward me so I could hop down from the car. Then he hugged me. I felt my puffy jacket flatten under his pressure. His robe was soft against my face and smelled of cigarette smoke. I had promised Aunt Samia I would kiss his hand, but in the moment, I couldn't bring myself to do it. I stared at my father as he hugged my mother and Alia. I noticed for the first time that my mother looked significantly younger than him.

His appearance didn't seem to fit with the voice I knew, and although I'd been told many times I looked like him, it wasn't the case at all. This can't be him, I thought. I was surprised to hear my own voice ask the question aloud before I could stop myself: "Are you really my father?"

My mother stared at me, her eyes wide, and bit her lower lip. Alia grabbed the man's hairy, wrinkled hand and kissed it. After a beat of silence, he laughed.

"Yes, unfortunately," he said. "I am your father."

FOR THE FIRST FEW DAYS of our visit, he was largely absent. Work was keeping him busy, he said. I didn't understand his job; I only saw his business cards lying around. Alongside his name was an image of a ship with the letter *M*, for Mrie. My father and uncles owned many ships that sailed between Tartus, Syria, and the port of Odesa, Ukraine. I never found out what was shipped from Odesa. All I knew was that one of my uncles in Syria was president of the Tartus Chamber of Commerce and Industry and had complete control over the free zone of Tartus.

At night, if my father wasn't busy working, he would invite us to have dinner in what he called "his section" of the house. This area was separated from our rooms by a large living room, a hallway, and multiple sets of stairs. The maid would come and place plates in silence, expertly navigating around the couch so as not to block Jawdat's view of the television. We would sit next to him as he chewed loudly and watched the news. I always felt a knot in my stomach, not knowing what to say to him. I remember him repeatedly asking if I visited his mother and whether I liked her more than our mother's mother. It was clear what the correct answer was. So, like a good daughter, I told him that Grandmother Tamra was my favorite.

ONE MORNING, MY MOTHER sent me to my father's section of the house to ask him if he would like to take us out for lunch. I tried to protest.

"He doesn't want to spend time with us," I said.

"He isn't used to having us here," my mother said. "We have to become part of his life. We have to make an effort."

Reluctantly, I walked through the living room, down the narrow hall, and up the stairs to my father's section of the house, stopping in front of the door to his room. He was wearing his glasses and reading through a stack of papers next to a big window overlooking the backyard, blanketed in white. I took a deep breath.

"Can you take us out for lunch?" I asked. My father lowered his glasses and gazed at me. His bald head shone in the bright sunlight. He stared at me so coldly for so long that I felt as if he were about to throw something at me. I stepped back and hid half of my body behind the door.

"Do you think I have time for this shit?" he said, erupting in anger. He yelled that my mother had turned me into a little sharmouta, a whore, teaching me about restaurants and wasting the money he sent us.

"I'm sorry," I said, lowering my eyes. "You're right." I slid out the door as quickly as I could and ran down the stairs, brimming with fury. It was all my mother's fault. Why did she make me go to him? It was even more humiliating than begging for money over the phone. Why did we even come here? I resolved that I would never speak to my father again, no matter what my mother said.

When I told her what had happened, she asked if I'd first kissed his hand. "He isn't used to having you and your sister around," she reminded me again. "You must approach him slowly. Be patient."

In the days that followed, she would hug me and tell me this was all for my future, that she wanted nothing but for us and my father to be in each other's lives.

AFTER THAT, MY FATHER stopped inviting us to dine with him. My mother told me I needed to apologize to make up for my mistake, but I refused. I had done nothing wrong.

Almost two weeks into the trip, my mother told me she had seen my father coming into the house with big white paper bags. "Maybe he has gifts for you," she said. My tenth birthday was coming up, and we were going to return to Syria in a few days. She insisted that I apologize to my father and try to connect with him again before we left. If I didn't, I might not receive my birthday gifts. Plus, she said, she had placed the charm Aunt Samia had given her under the doormat outside his room. The magic ought to be working by now. I never knew if my mother truly believed in Aunt Samia's spells or if she was simply desperate enough to try anything.

I was still reluctant, but my curiosity was piqued; I did want to see what my father had bought me. I wondered if my mother had told him that I wanted a remote-controlled car. My mother dressed me in the birthday outfit we'd brought from Syria, a red dress with little white teddy bears and thick white wool tights, in case he wanted to take us out after he gave me my gifts.

She made me recite the exact words I was supposed to say to my father: "Baba, I know you are busy, and may God bless your hands. But if you finish your work early, would you take us for dinner? I want to celebrate with you. It's my first birthday with us together."

I was nervous to bring up a restaurant again after what had happened, but I practiced these lines as my mother braided my hair, and when I was able to deliver them to my mother's satisfaction, I climbed the stairs again to my father's wing of the house. The maid saw me and said something in a language I didn't understand, but from the way she smiled, I suspected it meant I looked beautiful.

Scared, I stood on the brown doormat outside my father's door, feeling its coarse fabric through my wool socks, practicing my lines one last time in my head. Under the mat lay Aunt Samia's spell. Maybe it worked after all. I smoothed my dress, opened the door, and stepped into the room.

My father was in his bathrobe, talking on the phone, the TV blaring behind him. As I looked around the room, searching in vain for the bags my mother had mentioned, my father turned to me.

The way he looked at my dress remains burned in my memory after all these years. He slid his glasses down and, raising his eyebrows, tightened his lips as if he was holding back laughter. He placed his hand over the phone receiver. "Don't you know how to knock? And what is this you're wearing?"

Shame emptied my brain. I opened my mouth, but the words were trapped inside. The voice of the man on the television droned on as my father waited for me to speak. I felt my knees trembling. I tried again, but the words refused to come.

"Did your mother send you here to spy on me?"

"I am turning ten," I whispered. "It is my birthday. May God bless your hands."

"Do you think I have time for this?" He shouted so loudly that I took a step back. "Can't you see I am busy?"

From now on, he said, no one was allowed to enter his room. I should tell my mother that if we needed something, we had to call him first. Then he waved his hand, dismissing me.

On the other side of the door, my whole body shook. I was even more humiliated and angry than before. I suddenly realized that my mother had lied to me. There were no bags. She had tricked me into apologizing to him, and for what? It had only made things worse. I lifted the doormat and removed Aunt Samia's spell. By the time I reached the bottom of the stairs, I had ripped it to shreds.

FOUR

Six months later, in the summer of 2000, my mother, Alia, and I visited Aunt Khuzama, my mother's sister, in Prague, where she was working at the Syrian embassy.

Shortly after our arrival, I was in the small park behind my aunt's house collecting leaves to press and dry, planning to show them off at school as evidence of my trip. Most of my classmates had never left Jableh and its mountains. A few had traveled to Damascus and Aleppo, but I didn't know anyone who'd traveled internationally. I imagined myself on the first day of fifth grade, opening my bag and displaying the leaves on my desk. My classmates would gather around, asking how I got them. Then I would mention my summer in Prague, and they would be jealous because Wael Kfoury, a famous Lebanese singer, had shot his latest music video there. I couldn't wait.

Alia, then eleven years old, yelled from my aunt's balcony, interrupting my reverie.

"Come upstairs right now!"

DEFIANCE

I ignored her and continued filling my bag with leaves.

"Come upstairs," she yelled again. "Baba Assad has died." By the time I looked up, she had already disappeared inside.

I dropped the bag of leaves and sprinted up the stairs. A shiver ran through me as I entered the living room. My mother, my aunt, and Alia were all sitting on the edge of the couch, their eyes glued to the television screen. On Syrian state TV, a man in a gray suit was holding a white piece of paper, which trembled in his hands.

"He was our leader, our father, our brother, our comrade," he said. "Today, we are orphans. We all are orphans. We have lost our protector."

It didn't make sense. Hafez couldn't die. He doesn't die like the rest of us. He was stronger than death. The mere thought that he might be gone made me feel like a bad, unfaithful Syrian. We called him "the immortal," "the eternal." Even at that moment, the man in gray announcing Hafez's death on TV was referring to him as our "immortal leader."

I looked to my mother for reassurance. But her green eyes were filled with tears, fixed on the screen. She sat so still I couldn't tell if she was breathing. Next to her, Aunt Khuzama had covered her face with her hands, leaning back on the couch. I could hear Ibrahim, Khuzama's husband, weeping inconsolably in their bedroom. As the reality that the president had really died began to sink in, I started crying, too. Baba Assad was gone.

I would later learn that when the news broke, Alawite shopkeepers and families across Jableh packed whatever they could carry and drove up into the mountains again, fearing that Assad's death meant we were no longer safe. The streets were flooded with Syrians in mourning. Hafez was the only president anyone under thirty had ever known. Everyone in my generation remembers where they were when they found out the president had died. It was the first significant political event of our lifetimes.

The announcement ended, and a transmission to an emergency session of parliament began. The officials—who, I'd eventually come to understand, had all been granted their roles as the result of bribery or favors—were sniffling into their white handkerchiefs. One man was beating his chest with his fists. Eventually, the president of the parliament appeared on the screen and addressed the room, a portrait of the late president towering behind him. After expressing his devastation and sadness, he announced that the purpose of this session of parliament was to vote on a constitutional amendment. The minimum age to become the president of Syria was forty years old. Bashar al-Assad, the only person eligible to inherit the presidency, was only thirty-four. Half an hour later, 98 percent of parliament voted to pass an amendment that lowered the age restriction.

That night, Grandmother Wadia called us from Damascus and swore that Hafez's face appeared in the moon. Although Bashar's confirmation had already been scheduled to take place less than a month later, Syrian state TV encouraged Syrians to exercise their democratic rights by formally voting for the late president's son. Pundits said that Israel could attack Syria at any moment because Hafez was no longer in power, and that only his son, Bashar, could defeat Israel and all the imperialist powers combined.

Days later, voting centers opened. People stood outside waving pictures and flags while chanting, "Even if they mounted us on an iron spike, we would not choose anyone but Bashar." Inside, some voters, to emphasize their unwavering support, pricked their fingers with needles and marked their "yes" ballots in blood before casting them, as they had for Hafez.

Everyone had to vote, even Bashar himself. I watched him on TV pushing his way through the crowds at a voting center, surrounded by bodyguards. He placed his ballot into a box with his portrait hanging on the wall behind him. He left amid voters chanting, "We will sacrifice our blood and souls for you, Bashar." Banners hung in the streets and on every government building, congratulating the new president on his election well before the voting had concluded. When the results were announced, they showed that 99.7 percent of Syrians agreed that Bashar al-Assad should be the next president.

WE WERE BACK IN JABLEH when our new president appeared on TV and swore on the Quran to defend the country. He thanked the Syrian people for voting for him, stating that the trust and faith we had placed in him made him confident and hopeful for Syria's future, and that he would gladly follow our will.

He went on to say that, in a way, his mission would be easy, because his father, the immortal leader, had laid a solid foundation for Syria's future. On the other hand, it would be extremely difficult to replicate his father's extraordinary approach to governing. An hour into his speech, I started to worry that his remarks would appear in the next national education textbook. How could I possibly memorize all of this?

When my mother stood up and went to the kitchen, I changed the channel to Spacetoon. But I could still hear the president's voice; the whole neighborhood was watching the speech. Feeling guilty, I turned the channel back to the news.

As the president concluded his speech, the members of the parliament stood, clapped, and chanted. The camera followed him as he walked out of the building, surrounded by bodyguards. Crowds outside the parliament were chanting and crying. He waved to them and got into his black car.

The next day, shop windows were covered with portraits of the new leader. Families throughout the city hung banners adorned with quotations from Bashar's presidential address. Ours read, "We Are Beside Doctor Bashar on the Path of Reform!" We hung it between our balcony and my grandmother's roof across the street. In the lower right corner, it said, "Given by the Mrie Family."

I couldn't remember a time when the community had ever seemed so hopeful. Everywhere, shopkeepers, customers, and vegetable sellers discussed how much Syria would change, for the better, of course, under the new president's leadership. My neighbor said he'd heard we might even have a mall in Jableh. An expensive car with a Saudi plate was seen on the corniche. They must be investors, the neighbor said. They were going to fix the park near my house and install swings. I even heard that the internet would soon be available to all Syrians, since Doctor Bashar had been chairman of the Syrian Computer Society. I loved the new president.

A few weeks later, at Grandmother Tamra's house, my aunts Fadia and Samia were on the balcony, drinking maté out of tea glasses with metal straws and discussing why Bashar was still single. He was British educated, a doctor, tall with green eyes, and the son of Hafez. He was now the president of Syria. What was he waiting for? Samia wondered. He needed a good Alawite wife to support him. His father could never have done his job without his wife, Anissa. She looked to Aunt Fadia for her opinion on this important matter.

Aunt Fadia reasoned that Bashar had been busy since his brother Bassel died. Bashar didn't have time to think about marriage then or before. When he was in the UK, there were hardly any Alawites. Bashar couldn't marry just anyone. It was only a matter of time, Aunt Fadia said, before he drove to Qurdaha—fifteen miles from Jableh—to visit the graves of his father and brother; maybe he'd meet someone there.

"Qurdaha and the nearby villages are known for the beauty of their women. They all have fair skin. Some are even blonde." Or he would find the right one in Jableh, she said. "He comes here often."

Aunt Samia nodded. "Bashar was seen driving along Jableh's corniche last Saturday. All the women were talking about it."

"Exactly!" Fadia interjected. "He was driving on the corniche looking for a wife." Samia had never thought of that. Aunt Fadia paused. "What if while driving around Jableh, he saw Louly?" Fadia's daughter Leen, whom she affectionately called Louly, was beautiful. "Any man would kill to be with her," Fadia said. Samia nodded in agreement, both of them brightening at the thought of it.

"Think of how many black Mercedes will line up outside the house when Bashar and his mother come to ask the family for Leen's hand," Fadia said, pointing all the way down to the next block. Samia and I followed her finger.

"Everyone will know that the president is in our house," Fadia said, imagining how jealous my uncles' wives would be to learn that Bashar was going to marry one of her daughters and not one of theirs. Fadia might even get a Mercedes herself.

We listened in silence. I pictured Bashar with his long legs sitting on the yellow sofa under my father's picture. Our new president would sit next to the TV, the big loquat tree behind him in the window.

"No!" Aunt Fadia exclaimed suddenly, slamming her glass down on the silver tray. "I will not allow it. Not before Louly finishes ninth grade at least."

Samia agreed. "Even if you accepted, Leen's father would never give his permission," she said. She reminded Fadia that her daughter hadn't even gotten her period yet; Leen was ten years old.

LATER THAT FALL, when I had been in fourth grade a couple of months, Aunt Samia moved into Grandmother Tamra's house. My grandmother's health was declining, and she couldn't remember her medication or administer injections by herself. Often, before I'd even had a chance to change after school, my mother would ask me to run across the street to deliver a plate of whatever food she had cooked that day to Aunt Samia.

Most days, my aunt would ask me to eat with her at the kitchen table to keep her company; she didn't want to eat alone. Although I hated the smell of my grandmother's kitchen and disliked how Aunt Samia often planted a kiss on my cheek, leaving behind a revolting smear of sticky, wet grease, I never let my disgust show. My mother had taught me always to be kind to my aunts and show them respect. By that age, I listened, and often I would have my post-school meals at my grandmother's.

One afternoon as we were eating, there was a knock at the door. I ran to open it and found a woman with a baby in her arms. She said she was a tenant of Oum Jawdat, my grandmother, and that she wanted to see her. I had learned that when a renter showed up asking to see my grandmother, it meant that they were not going to pay.

"Whose daughter are you?" the woman asked.

"Jawdat's," I answered.

She hugged me and said that I must be my grandmother's favorite. I walked her to my grandmother's bed and returned to the kitchen. As I was sliding into my chair, I could hear the woman weeping loudly, almost performatively. I looked at my aunt. "Why is she crying?" I asked.

"Crocodile tears," Aunt Samia said, shoving a slice of tomato into her mouth. She reminded me that I was ten years old and should know by now that if I believed everyone, I would have a very hard time in life. "This woman hasn't paid the rent in months. She thinks she is smart enough to scam Grandmother. But she is wrong. Grandmother is sick, yes, but she is still sharp as a fox."

A few months earlier, the woman had claimed that her husband, who worked as a construction worker in Lebanon, had fallen from a building and broke both his legs. This was her excuse for not paying rent. We heard the door slam and Aunt Samia rushed toward Grandmother Tamra's room.

"She says her husband has to put metal in his legs, but I can tell from her eyes that she's lying," my grandmother said, her voice shaking with anger.

DEFIANCE

"This is not good for your blood pressure. Please calm down," Aunt Samia said, stroking Grandmother's leg.

"Bla marba!" my grandmother shouted. I had never heard her voice that loud before. "No honor, no honor. If this was true, she'd be calling from Lebanon where she'd be taking care of her husband. What is she doing here? Every month she comes up with a new excuse. She says she can't leave because her children go to the school nearby."

"She is a whore!" my aunt said. Then she begged my grandmother to take deep breaths. "The doctor told you not to get angry. Trust me, I will deal with her."

My aunt pulled something from the medicine bag and told me to bring some water with a few drops of rosewater to calm Grandmother Tamra down. I was scared. I had never seen my grandmother this angry.

"She is a snake! She knows we can't do anything, or people will say we're kicking some poor woman and her children out onto the street," Aunt Samia exclaimed. She placed a pill into Grandmother's mouth, who then allowed her head to sink back into her pillow as she closed her eyes. I felt sad that people were taking advantage of my grandmother because of her illness.

WEEKS PASSED, AND I mostly forgot about the woman and the entire drama. My mother, Alia, and I were watching television when we heard screaming outside. My mother quickly muted the television, and the three of us listened closely to try to figure out what was happening.

"This is your Aunt Samia's voice!" my mother exclaimed, jumping from the couch. She hurried to her bedroom, rolled up the wooden jalousie shade, and the three of us stepped onto the balcony. From there, we could see Aunt Samia in her bedroom robe with a few policemen standing beside her. Neighbors were watching from almost every balcony on the street.

"What happened?" my mother shouted down.

"We are doing this to protect our children," Aunt Samia said, looking up and shading her eyes from the bright light of the streetlamp.

"There is no one inside! Please, I beg you!" The woman I had seen at my grandmother's house was trying to kiss Aunt Samia's hand. Aunt Samia yanked her hand away. "We don't want you ruining the reputation of our neighborhood."

"There was no one inside! I swear!" The woman was weeping.

We found out later that Aunt Samia had called the police to report complaints from neighbors in the building that the tenant was turning my grandmother's property into a whorehouse.

I was horrified. I had heard my aunt promise my grandmother she'd take care of it, but I never thought it would be like this. When I told my mother what I had witnessed, she started to cry.

"Isn't she terrified of how horrible she is? Isn't she concerned about her horrible behavior?"

Not long after, we watched the woman and her family pack their belongings in a truck and drive away. A new family moved in, and everyone on the street seemed to forget her and what had happened. If anything, my aunt was praised for protecting our neighborhood. But something shifted in my mother in the weeks that followed. She stopped sending plates of food with me to Aunt Samia. When she called, my mother would not pick up. And I didn't mind; I preferred to eat in the warmth of my home, not in my grandmother's kitchen with Aunt Samia.

I SPENT MOST DAYS after school in third and fourth grade playing with my cousins, Leen and Lama, Aunt Fadia's two daughters. Their phone number was the first one I memorized in Jableh, even before my home number. My mother never minded. It reassured her that we were finding our place in the large family we had abruptly become a part of.

DEFIANCE

One day after school, Lama called and asked if I was alone. I assured her that there was no one else around. "Good," she said. She told me her neighbor, Suliman, whose family rented their apartment from my grandmother and whose father was a construction worker in Lebanon, could get us real live Pokémon characters.

"He asked me what I wanted, and he said his father will bring it back with him on his next trip to Jableh," she said, and advised me not to tell my mother because she would tell Aunt Fadia.

"Of course, I won't," I whispered. My mother hated the idea of having pets. She always said she didn't need more chores because she knew whatever pets we got would become her responsibility.

"I will hide the ball inside my clothes," I said, and my cousin said she was going to do the same. We should be smart, we decided, and avoid Pokémon characters that spray water or spit fire, which would be extremely difficult to hide. We were not professionals yet; we might end up burning down our houses.

That night, when my mother was busy cleaning up the kitchen, I brought out my brown clay piggy bank, wrapped it in my comforter, and hit it against the wall as quietly as I could. I counted out 400 liras in coins and small bills and stuffed them deep into a sock. The next morning at school, I found Suliman.

"I want Pidgeotto. The flying one," I said, holding out the sock.

"Good choice!" Suliman whispered. "Pidgeotto's the best." He slipped the 400 liras into his jacket.

The week dragged on. I woke up each morning counting the days left until Suliman's father returned. When the day arrived, Suliman said his father had to postpone his trip. A few more days passed, and still I heard nothing, so I called him. "Tomorrow," I demanded, and he promised to meet me after school.

That afternoon, Suliman was indeed waiting for me at the rusty gate, but his hands were empty.

"On his way to Jableh, the car got into an accident, and the balls rolled down the street, and all the Pokémon escaped." He swore on his life and his little sister's life that this was true.

I was furious. "I want my four hundred liras back," I said.

"Impossible! My father bought them, but they escaped. I don't have the money."

I remembered what Aunt Samia said: that if I was scammed, it would be on me. Smart people don't get scammed; only the stupid ones do, and I refused to be one of them.

"If you don't give me my money tonight, I will tell my grandmother to kick you, your mother, and your sister out of your house," I threatened.

Suliman's eyes widened. "Please don't do this," he pleaded.

"I will do it," I said. "If you don't give me back my money."

Starting to cry, Suliman turned and ran home. I watched his yellow backpack bouncing up and down behind him.

LATER THAT DAY, I was in my room doing my homework when my mother opened the door so hard it hit the wall and bounced back. "What did you say to Suliman?" she shouted, hands on hips, glaring at me.

"Suliman? Who is Suliman?" I hoped I was convincing enough.

"Aunt Fadia's neighbor!"

"I didn't say anything."

My mother strode over to my bed, took hold of my hair, and pressed my face into my book, the paper soft against my nose.

"Don't lie to me!" she shouted.

"He stole four hundred liras from me, and I have no money left." I pushed her hand away, opened my closet door, and took out the pieces of broken clay. "He stole my money!"

"You told him you were going to kick him out of his house? You are just like your aunt!" she screamed as she yanked a clothes hanger from my closet and hit me with it so hard it left stinging welts and bruises on my arms. "If you ever threaten anyone again, I will burn your tongue with a lighter." She forced me to call Suliman and apologize.

That night, my mother stayed in the kitchen. I opened the door and found her crying. Thick streaks of cigarette smoke hung in the still air.

"I apologized to Suliman. What else do you want me to do? Stop crying!" I begged.

"Get out and close the door behind you," she whispered.

It took a while for her to reemerge from the kitchen. Then she told me something I had never heard her say before. She said that she had brought us here because she thought it would be better for our upbringing, but she was mistaken.

FIVE

In late fall 2001, when I was in fifth grade and Alia in sixth, the phone rang as we were eating dinner with our mother in front of the TV. I quickly set my plate down, jumped from the carpet, wiped my hands, and answered the call. It was my father.

"What are you doing?" he asked.

"We're eating dinner," I answered. "Chards and onions with lemon."

"Can I join you? I'm hungry."

"By the time you get here, we won't have any food left."

My mother stood up and tapped her hand on her mouth to silence me.

"I mean, you should come! Mama will make more. But I have school tomorrow, and I'll be asleep by the time you arrive."

My mother's eyes widened, and she started gesturing at me aggressively. Without another word, my father hung up. The moment I replaced the phone on its cradle, my mother began to shout at me from across the room.

"You are so disrespectful! Your father is trying to be nice, and you embarrassed him. Call him back and say you're sorry," she said. I refused.

Since our visit to Ukraine, my father had sent money more regularly, but he rarely called. I had a feeling that he had decided we were not good enough for him. Aunt Samia said that it must have been something we did or said, and that she was disappointed we had ruined our chance with him. In private, though, my mother insisted that my father's attitude had nothing to do with us.

"Of course he loves you! There isn't a father who does not love his daughters," she would say, reminding us that, unlike her, my father was not used to having Alia and me around, and that he was old and had a bad temper. She also told us that he had paid for the tickets to Ukraine; he clearly wanted us there, even if he wasn't good at expressing it. (Later, I realized that this was not the case—my mother had sold a piece of gold she had saved to buy the tickets.)

"I forbid you to eat until you apologize," my mother said. I started crying.

When the phone rang again, my mother picked it up. I heard my father's voice, but it wasn't coming from the phone. It came from outside our front door.

"He's here. My father is here!" I said, wiping my tears with my sleeves. In one leap, I opened the door. There was my father, hunched over a dark leather suitcase with a cell phone to his ear, still talking to my mother on the line a few feet away.

"I thought you were going to sleep?" he said, opening his arms for me. "I came here to see you." As we hugged, I grabbed his hand and kissed it. I was still processing what had just happened, wondering if my mother had been right all along, that he did love us and only needed time to adjust.

"Allah yerda aliki," he said. "May God bless you." Then he lifted his suitcase and entered our apartment for the first time ever. He embraced my mother and scanned the home she had made for us.

I followed his gaze. My books and notebooks were scattered on the floor. The tray of food was on the carpet. Our laundry was drying on a rack near the heater. I'd always found our home pretty and its smell comforting, but at that moment, seeing it through my father's eyes and comparing it with his opulent home in Odesa, it seemed ugly and embarrassing. With my frizzy hair and ink-stained pajamas, I was no better.

But it didn't matter. Watching him bring his bag inside and close the door behind him made me happy. It was what my mother always wanted: the four of us reunited at home in Syria.

UNFORTUNATELY, IT ONLY took a few days to realize this arrangement would be no easier than the others. Though I understood by then the importance of having a father in our lives, his presence quickly began to feel like a punishment I did not deserve.

Alia and I could no longer do our homework in the living room, nor could I watch my new favorite cartoon, *Detective Conan*, a Japanese show dubbed into Arabic. My father had taken over the living room couch, where he began spending his entire day. He didn't even watch TV; his ear was always glued to the telephone. He would shout angrily in French and Russian. When he spoke Arabic, I caught fragmented phrases about money, ships, and papers being signed or not signed. Sometimes, he would slam down the phone so hard I worried it would break.

When he was upset, we knew we should just steer clear of him and hide in our rooms. Just like when we were in Ukraine, whenever he ate dinner with us, it was across from the TV, and we had to chew as quietly as possible so as not to disturb him. With my father there, home no longer felt like home. We couldn't relax or be ourselves. Even when we tried to do everything right, we always seemed to have done something wrong.

"I should have stayed with one of my brothers," he would exclaim for the smallest reasons, like my mother forgetting that he only ate his eggs sunny-side up or the fact that we didn't have central heating.

My mother never responded to these outbursts or attempted to defend herself. "The big bowl fits the small bowl," she would tell us—being the bigger person and not letting an argument escalate is always better than shouting back.

But one day, she broke her own rule. Their fight began when my father saw my mother hanging his clothes on the rack near the heater. Though he had been staying with us for two weeks at that point and should have realized we didn't have a dryer, he was upset that his clothes wouldn't be ready in time for his next appointment.

"I have to leave in an hour!" he shouted. He called my mother the worst whore the earth had ever seen.

At first, my mother remained silent. She set up the ironing board and spent the next half hour sobbing, hunched over the hot iron, attempting to dry the clothes he needed.

Meanwhile, from his spot on the couch in the living room, my father called Aunt Samia and, in a very loud voice, told her how much he regretted staying with us. It seemed like Aunt Samia was agreeing with him, which only stoked the flames of his anger. He called my sister and me brats, complaining that he never once saw us doing dishes or chores. He accused my mother, who was just a few feet away, of spoiling us and making us believe we could become successful in life if we went to school and studied.

At that moment, my mother threw his clothes on the floor and told him to dry them himself. "I am not your maid," she said. "You should go and stay at your brother's house if that's what you want to do." I had never seen her so furious.

He yanked the phone off the wall by its cord and threw it at her. She ducked, and it crashed into the wall behind her. He stood up and launched himself toward her. Alia and I started screaming, sure he was going to hit her. But my mother stood her ground, shouting that he must talk about her daughters with respect.

"I didn't raise them just for you to come and insult them in front of people," she yelled. I was horrified. I had never seen my mother speak to him this way. She didn't flinch, even when he was just inches from her face. Then he bent down, picked up the half-dry clothes from the floor, and got dressed.

Before he left, he shouted at her that he didn't know if he was coming back for dinner or if he was coming back at all. Then he slammed the door so hard the whole apartment shook. My mother wept through the evening, smoking one cigarette after another. I kept going to the stove to light them for her. I hoped his threat was sincere and that he would never return.

"Do you love Baba?" I asked her later that night as she set a place for him at the dinner table, still hoping he was on his way.

"Of course," she said. "He loves us, too. He's just angry. He has a temper." When I told her we shouldn't let him back in, she told me to be quiet.

In retrospect, I wonder if there were deeper reasons, emotional ones, beyond the financial support and the societal stigma faced by fatherless Syrian girls, that made her so determined to keep him in our lives. Perhaps my mother had once glimpsed the genuinely loving side of my father and clung to the hope that it might reemerge. At the time, though, it was unfathomable to me that he could ever have brought her happiness.

Despite everything, she remained hopeful; I could hear it in her voice when she came into our room to see if we were awake when he returned later that night. She asked us to get up to kiss our father's hand and welcome him home. I pretended to be asleep.

My father stayed with us until the end of that year. Though I still resented the space he occupied in our home and how he treated my mother, I must admit that his presence had some tangible benefits. When I brought home my report card that December, just as the semester was about to end, for the first time in my life I had the opportunity to choose which of my parents would sign, and I chose for it to be my father.

As a reward for my good scores, he gave me two 500-lira bills. My daily allowance in fifth grade was ten liras. My mother tried to take the money from me, saying that going to school with huge bills would hurt the feelings of poorer students.

At school the following day, I couldn't stop smiling. I kept my signed report card open on my desk. I wanted everyone to see my father's signature.

JUST BEFORE NEW YEAR'S EVE, my father announced that he would not be returning to Ukraine. Instead, he planned to stay in Syria and live in the mountain villa he'd built for his mother, which she had used as a summer house until her health worsened.

"You and your sister will have an entire floor in the villa. You can visit me on weekends whenever you want," he told us.

This seemed like the best possible outcome. It was a relief to finally reclaim our home, our routines, the scattered orange peels on the heater, and our personal space, but we could also visit our father. His presence in our lives wouldn't force us to give up our home anymore; at last, we might have found the right balance.

Less than a month later, we took our first trip to my father's new home. He called one morning and said it had been snowing all night. He knew his little Loubna loved snow.

"Would you like to spend the day here and stay for the night?"

"Of course!" I answered without hesitation, even though my sister and I had never spent a night alone with our father. By the time I hung up the phone, my mother was packing a small bag, and Alia was digging through our socks and gloves, trying to find two matching pairs.

About an hour later, my dad honked outside the entrance to our building. Alia sat up front and I climbed into the back. We drove up into the highlands. As we ascended, patches of snow appeared on the mountainside, growing deeper and fresher, eventually covering the road and weighing down the pine trees. Gusts of wind caught freshly fallen flakes and cast them into the air.

We drove through the string of villages that we passed on our way to visit Grandmother Tamra in the summertime. But now, our father slowed down to point out surnames of families Alia and I didn't recognize and explain who they were and how they were connected to us. I understood for the first time the true essence of a village, of a hometown in the Alawite mountains, where our family had lived for generations and where it seemed like everyone was somehow related.

He put on music and started singing along in French. I hid my face behind Alia's seat, poked her from behind, and chuckled. When he noticed we were snickering, he sang louder and turned up the volume. His eyes smiled at me in the rearview mirror as we laughed louder. I had never seen my father so happy and carefree. I felt I was finally catching a glimpse of what it was that my mother had loved about him.

He parked the car on a bluff overlooking a valley dotted with patches of olive trees, and we got out. I kneeled and dug my fingers into the snow, feeling the same cold burn I'd felt in Ukraine.

"Look down!" my father said, gesturing at a grove of pine trees hundreds of feet below us. "That's the village's spring. Its soul. The water in our mountains is sacred. People here live longer thanks to it."

I asked if we could drive down and see the spring, but he explained that the road was too dangerous in the snow. If we wanted to see it, we'd have to walk down.

"Our ancestors used to walk this road every morning," he told us, "filling sheep- or donkey-skin sacks with water and climbing all the way back uphill with the loads on their heads. This spring was their only source of water. You should be grateful you're living in different times now. You don't understand how hard life was for your great-grandparents."

He reminisced about coming here with his brothers in the summer, building small dams with rocks to cool peaches and pears while they swam. "I've seen the most beautiful lakes in France, but nothing compares to this water. This spring. I've missed it."

"What else did you miss?" I asked, hoping he would mention us. To my surprise, he started tearing up. I watched him gaze up at the mountain, sucking on the plastic filter of his cigarette. In that moment, he suddenly seemed old, broken, and weak.

My mother was right. My father was cold and mean sometimes because he'd lived away for too long. I couldn't imagine how hard it must have been for him to leave behind my grandmother, his eight younger siblings, and these mountains he loved so much.

"Muhammara on saj!" he exclaimed. "There is nothing like the taste of the fresh bread with olive oil. No meal in this world compares to muhammara on saj, especially when it's made with oil from these olives." He swept his hand across the rolling olive groves.

"Three hundred thousand olive trees," he said.

"All of them?" I asked. He nodded, his eyes still fixed on the valley. I gazed at the trees and realized for the first time how rich we were. I didn't know anyone else whose family had thousands of olive trees securing their future.

IT WAS ALMOST SUNSET when we arrived at the house. On the third floor, which Alia and I would occupy, was a master bedroom with a massive terrace overlooking the mountains. In the kitchen, my father threw steaks in a heated pan, causing a puff of steam and grease to rise. He said he was going to have to teach us how to cook since my mother wouldn't, and showed us how to make his favorite salad. We were not young anymore, he added; in the blink of an eye, we would be housewives ourselves, and we needed to know these things. We peeled garlic cloves, smashed them, and mixed them with diced tomatoes, a wild purslane we call bakleh, lemon, and olive oil.

After dinner, my father sat down in front of the television, rested his leg on an ottoman, leaned his head back, and closed his eyes. He told us he was in pain and sent me to get a blue tube of cream from his bedside table. Then he lifted his gray woolen pants, revealing a circle of dark, wrinkled skin in the middle of his left thigh, and began massaging the cream into it. Alia and I exchanged a glance, our eyes widening slightly in surprise. We had never known he had such a hideous scar.

"Does it hurt?" I asked.

"Only in the cold," he said.

LATER THAT EVENING, after we had made our bed, we called our mother to tell her how great the day had been.

"I told you!" she exclaimed. "Your father loves you."

We turned off the lights. I lay my head on the pillow and closed my eyes but couldn't sleep; the sharp taste of garlic from the salad lingered in my mouth. I stood up and searched our bag and the bathroom cabinets for toothpaste but couldn't find any.

"Are you asleep?" I poked Alia.

"Yes."

"No, you're not! Can you please come downstairs with me? I need toothpaste."

"It's late. Can't you just go to sleep? Stop being annoying!" She pulled the pillow over her head.

Throughout our childhood, I never understood how Alia managed to fall asleep the second she laid her head down. I kept staring into the darkness, feeling the itch of the garlic in my mouth, until I finally rolled out of bed.

The cold marble under my feet made me shiver as I padded downstairs to my father's floor. I turned the handle to his door at the bottom of the stairs, but it wouldn't open. I pushed harder. Nothing. The automatic lights in the stairwell turned off. I leaned with all my weight and pushed the door one more time.

Suddenly, it flew open. I tumbled onto the floor, falling right at my father's feet. I looked up and saw a silver gun pointed at my forehead. I felt the cold radiating from the metal between my eyes.

"Ylaan Rabik!" my father screamed so loudly that it filled the dark hallway and reverberated off the walls of the stairwell. "Fuck your god. I almost shot you!"

"I'm so sorry!" I said, my voice shaking. "I only wanted toothpaste!"

My father lowered the gun. It clicked.

"Come," he said, sighing, and walked to his bathroom. I picked myself up off the ground and followed him. He placed the gun on top of a cabinet. I avoided looking at it. His wrinkled hands trembled as he shuffled through packs of razors and soap. Finally, he handed me a spare tube of toothpaste.

"Keep it upstairs," he said.

I didn't tell my mother about the gun. I worried she might be disappointed in me for ruining our time with our father yet again. I was surprised and relieved the next morning when he didn't yell, only quizzed us on what he had taught us the night before about how to make his favorite salad, telling us we should memorize all of his favorite dishes if we wanted to visit him more often, which he knew we did.

LOUBNA MRIE

. . .

As pleased as my mother was with the outcome of this first visit, our trips to the mountains were often fraught and overshadowed by obligation. My mother continued to make us call our father at the end of each month to remind him that he was supposed to send us money for the next month like he'd promised. When he wouldn't answer, my mother would call my uncles and ask for their help. Embarrassed that his brothers knew he was shirking his responsibilities, my father would lose his temper and shout that we were the ones embarrassing him. Then he'd demand that we visit him immediately to apologize before giving us a single lira, even if it was a school night.

On these occasions, I would go alone to retrieve the money so that Alia, who was an excellent student, wouldn't have to miss school. While my sixth-grade classmates were learning, I would spend the day alone watching television until my father returned home. As much as I dreaded my lessons, being trapped alone at my father's house with nothing to do and no one to talk to was even more miserable.

Some nights, when he was miraculously in a good mood, we would talk or play cards. I would let him win so we could finish quickly, and he'd give me the money so I could get back home in time for school the next day.

Other nights, he would suddenly erupt in an inexplicable rage. I found myself apologizing for things I did not know were out of bounds, like flushing the toilet upstairs during the night or eating too fast. On those evenings when he was, in his words, too angry to be around me, he would ask me to grab his coat from his closet because he was leaving again, meaning I would have to stay over again and miss another day of school.

One night, after dinner, when my father asked me to retrieve his coat from his closet, I spotted a few rifles leaning against the wall. At the sight of their gray metal barrels and the dark cherry wood of the gunstocks, my heart dropped. I felt the same icy fear I had felt staring into the barrel of his silver handgun. I gave my father his wool coat with trembling hands. I thought I had buried my terror, but it seemed to have nested somewhere in my body.

Over time, though, my fear of the guns dissipated. Eventually, the knowledge that my father owned them and knew how to use them made me feel powerful, somehow. I felt the same way when I heard my father get angry with someone on the phone and say, "I will let you walk in your son's funeral!" When his anger was directed outward, and not at our family, I could admire his strength and view him as a protector.

I did not know then that this was no idle threat—it would be years before I understood that my father's ability to end lives was what had lifted him and his brothers out of poverty. Back then, sensing that my father was someone to be feared made me proud to carry his name. When I learned that the scar on his thigh was from a gunshot, I asked him repeatedly to show it to me. I even told my friends at school about it. I didn't need to investigate the details of his work; I was proud just knowing that he was important enough for someone to have tried to kill him.

SIX

In the summer of 2002, as I had finished the sixth grade and was about to enter seventh, broader societal expectations for maturity and responsibility became more pressing. Schools transitioned from mixed classrooms to segregated ones—a time, my father said, when my actions would be noticed and could bring shame to his name.

In my effort to prove I was a good daughter, I felt obligated to visit my grandmother Tamra, though by this point, her health was declining rapidly, and she did not seem to know who I was. Sometimes, as I sat by her bed, she would ask who I was, and when I said "Loubna," she looked confused. But when I said "Jawdat's daughter," she would nod. Other times, she mistook me for Ali, the only son of my uncle Wahib, my father's brother who had become the president of the Tartus Chamber of Commerce and Industry. My grandmother worshipped my father, but Ali and Uncle Wahib were everyone else's favorites.

Twice a year, on the first day of each Eid, our whole family would gather at my grandmother's house to kiss her hand. I don't recall much of those days, but I distinctly remember the atmosphere crackling whenever Uncle Wahib stepped into the room. My aunts would rush toward him, eager to kiss his hand and compliment his wife's clothes, lavishing his children with kisses—Ali, in particular, would receive prayers for a long life.

On these occasions, we would receive Eidiyah, a sum of money from my uncles, after wishing them a happy Eid. Uncle Wahib always handed out the thickest wad of cash. I remember one Eid, standing just outside my grandmother's door and counting my bills. It was 18,000 liras—6,000 of which were from Uncle Wahib alone.

But outside the family's walls, I was confronted with questions about him that I did not know how to answer. In school, kids would ask me if I knew that Wahib was a welder who never finished ninth grade and couldn't read. I often told these kids to shut their mouths or told the teachers they were insulting me. In truth, although I knew my family had been poor just a generation ago, I didn't know the details of their rise to prominence; all I knew was that I had to defend the family name.

When I asked my father if the rumors about Uncle Wahib were true, he burst out with fury and demanded to know who was saying such things.

"Some kids at school I don't know," I said, vaguely. "They commute from the villages."

My father nodded. "Poor people are just jealous of us."

I accepted this. Who cared if my uncle had dropped out of school? By that time, he monopolized the steel market in Syria and was referred to as the king of steel. His factory and ships provided work for hundreds of young men and women with college degrees. "May God bless his hands" and "He never turned away anyone in need" were phrases repeated whenever I mentioned my full name and was asked if I was related to Wahib. Then they would pray for his and Ali's health, just as my aunts did.

Though Ali and I had grown closer thanks to the time we spent together at our grandmother's, certain aspects of his attitude unnerved me. He seemed to move through the world with impunity. As soon as he wanted something, it seemed to appear; it was as if the rules that governed the rest of us didn't apply to him. When I was with Ali, whatever food he was craving would magically appear, delivered by his family's driver; we could summon a car at any time to take us wherever we wished.

On one particularly memorable night, Ali declared he wanted to go to the amusement park, though it was after hours and surely closed. I watched in fascination as his driver stepped out of earshot to make a phone call. Twenty minutes later, we were through the park gates, finding that all the park's attractions were up and running just for us to enjoy for as long as we wanted.

Later, still buzzing from the spinning rides and the bumper cars, I asked Ali how this was possible.

"I am the son of Wahib Mrie, and no one says no to me," he said.

Over time, I began to realize that Ali didn't quite view me and his sisters as his friends—we were more like toys for him to play with. His favorite game involved picking chewed food from between his teeth and flicking it into our hair. One night, when his sister Heba refused to participate, he locked us out on the balcony, went inside, and turned off the lights. She shouted to the guards for help, but they ignored her. When we realized Ali wasn't coming back and intended to leave us outside all night, Heba began screaming as loud as she could and threatening to break the glass, until the neighbors turned on their lights and came out onto their own balconies.

Ali stalked back into the room and opened the door, but once Heba was inside, he tackled her to the ground and pressed her head under his

DEFIANCE

foot while he ranted and berated her, calling her hideous names. The maid watched as Ali pulled Heba's hair and beat her but did nothing to intervene, remaining silent until his tirade was over. When their mother learned what had happened, she was more concerned that the neighbors had been disturbed than about whether her daughter was seriously injured.

After that incident, I kept my distance from Ali. It was fun to pretend that I, too, was above the rules when I was in his good graces, but now that I had a taste of what it was like to be on the receiving end of his cruelty, I was afraid of him. My mother told me that I was old enough to know my worth and reassured me that I didn't have to be friends with anyone who treated people the way Ali did, no matter what the rest of the family might say. I stopped returning his calls.

GRANDMOTHER TAMRA DIED a few weeks later. It was my first genuine encounter with death, a concept I had never truly grasped before, and it was surreal. One day she was there, the next her bed was empty. I felt guilty for not visiting her more often in her final weeks while I was avoiding Ali.

At the wake, Aunt Samia interrogated me about why Ali and I weren't friends anymore. When I told her I was afraid of him because of what I saw him do to Heba, she scoffed, claiming that boys simply play rougher. I should consider myself lucky that Ali had taken an interest in being my friend; he was the family's favorite, after all, and here I was making a big deal about nothing. Out of love and respect for Uncle Wahib and his only son, I should forget that anything had ever happened and apologize for ignoring Ali.

Though it infuriated Aunt Samia, I refused. My mother's words had given me courage and comfort; I was beginning to understand that I had the power to say no, even to the men in my family. Still, I hated how worthless and small I felt. I hated being a girl. I knew that things would have been different if I were a boy. It didn't matter what had happened that night; Ali was a boy, and Heba and I were just girls. We all shared the same last name, but only Ali could pass it on. Only he mattered. My being a girl was probably why my grandmother didn't remember me as I sat by her deathbed day after day. I wasn't significant enough to be etched into the part of her memory where precious boys were imprinted. At that moment, I hated my grandmother so much that I wished she had died sooner.

After my grandmother died, my uncles inherited her house and the rental properties my aunt Samia had managed for years. They sat vacant. Syrian law entitles male relatives to inherit twice as much as their female counterparts. With six brothers whose claims came ahead of theirs, my four aunts, despite their struggles to make ends meet, received almost nothing.

As Alia and I grew from girls into teenagers, the importance of securing our inheritance, our werteh, became ever clearer to us and we knew we had to keep our father happy to protect our future. And he was aware of this dynamic, and took advantage of it. Whenever an argument grew heated, no matter its cause, he would invoke the werteh and threaten to cut us off. Anytime I had the urge to oppose my father, I would ask myself, "Is it worth risking my werteh? Is it that important?" The werteh was not just my future; with my father owning our house, the werteh also secured a home for my mother and Alia. So, no matter how I felt, I always defaulted to deference, apologies, and gratefulness toward my father. I tried to remember to "shorten my tongue" and refrain from asking questions.

But there were so many things I wanted to know: Why did people refer to him as "the Doctor"—doctor of what, exactly? Who shot him in the leg? Why was his closet packed with guns? How was it that, when we went to Lebanon one summer, he only showed the border control officer a permit that said "Air Force Intelligence," and we didn't have to present our ID to cross over from Syria? I knew I wasn't allowed the answers to these questions. They were sacred, shrouded secrets I could not risk uncovering. Besides, my werteh was far more important than any answer my father might give me.

As I approached high school, he began to weave the topic of marriage into our conversations. Unlike my mother, who prioritized education, my father saw marriage not just as a priority but as a mandate. He once explained that even if I became the most famous doctor in Syria, without a husband, I would be referred to as a spinster, not a doctor—and no daughter of his would be a spinster. He would remind me that I couldn't marry just anyone. My husband had to be an Alawite with a last name my father recognized. A poor man would only be after my father's money, and no one takes advantage of Doctor Jawdat.

These conversations upset my mother, for whom talks of marriage could wait until Alia and I had graduated from college. She knew the value of education; it was the reason she had been able to work to support us when we lived with her mother in Damascus. She knew the only way for us to gain true independence from my father was to focus on our education, not to step into another man's shadow.

But no matter how many times my mother hammered this point, the fact remained that I struggled in school. Memorization—which was the foundation of Syria's educational system—had always been extremely difficult for me. Grades were not based on writing papers, undertaking research, or participating in class discussions. Arguing with a teacher, or even questioning one—"acting smart," as they called it—was considered a punishable offense.

At home, Alia and I had to keep studying until we had memorized all the material we were assigned. Sometimes, my mother would be in the living room, watching TV, and when I heard her laugh, I would run to see what she was watching, promising her that I had memorized my lessons and could recite them when the episode was over. I would lay my head on her lap, feeling her whole body shake as she laughed, happy to have sneaked in a break. More often, though, she sent me back to my room until she could come check on me and make me recite my lessons.

If there is one image etched in my mind from those evenings, it is my mother, with her beautiful green eyes, sitting on my bed with my book open in her hands. She would lift her eyebrows occasionally to signal whether I was right or wrong. She was not fixated on word-for-word memorization; if I grasped the general idea, it was enough for her. My teachers were another story.

Like most of my classmates, I resorted to cheating. Sharing answers and trading tips were the only times we, as students, felt truly united. And when cheating was impossible, we turned to gifts, which teachers not only expected but encouraged. Principal Jameela used to write her shoe size on the chalkboard before Teacher's Day, when parents and students visited teachers in their homes. My mother would gift my teachers nice sets of coffee cups or tableware. Sometimes, during the year, when exams were approaching, I would visit Principal Jameela with my mother and sit in the corner as she opened her gifts and told my mother how smart I was. I was just "distracted," she said, to which my mother would nod. I was her youngest, she said, so she wasn't as hard on me as she was on Alia. She blamed herself.

Most nights before my exams, Principal Jameela would call my house and suggest lessons and page numbers for me to review, her way of hinting at the exam questions. Often, after the call ended, my mother would be furious and embarrassed.

"Can't you just memorize your lessons like everyone else?" she would say. "Jameela won't be there to help when you reach ninth grade!"

Seventh- and eighth-grade exams tested the student's knowledge on a quarter or half of the textbook required for each subject.

DEFIANCE

The ninth-grade exam was the first milestone in the Syrian educational system and required word-for-word memorization of the entire textbook for each subject—which included Syrian geography, history, Arabic grammar, and poetry. Questions were printed and distributed by the Ministry of Education to ensure they were not leaked beforehand, and exam papers were corrected in a different city to avoid any bribes or connections to graders. We often prayed our papers would not be graded in the far south, in places like Deir ez-Zur, because we had been told that people there hated Jableh and Alawites, and would fail us on purpose.

Students began familiarizing themselves with the books the summer before the school year started, spending the year memorizing. Two months before the ninth-grade exams, which were held in June, it was easy to tell which households had ninth graders. They were the ones where students paced back and forth on balconies from early morning until after midnight, open books in hand, reciting endless passages, terrified that their memory would fail them.

Ninth grade is not just an educational milestone in Syria. It is also the year when girls officially become teenagers, little women. In the conservative areas of the country, it is the year young women are forced to drop out of school to get married.

In the summer of 2004, Alia graduated from ninth grade with a score of 288 out of 290 on her exam. Her score was the second-highest in all of Syria—even higher than that of cousin Ali, who had his driver posted at the entrance of the exam center with a bag of cash for the exam supervisors to grab handfuls of before they went in to help him. When the results were announced, Ali was hurt that he didn't score higher, and his father bought him a Hummer to cheer him up. It was one of three Hummers in Syria back then. Alia may not have received a car as a reward, but her score was the talk of the family and neighbors.

I had never seen my mother so proud. In a country where women were told that girls raised by their mothers alone could not succeed, my mother and Alia had proven them wrong. My mother was enough—more than enough.

People descended upon our house with gifts—makeup, hair products—suitable for someone entering high school. They came to congratulate my sister, drink coffee, and eat chocolate. "Are you going to score even higher than Alia? Are you as smart as your sister? I bet you're even smarter!" they would say. I would just nod.

Now that Alia was officially a teenager, she began to experiment with more grown-up things like makeup, underwire bras, and—most important—taking walks with her friends along the corniche, for which I tagged along.

When we first moved to Jableh, I loved the corniche during the summer, with its smell of toasted nuts and the fishing boats that glimmered in the distance like stars. I was too young at the time to realize it was also a place where single people came to search for a potential spouse. Intelligence officers and commanders who served in the government in Damascus and other big cities would return to Jableh to spend summer with their extended families: When it came time to find a wife, they looked for an Alawite woman back at home.

Every evening, Jableh's corniche turned into a parade of cars: expensive vehicles with polished chrome, tinted windows, and no license plates, a sign of high-level security approval. The sidewalks would be packed with young women looking their best, their hair reeking of hair spray as they battled the heavy humidity to keep it straight. They walked as slowly as possible, surveying the cars as they cruised by, searching for an eligible suitor. It didn't matter that they could hardly see through the car's tinted windows; what mattered were the cars themselves and the wealth and power they signified. The better the car, the higher the probability that the guy would get the girl's number if he stopped to talk to her.

When we returned home, like almost every family in the neighborhood, we continued the night on our balcony, where my mother would join us to escape the stuffiness that had built up in the apartment over the course of the day. During summer in Jableh, no matter how hot the day or early evening was, a breeze would rise close to midnight. I had noticed it the first summer we moved there, a breeze damp with sea moisture, loaded with the smell of brine, the sweet fragrance of night-blooming jasmine, and the scent of flavored tobacco wafting from the nearby balconies. Although most people kept their lights off, you could see the glowing coals of hookahs being kindled. Men placed them in copper holders and swirled them in a hypnotic motion, casting ephemeral trails like shooting stars. The night air was filled with distant murmurs and laughter, the soothing gurgle of the hookahs, and music drifting from radios or cars that had earlier paraded along the corniche. Some men, when they spotted a girl they liked, would cruise under her balcony at night, hoping to catch more glimpses of her.

One evening, as we were walking home, the son of a parliament representative spotted me and followed me home in his car. His name was Jaafar, and he was twenty-three. He made a habit of driving back and forth below our balcony, blasting romantic songs as loudly as possible. When I happened to be outside, I would peer over the edge of the balcony and see his hair, slicked down with copious amounts of gel, shining under the streetlights as he slowed down to look up and smile at me.

Even though I had no interest in him, I enjoyed his efforts and smiled back. The blasting music under my home announced to the neighborhood and to me that someone with an expensive car desired me. It was something to be proud of. I had value.

For my mother, though, this man was nothing but an unwelcome distraction. "You should be preparing for the ninth-grade exam!" She reminded me that most students my age had probably started memorizing already. She would recite Alia's score and her usual point about how it was education, not marriage, that would bring me independence. That line, among many others, was repeated throughout the school year as she fed me bowls of walnuts, honey, and sesame seeds, which were supposed to strengthen my memory. But no amount of walnuts could help. I knew I couldn't memorize, so I didn't even try.

WHEN THE EXAM RESULTS for my year were announced, I found that I had scored 164 out of 290—barely passing. Just as Alia's high score the previous year had been my mother's achievement, my failure was hers. She was furious.

"Of course!" my mother said. "All girls lose their minds after ninth grade, but you and your sister lost yours at the same time." I tried to blame it on the town where my exam was corrected; maybe I was targeted. My mother told me to shut up and call my father to tell him what happened.

"Please, you call him," I begged my mother. I was terrified.

"I'm not dealing with this," she responded. "You should call him as soon as possible before he hears the news from someone else."

I dialed his number and held my breath. He answered.

"The results are out," I said. I braced myself and told him my score.

"Mabrook!" he shouted. "Congrats! That's great! You're so smart, just like your father."

"But Baba," I said in a low voice, holding my breath. "It's 164, not 264. It's 164 out of 290. I was three points away from failing and having to repeat the whole year."

I felt my heart pounding as my mother stood still, her eyes fixated on me, waiting for my father's reaction, expecting it would align with hers and confirm to me that I should feel ashamed of myself.

But he just laughed and told me he would call back later. Then the line went silent.

This infuriated her. She said that my father must have been dining with people and probably did not want to say anything mean to me in front of them. But when he called back later that evening, all he asked was what I wanted as a gift.

THAT SUMMER, while girls my age were just beginning to do what I had begun doing the year before with Alia, my mother was still so angry with me that even stepping out of the house was torture. She reminded me daily that she was glad Alia had scored high so people would know my failure was not because of her. I should be ashamed to show my face in public and go into hiding until people forgot how low I scored.

But my father remained quite the opposite. One day, he even came to pick me up for lunch and bought me a piece of gold.

"School is worthless," he reminded me. "It's not a big deal. Only people who need to get jobs care about it. You're the daughter of Doctor Jawdat. You don't need to work. You'll have a husband. That's why I always tell you to be careful who you choose. Your husband must be respectful with money, and you'll have your werteh."

When he dropped me off, he told me I should remind my mother that her own education was worthless, and without him, she would starve to death.

I don't remember exactly why I told my mother what my father said. Maybe she was lecturing me again or refusing to allow me to go out. Whatever the reason, I was angry. As soon as I relayed his message, she picked up the phone, shaking, and dialed his number.

"You criminal! You and your family are illiterate, and you want my daughters to become just like you! You're afraid you won't be able to control them, and that's why you're undermining everything I'm trying to teach them." I had never seen her so angry.

I stopped paying attention to what she was saying and moved closer, desperate to unplug the telephone cord and end the call. I was terrified, knowing that in two weeks we would have to call him to send us the money for the month. I wasn't wrong. When the time came, he dragged it out for days, ignoring our calls. When he finally picked up, he ordered me to put my mother on the line so she could apologize for what she had said.

As she held the phone, I heard her whisper, "May God bless your hands."

Her surrender proved to me that my father was right. Education was secondary. Without his money and approval, we had nothing. I had nothing.

SEVEN

Bakaloria is the second milestone in the Syrian educational system, structurally similar to the ninth-grade exam but covering almost double the volume of books. The score a student achieves on this final exam determines the field of study they will pursue. Some students retake the exam multiple times to achieve a high enough score to join their desired department. However, most students, unwilling to endure the stress again, settle for whatever field their original score gives them access to.

In the summer of 2007, when I was sixteen, Alia scored high enough on her Bakaloria to be admitted to law school at Latakia University, which was a thirty-minute bus ride from Jableh. The following fall, she was barely home during the day. Almost every night at dinner, she talked about how fun, big, and different Latakia and its university were compared to Jableh. I longed to join her there and did my best to improve my memorization. My mother hired private tutors to support me throughout the year. "Even if we don't eat this year, you must pass," she would repeat at the beginning of every month when, from the stack of cash my father sent to the house, she would count out a dense chunk for my lessons. She wanted the teachers to sit with me at our round dining table in the living room while she, in the kitchen, often listened to ensure I followed along and that we were not wasting the paid hour on random conversations.

Although I studied harder than I ever had before, I still relied on cheating. To my surprise, the teachers supervising the Bakaloria exam process were not strict. Maybe they knew the outcome would shape our destinies, so in the last ten minutes they allowed us to open whatever aid materials we brought.

When the results came in, my overall score was not bad, but my English grade in particular was high enough for me to be admitted to the English literature department at Latakia University if I paid around $700 a year in tuition.

Although my father offered to cover the yearly fee, my mother cautioned me against entering a program that would be contingent on his money. She worried about what I would do if, for one reason or another, he withdrew his support. But I refused to listen to her and submitted my papers.

As a reward for my loyalty to him, my father significantly increased my allowance—it was almost half as much as he sent our household for the whole month, more than even I could spend. "You are Doctor Jawdat's daughter," he would say, counting out the bills. "Go take your friends out to eat."

During my first year at university in 2009, I met students from areas across Syria, including Idlib, Deir ez-Zur, the Sunni part of Jableh and Latakia, and the Kurdish region in the northeast. Despite this diversity, I rarely stepped outside my comfortable bubble.

MAIS, ONE OF MY FRIENDS from elementary school, lived nearby and had also enrolled in the English literature department. Every morning, we would take the thirty-minute bus ride to Latakia and spend the day at the university gossiping about other girls and their outfits or debating where to eat. We rarely attended lectures.

In public universities, especially in the overcrowded humanities departments, the number of admitted students far exceeded the seats in the auditorium. As a result, it was common to skip classes all year and simply purchase printed lecture notes from students who made a living by showing up early to lectures and diligently transcribing everything the professor said. These notes would then be memorized before exams.

To PROVE TO MY FATHER that I was worthy of my new allowance, I started spending every weekend at his house. That was the first time I felt a growing distance between my mother and me. I didn't realize then that she might have felt unfairly sidelined—that despite her encouraging me to spend more time with him over the years, my father didn't want to be involved during the hard times, and now that I had made it to college and the work of raising me was done, he was reclaiming his place in my life.

Alia didn't want to join me. She was too busy with her schoolwork, and she saw my trips as an opportunity to enjoy our bedroom in Jableh by herself. I didn't mind; I wanted to go alone to show my father that I was willing to choose him over weekends with my friends. In return, he would see that I deserved his money. I cannot recall one time my father ever said something kind to me during my childhood or adulthood, but I do remember the smell of the bills he handed me, still warm from his pocket. The more time and attention I gave him, the more cash I received. Money was his love language, and it became mine.

"Baba, everyone knows you!" I would tell him. "My professors, when they see my name, always ask if I am related to you!" (That happened only once—I was rarely in class—but I knew that telling him this would make him more inclined to show off his wealth through me.)

We fell into a routine. Every Thursday, Suhail, my father's driver, would take me the half hour uphill to my father's house. When we arrived, I'd run up the stairs to the kitchen to see what Salma, my father's longest-serving housekeeper, had prepared for dinner. Salma often made me the dishes my mother did not allow in her kitchen, like fried chicken and kibbeh nayeh—raw chopped lamb on bulgur, doused with olive oil and pomegranate sauce. My mother said eating raw meat could cause intestinal worms and the stench of fried chicken would linger for days in her hair and our curtains. After washing my hands, I would go straight to my father's chair, grab his hand, kiss it, and touch it to my forehead before sitting down to eat.

AROUND THAT TIME, my father constantly talked about "the project": a resort he was developing in an isolated nearby valley. By then, he had spent millions of Syrian liras on expanding the village spring into a small lake, and he planned to build a little restaurant and hotel next to it.

"Our Alawite mountains are no less beautiful than the Swiss or French Alps," he explained. "They simply need investment. It is a shame that all Alawite businessmen develop restaurants and malls in big cities and give nothing back to the mountains that offered refuge for our ancestors. They are ungrateful." Without these mountains and the protection they provided our ancestors, he often said, Alawites would have vanished from the face of the earth. My mother called his project a midlife crisis.

After dinner, my father and I would sit in front of the television. He often switched between Lebanese and Syrian news channels, and when he began to snore, I would switch off the TV, nudge my father to move to bed, and go upstairs to my room on the third floor. When I couldn't fall asleep, I would lie on the chaise longue on the terrace, covered with blankets, and gaze at the stars. We were the highest house for miles around, and the sky was not polluted with light.

DEFIANCE

Most weekends, my father and I would tour the project's construction site. "This is so beautiful," I would repeat as my father pointed to random jumbles of rocks from the window while driving down the steep hill toward the spring—the soul of the village, as my father called it. I struggled to grasp my father's vision. It was hard for me to see our village and my trips there as anything more than a burden I endured for his approval, let alone a place that could attract tourists someday. I despised how much money my father was wasting and how the project absorbed all his attention.

Some weekends, I succeeded in avoiding the trip to the construction site and stayed home with Salma. Though my father would beat her, sometimes on a weekly basis, and she would leave the house with a bruised arm or eye, she always returned. I once asked her why. "The Doctor is generous with me," Salma told me. "He could easily replace me with a maid from Ethiopia like your uncles did. But your father chooses to support us. He is loyal to the people of these mountains—wlad al balad—despite the years he spent in France." I nodded quietly, knowing that my father didn't hire a foreign maid out of loyalty to wlad al balad, but because he believed Black people brought bad luck.

Some Fridays, other guests would visit. This was fine by me, so long as they stayed away from the third floor, which I considered my domain. The most frequent guest was a woman named Hanan, who would arrive with her daughter, Nour, early on Friday mornings, and leave the next day. She said Nour had to go to school on Sundays. I didn't like Hanan, but not because it was clear that she was my father's mistress. After all, she was not the first, and I knew that one day he wanted to remarry and eventually have the boy that would carry his name. It didn't bother me; if anything, I appreciated that during the times he had a woman in his life, he would send money without Alia and me being forced to call or visit him.

The only thing that disturbed me about his mistresses was how young they were—often in their early to mid-twenties or even their late teens. The affairs always ended with my father moving on to a new mistress, leaving the other young woman distraught. I felt bad for these women but accepted the idea that their unhappiness was ultimately their fault because, as we say in Arabic, "nothing disgraces a man"—or, as some would add, nothing disgraces a man except his pockets. As long as a man provides for his family, he is free to do as he pleases. My father was no exception. If the man is married, it is his wife's responsibility to turn a blind eye, because anything else would risk the destruction of her life and family, which it is her job to protect.

But Hanan was different from my father's other mistresses. She would strut around the house wearing a shiny black nightgown and shout from the kitchen balcony, instructing the drivers to bring things from the village grocery because she, not Salma, was going to cook for Doctor Jawdat. She spoke to me in a high-pitched voice as if I were a child. "Oh, your eyes are just like the Doctor's," she would say. She often tried to bond with me by giving me skincare advice and explaining how simple habits like eating lettuce, especially before going to bed, slowed down aging. "You should start now. You will regret it later if you don't!"

What made me despise Hanan the most, though, was the way she treated her twelve-year-old daughter, Nour, who was always by her side.

I felt bad for Nour. She would sit on the balcony alone, which reminded me of the many days I had spent there waiting for my father to come and give me money. I often tried to talk to her or offer her my makeup bag to play with, or turn on the TV, handing her the remote control so she could choose the channel. But all she wanted to do was sit quietly on the balcony and gaze at the evergreens growing out of the white limestone mountainsides.

I admired that my father was generous enough to allow his mistress's daughter to stay at the villa. What if she had no one to take care of her back home? At least at my father's house, she was being fed. When Hanan,

Nour, my father, and I would eat dinner together, as usual, "the project" was the main topic of conversation. Hanan would say that the village should erect a statue of Doctor Jawdat to thank him for investing locally. "If all Alawite businessmen did what your father is doing, these mountains would become the largest tourist destination in the world!" I would nod, happy at least that someone else was there to entertain my father during and after dinner.

ONE NIGHT, WHEN HANAN and her daughter were visiting in late winter, I was getting into bed when I realized that I'd left my phone charger in the kitchen. I tiptoed downstairs and switched on the lights. A woman shrieked.

"You scared me!" Hanan shouted. She had been sitting in the dark at the table alone and stared at me as if she had seen a ghost.

"Sorry," I said, collecting my charger from underneath the table. When I stood up, Hanan was right beside me. "Go back upstairs!" she said firmly before her voice resumed its usual saccharine tone. "Your father won't be happy if he finds out you're still awake!" She placed both her hands on my shoulders, and steered me to the door.

"My father doesn't care what time I go to sleep! I'm not a child," I protested, swatting her hands away, irritated by this fake motherly imposition. Just then, I heard a loud noise coming from my father's room. Both Hanan and I froze. She cast her eyes downward, avoiding mine.

Another sound erupted, a groan—almost a scream. I couldn't tell if it was pleasure or pain. But I recognized that voice. I knew that voice. I felt blood rushing to my face. I stood still. Hanan pushed me out of the kitchen, into the corridor, and firmly shut the door behind me. I stood there, my back to the door, motionless long enough that the hallway light turned off. My heartbeat throbbed in my ears. My father was not sleeping with Hanan—but with her twelve-year-old daughter.

I returned to bed, but sleep was inconceivable. It felt like I had entered an alternate reality. I tried in vain to remember that nothing disgraces a man—but this was not nothing. Nour was a child. I was so disgusted by my father that I worried I might not be able to hide it. I wanted to call someone. I thought of my mother, but I knew she would tell me exactly what she had been trying to say since I went to college—that I should distance myself from him.

I woke up exhausted the next morning, as if I hadn't slept at all. I stayed in bed until I heard my father's car drive away. I went downstairs and found Salma, who said Nour and Hanan had left with my father. When I told Salma what had happened during the night, I was horrified to learn that she already knew.

"Her mother is a horrible person!" Salma said. "Poor Nour. It's all her mother's fault. Your father is not the only one."

Salma explained that Hanan had wanted to leave her village and move to Jableh, and had convinced my father to give her the house that had once belonged to and been rented out by Grandmother Tamra, the one right across the street from my mother's house that Aunt Samia had spent years collecting rent to maintain. Around that time, Aunt Samia's husband had died, and she had asked my father to give her one of Grandmother Tamra's houses, but he had refused. I couldn't believe what Salma was telling me.

In the evening, my father returned home from the valley and called for me. I hesitated. I feared that Salma had told him about our conversation and that I knew about Nour. My father would always say that Salma was his eyes and ears when he was away; it was why he would never replace her.

I went downstairs to his room, where I found him lying on his bed, his eyes locked on the television screen. He handed me a thick white envelope and asked me to help him count the money inside and then return it to him when I was finished. I left the room and completed the task. The envelope was filled with hundred-dollar bills. Two hundred of them. Twenty thousand dollars; a million Syrian liras. I put the money back in the envelope and weighed it on my palm. I had never held that much cash before. I walked to my father's room and gave him the envelope. "Twenty thousand dollars," I said. My father opened the envelope, removed four bills, and extended his hand in my direction without looking at me.

That was $400; 20,000 Syrian liras. I looked at the money in my father's hand. I knew exactly what he was trying to do: He was forcing me to see and feel between my fingers what I would be losing if I turned against him or judged him. He was reminding me again, just as he had throughout my childhood, that he had the power.

I took the crisp bills, folded them gently and silently, and slid them into my pocket. Then I bent over and took my father's hand, cupping it between mine. I kissed it and placed it on my forehead multiple times.

"You are the best father in the world," I said, and he slowly slid his hand away and tapped me on the head.

Over the years, I had learned not only to conceal my disagreements with my father but also to tame my inner resistance to him. I was so terrified of him, so conditioned to submitting to his will, that even silent resentment felt dangerously out of line. But with Hanan and Nour, I couldn't do it. I couldn't push that night away. Knowing that Nour was a child my father relentlessly assaulted, and that my aunt couldn't live in the house across the street that once belonged to my grandmother because of the deal he had struck with Hanan, made every step I took past their house torture. I would walk fast, my heartbeat loud in my ears, hoping and praying that I looked normal. But I couldn't deny it any longer: I hated my father to a degree I hadn't previously known was possible.

I stopped spending weekends at his house. Whenever he called me, I would use Alia's excuse: I had to study; my exams were approaching. My allowance shrank, but it didn't matter. Whatever I could buy with the money paled in comparison to the rage that stirred within me whenever I saw his number on my phone or his car parked outside Hanan and Nour's house, just across from ours. He knew I was lying about studying when my exam scores showed that I had failed four classes out of eight. I was one class short of repeating the entire first year. When my mother saw my grades, she was so angry that she sent me to my father's house for the night as punishment, knowing I had been avoiding him.

As usual, my father was not concerned about my education. He was concerned about my hair, which I still wore curly. "You are now at an age when you should take better care of your looks. Can you fix your hair like your cousins?" he would ask.

Throughout my childhood, for family events, my mother would bring me to a salon to have my hair straightened, a process I dreaded, though I was often mocked for having such tight curls. Even to my face, kids at school called me Scotch-Brite—a squiggly stainless steel pot scrubber. My cousins called me Jessie, after the Ethiopian woman who did housekeeping for my uncle. Aunt Samia would comfort me by saying that, unlike Jessie, I had fair skin, and when I was old enough, my hair could be more permanently straightened with keratin. "Look at the hair of Uncle Wahib's daughters!" she would say. "Their hair was curlier than yours and now it is so soft and straight you would think they were born in France." And it wasn't just my hair—my father had promised me a nose job as a gift, believing it would improve my marriage prospects.

I was the only one in my generation of the family without plastic surgery. All of Uncle Wahib's children, including Ali, went to the same doctor and got the same nose, gradually morphing into carbon copies of each other. It never made any sense to me why their natural features were considered ugly and needed to be "fixed." I was against changing anything about my hair and my face. At the time, I didn't have the right words to vocalize that I did not want to be a clone. I wanted to be my own person.

Still, I never dared to challenge my father because the fact remained that he funded my life and my tuition. I couldn't afford to express my disgust or disapproval. If I didn't want my life to change—if I didn't want to jeopardize my future—I had to remain silent.

EIGHT

After my allowance dwindled, keeping up with Mais became challenging, and we gradually spent less time together. During the second year, she continued her routine of exploring new restaurants, while I, driven by boredom, finally began attending my lectures. With four classes to carry over from the previous year, I had plenty of work to catch up on.

Sometimes, after class, I would take my notes to one of the affordable coffee shops around campus. Most of them were dark and humid, smelling of stale hookah smoke, playing loud music. My favorite was called Prose Verse. Unlike the others, it was sunny, with large windows and colorful plastic tables. You could borrow books from their library and order maté served with a pot of hot water that could fuel a couple of hours of studying. I would open my laptop to translate unfamiliar words and phrases.

In Syria, the English literature department, much like the broader educational system, was based on memorization. However, instead of learning by heart as was required in school, we were now expected to understand and rephrase the professors' main ideas. I genuinely enjoyed reading, even though we mostly read old novels and short stories about eighteenth- and nineteenth-century British society, like *Anna of the Five Towns* and *Moll Flanders*. I loved learning new words. I would stay hunched over my laptop until my growling stomach reminded me it was time to catch the bus back to Jableh to eat whatever my mother had prepared for dinner.

Every day when I came home, she would hug me and tell me she still couldn't believe I had made it to college, reminding me of how proud she was that I was, as she put it, "back to my senses and studying."

In my second year, my grades improved; I even scored 96 out of 100 in writing. It was the first time in my life that I had done well without cheating. I maintained a similar discipline as I moved into my third year, spending hours studying on my laptop. However, as we reached the last months of 2010, something other than my schoolwork was keeping me glued to my screen: the Arab Spring.

IN THE LATE WINTER OF 2010, a series of popular revolts swept across the Arab world, sending authoritarian and corrupt governments up in smoke. The first occurred in Tunisia, one of the Arab world's most developed yet oppressed countries. That fall, rising unemployment and inflation were testing the patience of a population already weary of routine corruption. One morning in December, a police officer seized the pushcart of a twenty-six-year-old vegetable seller named Mohamed Bouazizi, claiming he didn't have a permit.

Bouazizi held on to his cart until additional police officers arrived and overturned it, causing his vegetables to scatter on the ground, and then beat him. Bouazizi tried to plead his case with the local officials. He was dismissed once, and when his case got dismissed a second time, Bouazizi grabbed a gasoline canister and set himself on fire. His self-immolation sparked mass demonstrations against then-president Zine El Abidine Ben Ali; thousands of people took to the streets of Tunisia, chanting Bouazizi's name.

While flipping through the channels at home around that time, I sometimes happened upon broadcasts of the protests in Tunisia, but I never paused to watch; at the age of nineteen, I didn't know anything about the country and couldn't have cared less about its anti-government protests. I did not pay much attention to politics then.

But one night in mid-January 2011, a blurry video from Tunisia appeared on the television screen, and I didn't change the channel. The segment showed a street after curfew, empty of people except for a white-haired man wearing a sport jacket, reflecting the orange glow of the streetlight. "Ben Ali has fled," he said in disbelief. "The people of Tunis are free. We are free. Tunis is free from its dictatorship."

I was transfixed. I had never seen anything like this before. Was it really possible for people to make such statements in public? Increasingly, it seemed that it was. What's more, their collective voice had an impact; they did overthrow the government.

Meanwhile, in Egypt, activists were using social media platforms to organize what they called a "Day of Rage" to protest after the death of Khaled Said, a twenty-three-year-old computer science graduate who had refused to be searched without a warrant outside an internet café and was beaten by security forces. This time, I followed the news. Unlike Tunisia, Egypt was familiar—I had grown up watching its soap operas and movies, and my phone was filled with music by the singers who were now in the crowds of people marching through the country's streets, chanting slogans and demanding that President Hosni Mubarak step down after thirty years in power.

Other countries followed: Soon Bahrain witnessed its first mass protests with its own Day of Rage, while Saudi Arabia banned public demonstrations. In Yemen, the president pledged to create a parliamentary system in a desperate attempt to quell the floods of people taking to the streets. In Jordan, protesters set up camp in the main square of the capital, Amman.

Anticipation grew about which country would be next, and every week more cities across the Middle East experienced their first protests, many of which were organized on Facebook. Every day, a new demonstration was being live streamed, with the speed of online news outpacing that of traditional news agencies. Facebook and Twitter had become the go-to sources for updates. While studying, I would keep a Facebook tab open and occasionally scroll through for the latest developments.

It was captivating to follow events in real time, reported directly by protesters on the ground, and inspiring to see people—often my age or even younger—standing against injustice, raising their voices, and risking their lives for what was right.

One day in March, while I am at the coffee shop after school, a video with "Syria" in its title stops my hand on the keyboard. It was shared by a Facebook page called "Syrian Revolution Against Bashar al-Assad."

I put my headphones on and click on the link. The video is blurry. A man begins to speak, announcing the time and location of the events—a common practice for protesters and amateur reporters so that news channels can play their videos. But I recognize the location immediately: It is the old covered market of Damascus, with its distinctive arched metal roof that stretches over the entire length of the thoroughfare. It is recognizable to anyone who has visited the city.

The protesters begin to chant "God, Syria, freedom, nothing else!" based off the chant we have been taught to repeat over the years: "God, Syria, Bashar, nothing else!" My heartbeat quickens as I bring my laptop closer and hide the screen in my lap. It feels like I am watching something I shouldn't. It's fine to follow protests in other countries, but seeing protests in Syria is surreal. It feels wrong.

I look around and wonder whether other people in the café, those whose eyes are fixed on their laptops, are watching the same images. I turn down my volume, worried that the sound is leaking out of my earbuds. "God, Syria, freedom, nothing else!" The demonstrators attempt to rally the market-goers, yet the crowd remains small and the protest quickly disbands, melting away into the adjacent alleyways.

I copy and paste the link and send it to Emad, a guy I've become friends with here at the coffee shop. He comes from a well-known Christian family and often spends his summers traveling around Lebanon with the church. He's smart and insightful—if a bit of a know-it-all—and always has something to say. I'm curious about his opinion.

"This is so stupid. I've seen it before," he replies.

"Why do you think it's stupid?" I type. "I don't see anything wrong with it."

His next message is longer: "What kind of freedom do they want? We already have all the freedom we need. We can drink, stay out late, and party, and no one will stop us. Education and healthcare are free."

"Maybe they mean free elections?" I type, repeating a term I've read across the platforms.

Emad then asks, "Do you know what a free election means? Free elections are a Western term. The West invaded Iraq to bring them 'freedom' and free elections. Look at Iraq. Do you want Syria to become Iraq? Don't be stupid. Don't fall for this."

As proof, he brings up the name of the Facebook page that posted the video, writing, "'The Syrian Revolution Against Bashar al-Assad'—look at the names who follow the page! They are all fake names, and probably none of them are even Syrian." He forgets that, in Syria, it would be very dangerous to engage in any political activity under one's real name.

DEFIANCE

Emad tells me that Bashar al-Assad is not like Mubarak. Mubarak closed the tunnels between Gaza and Egypt. Emad says we should be supporting the Egyptian uprising as an extension of our support for Palestine. Then he repeats the line I've heard before: Among all the Arab leaders, Bashar al-Assad is the last one standing against Israel and America. Emad tells me I should keep in mind that Egyptian politics are also more complex. They have so many political parties, while here in Syria the opposition we have is either the Muslim Brotherhood or a handful of American-infiltrated groups. I don't push the issue further.

No longer spending my weekends at my father's house, I am glad to resume the Friday routine of my childhood. My mother gets up, makes herself coffee, then calls the Jableh fish market to inquire about the morning catch. A voice on the other end of the line tells her what they netted before dawn. She places her order, which will be delivered to our home by noon. Then she turns the TV on to the news, and sips her coffee, black and sweet. I have always loved these Fridays, when I would stay in bed until noon.

But on the morning of March 18, I can't. The television is too loud. I squeeze my pillow against my ears. I can hear a woman's voice, a news reporter, asking questions. A muffled male voice is answering. I drag myself from bed to go turn it down.

"Police Forces Fire at Protests in Daraa" is written at the bottom of the screen. I pause, then open my computer, log into Facebook, and type: "Syrian Revolution Against Bashar al-Assad." The page has nearly four thousand likes now. I read through the posts and comments and scan the photos. Days earlier, in Daraa, just a few hours' drive south of Jableh, the school principal went to work and found graffiti painted on the walls of the schoolyard: "It Is Your Turn, Doctor."

The principal called the police, who were shocked and furious. Why would anyone insult our president in this way? Even worse, why insult him on the walls of an institution he and the party had built for these ungrateful kids? The police couldn't return to their station empty-handed. They looked closely at the walls, which, like any school in Syria, were scribbled with the names of students, past and present.

The students arrived and lined up for the flag salute. The police officers picked thirteen of the names and took them away in gray military jeeps. The eldest was fifteen years old. When their families learned what had happened, they gathered at the governor's residence. The governor, Atef Najib, a cousin of the president, told them to go home and forget about their children.

The families were furious and devastated. They decided that on March 18, after the Juma'a prayer, they would march through Daraa's streets in protest. And they did, calling upon people to join them, and hundreds, maybe even thousands, did.

"We prefer death over humiliation," they chanted. "Our blood and soul we sacrificed for you, Daraa." The police arrived, raised their rifles, and ordered the protesters to disperse. When the protesters refused, bullets were fired, puncturing bodies in the crowd. And now, in front of the television, I read their names aloud, and my mother comes in from the kitchen, a scarf over her hair so it won't smell of sizzling oil and fish. She reads the names along with me.

"Do you think it's true?" I ask. "Have people been shot and killed?"

"If the president replaces Atef Najib, this might end," she says. "He is bound to do something." She rushes back to the kitchen.

This will end soon, I think. This is not serious. I change the channel, not knowing that those names are the first three of what will become thousands upon thousands of dead.

In the days that follow, the number of casualties increases: first thirteen, then twenty-five, then thirty. Yet that day, Syrian state television continues to air its regular Friday schedule without interruption. There's a cooking show followed by a talk show about the importance of fitness. It's only when it becomes impossible to ignore the severity of the news that they report on the situation. They claim that Islamists are crossing over from Jordan and terrorizing people, killing police officers and civilians.

Meanwhile, new Facebook pages begin posting the names of those who have been killed and detained, urging people not to believe the government's narrative. "We are not terrorists," they shout in their shaky footage. As they risk their lives to film those falling dead around them.

IN LATE MARCH, a week after the protest in Daraa, other small protests erupt across Syria. In Jableh, a group of people leave a mosque in the mostly Sunni old city and march their way through nearby alleys, chanting in support of Daraa. I check pro-government Facebook pages, which claim that the protesters chant, "Alawites to the grave, Christians to Lebanon." I click on a video of the Jableh demonstration and watch it several times. The video shows a group of men, their faces covered by Syrian flags, walking through the tight stone alleyways of Jableh's old city. I don't hear any sectarian slogans, only calls for Alawites to join them.

"This is a revolution for everyone. Don't let the government convince you this is a threat."

The next day, there are calls on Facebook to boycott Sunni businesses, accusing Sunni shop owners of funding the Daraa protests and those who chanted insults against Alawites; in Jableh, they are urging people not to give their money to businesses who wish them dead. Although no one knows who was behind the posts, they spread, and people follow.

Days later, our neighbor knocks on our door, out of breath, warning us: "Three women in burqas are going around, spraying drugs on people's faces and trying to kidnap them!" He advises us not to open the door to anyone. Rumors quickly spread that terrorists from Daraa have arrived in Jableh. Checkpoints appear at street entrances to stop and search every car, requiring IDs. The shopkeepers in our neighborhood, who often keep their businesses open past midnight, begin lowering their steel security shutters right after sunset.

My father calls repeatedly to urge us to keep our doors locked and stay away from the windows. He had heard that a car flying an Israeli flag was spotted roaming the streets, and they might fire at windows. Although no one I know has seen the Israeli car or the women spraying drugs, the armed soldiers outside my house make the danger feel real. No level of skepticism can outweigh the shouts of neighbors asking the soldiers if everything is safe. Every night before bed, we ensure our doors are locked.

Baseless rumors that incite fear aren't new to Jableh. In the spring of 2003, when Iraq was invaded and refugees started to pour into Syria, a rumor spread that Iraqi women—paid by the United States—were injecting bottles of ketchup across restaurants in Jableh and Latakia with HIV-infected blood. Most restaurants stopped putting out ketchup bottles, or the waiters would open the sealed bottles in front of the customers to prove they were safe. That same year, Aunt Samia called and instructed us to never, ever pick up the phone if we did not recognize the number. She told us that people all along the coast were receiving phone calls from the United States and Israel that triggered seizures. We didn't know anyone who had contracted AIDS from ketchup or suffered a seizure caused by sound waves, but it didn't matter. It was better to be safe than sorry.

Back then, rumors spread by word of mouth, but this time, in 2011, they are being broadcast on state television. Political analysts affirm that Qatar is sending pills, imprinted with the Al Jazeera logo, that are slipped into sandwiches to brainwash people into cursing the president. Others allege that the protests are staged in massive studios in Qatar and that, as good Syrians, we should delete all other channels to avoid misinformation and only watch Syrian state TV. They insist that there is no uprising in Syria; it is all fabricated by Al Jazeera. Consequently, across Jableh, Al Jazeera's yellow logo begins to appear on trash cans, suggesting that is where this channel belongs. Some political analysts on government channels suggest that the protesters are not even Syrian, while others disagree, claiming that the protesters are indeed Syrian, but they are being paid for every protest they attend.

WHEN SUMMER RETURNS, it restores some sense of normalcy with its familiar humidity, cruising cars along the corniche, and coffee shops staying open late. Screening relaxes at checkpoints, which turn into social gathering sites. Life goes on. This reinforces the state TV narrative that nothing alarming is really happening in Syria and that whatever other news channels and social media pages are claiming about deaths, protests, and detainments is a lie. "It ended, we succeeded" becomes a slogan hanging from balconies and painted on walls.

Occasionally, "love rallies" erupt, transforming public squares into dance parties with large loudspeakers blasting songs praising Assad and chants celebrating Jableh's resilience. Jableh, with its unwavering support for the president, would never succumb to the chaos and betrayal that plagues other cities. "This is a media war on Syria," state TV keeps repeating, but "Syria is protected by God." Whoever had tried to turn Syrians against their president had failed.

NINE

It isn't long before reality catches up with Jableh. Later in the summer, things take a dramatic turn. On my way to the university to take my third-year exam, we get stuck in stifling heat and never-ending traffic, prolonging the usual thirty-minute drive down the highway. The congestion is caused by ambulances, one after another, red brake lights flashing, sirens wailing. The news reports an attack by a group of protesters on a military base in the Idlib governorate, in a town called Jisr al-Shughur. Syrian state television claims that the soldiers were asleep at their base when protesters infiltrated and killed them all.

From the number of ambulances, it seems that the majority, if not all, of the dead are from the Alawite villages surrounding Jableh. Before the bodies are driven up the mountains for their burial, the funerals pass through Jableh slowly, solemnly, and sorrowfully. Women toss rice from balconies and their ululations echo off the walls of the surrounding apartment buildings. The prayers of muezzins resound from minaret speakers all over town.

DEFIANCE

State television hammers the story for days, repeatedly broadcasting images of the burial services, of mothers and fathers weeping and hugging caskets draped with the Syrian flag. This is a reminder for us Alawites that the minute anyone has the chance or power to, they will kill us all. Many draw parallels to what happened in the early 1980s when a militant wing of the Muslim Brotherhood–organized opposition carried out an attack on a government cadet school in Aleppo, killing dozens of young Alawite soldiers in their sleep. Without protection from our president, we would face the same persecution our ancestors endured under the Ottomans; our skulls would be piled up as a sign that we are not wanted, that we are infidels.

Everyone wants to believe that the so-called imperialist media war against Syria is over and that everything is fine, but we are shaken. For us Alawites, the latent fear of persecution is always more powerful than any anger or frustration toward the government and its state media. Even Alawites who are atheists and individuals whose Alawite legacy is preserved only in a distinctive dialect side against change. They feel they have to choose between freedom and existence itself. Whether we agree or disagree with the government, there seems to be no choice but to support it and work to prevent chaos for future generations. It is a collective effort to keep ourselves safe.

For many, this means reporting anyone expressing disloyalty to the government and its president, which is done by writing a Takrir, a security report, that will be sent to one of the twelve Mukhabarat intelligence branches across Syria. If you care about the country, you have to help the government catch those who express negative thoughts about the president. Anyone can and should write a Takrir: the beggar on the sidewalk, the guy behind the bakery counter, the seemingly inattentive coffee shop waitress, even the old men pushing wooden carts with steaming stainless steel pots filled with boiling ears of corn and fava beans that suffuse the corniche with hypnotizing scents of cumin and lemon. No one can ever know for certain who has reported them; it could have been a stranger, but it could also have been a neighbor or even a relative. It is best to assume that everyone is listening, that even the walls have ears.

Growing up, surveillance was a common theme on Syrian comedy shows, which were popular not just domestically but around the Arab world. They were lighthearted and so popular that their new seasons would premiere during Ramadan, becoming the shows families gathered around to watch after breaking their fasts. The government even funded their production to demonstrate that Syrians had freedom of speech.

One episode stayed with me for years. It started with a security agent telling his wife that the branch where he served had announced a prize for the best report: a new car. The guy was determined to write the best security report, so he took his small recorder with him as he walked around his neighborhood. He tried to encourage his neighbors and friends to complain about prices and corruption, but everyone stayed silent; they knew he was a secret agent. He spent days trying, to no avail. Then, hours before the deadline, he visited his father, recorder in his pocket, and recorded him criticizing the government. He rushed home, confident that he would win the car; no one else would snitch on their own father. But as he started writing his Takrir, a wave of guilt overcame him. He started crying, telling his wife how horrible he felt for having become so brainwashed by his job that he was willing to turn on his own father to prove his loyalty to the government. As the agent cursed the security branch, his wife sat next to him, holding his hand. "It's okay, tell me more," she cooed, as she pressed "record" on the tape recorder under her jacket.

The show never hinted at what would happen to the guy after his wife submitted the security report. No one dared to talk about prisons or jails like Tadmor, where eight hundred men and boys were killed in their cells by automatic rifle fire and hand grenades on a June day in 1980. I had never even heard of Saydnaya, the graves not so far out into the desert sands, or the brutal and inhumane warehouse torture chambers at Hama. Though I feared the security forces, it was inconceivable to me that such places existed in my country.

The only person I knew who had been to jail was my mother's uncle. He had spent years in prison because of his writings criticizing corruption and was released only after my grandmother personally appealed to the president. But no one spoke about the conditions there or what he might have been suffering. In our family, conversations about his incarceration often centered on his wife, who threw dinner parties and invited people over for poetry readings at her home throughout his incarceration. "The glass never left her hand!" my grandmother would say.

Besides, Mukhabarat agents were not foreign to me. They were my relatives and neighbors. They were family friends, like my father's cousin, Hikmat, who ran the Mukhabarat branch in As Suwayda, a governorate deep in southern Syria. When Hikmat died of a heart attack that summer of 2011, just a few months after the start of the uprising, his wife and other women referred to him as a martyr because, they said, it was probably triggered by the rising threats in the country. Were it not for men like Hikmat, these mountains would have been burned to ashes long ago. "May God bless their souls," the women repeated in unison. "May God bless their souls," I echoed, wiping my tears.

I have never visited As Suwayda myself, though I have always wanted to see that part of the country. So when I spot the announcement for a group hike there, I immediately call Emad to start planning for us to go. It was Emad who first introduced me to these long, organized hikes, called the Maseer, run by an old man named Father Frans, a Dutch Jesuit who came to Syria in 1966 and settled in Homs, where he established a community center near the city. Each trip is intended to bring people from various backgrounds together to explore different parts of Syria.

The first time I went to a Maseer with Emad was when I was nineteen, not long after we first met. Although it is not acceptable for women my age to sleep outside their homes, my mother encouraged me to go when I told her about it. She said it was a shame that we didn't explore other parts of Syria more often. I agreed. But to be honest, seeing other parts of Syria wasn't my motivation. Then, like most people my age, I was itching for any opportunity for independence. Alia had no interest in going and did not understand why I would sleep in a tent if I were not homeless.

I saw beautiful scenery on these trips that I had never realized existed in my country. But the real thrill was in meeting new people. There were many foreigners in Syria at the time, either studying Arabic or just touring and visiting ancient historical sites. I was afraid to talk to them—my father had once told me that all foreigners were spies. But I was fascinated by the other Syrians, especially the women. They seemed to live in a different universe, one where women lived alone, studied theater, pursued degrees I had never heard of, and supported themselves financially. Marriage wasn't their end goal, and what their neighbors said about them seemed irrelevant; they were the opposite of the women I was raised with in Jableh. Listening to them made me aware of how small a bubble Jableh is. I am grateful that my mother allows me to go on these trips. Perhaps she wants me to see for myself that there are life trajectories other than the path my father had always paved for me—there is a whole world outside of Jableh, a world she was once part of but was forced to abandon so she could raise us.

Emad tells me he will not accompany me to As Suwayda. He is concerned about our safety as an Alawite and a Christian traveling there. "No one knows where the terrorists are hiding," he says. Predictably, Alia also declines, seeing no value in walking for miles under the blazing sun. But I still feel it is worth it to go, so I set out alone.

It isn't long before I realize Alia was right about the weather: As Suwayda is like a desert—hot and dry, with no trees, just endless expanses of yellow and red soil. This time, there aren't many foreigners in the group, likely due to the protests. But there is one American woman who decided to remain in the country because her boyfriend is Syrian—not only that, but he is from Latakia. He is around my age and had moved to Damascus for college. His name is Walid.

I must admit, under different circumstances, if I had just met Walid in Latakia and learned which neighborhood he'd grown up in and that he was Sunni, I would have done what was expected of me and not engaged in conversation with him. He belongs to the exact class and people my father looks down upon. But over the following days, I decide to let my guard down. As we trek for miles side by side, I learn that Walid is a third-year political science student at Damascus University, supporting himself by teaching Arabic to foreign students—although there aren't many of them left in Damascus, either. In his free time, he is learning Turkish, a third language that will, he hopes, help him get accepted into a master's program in foreign affairs abroad after he finishes his undergraduate studies.

When our trip comes to an end, I am grateful for the chance to have gotten to know Walid. I admire his intelligence and persistence—he is paving his way in life, preparing to study abroad by learning two languages. His future will be the result of his own efforts. He has what I increasingly feel is missing from my own life: the belief that he can become whatever he wants to be without following the path his family has prescribed for him. When the trip ends, we promise to stay in touch.

LOUBNA MRIE

That year, we celebrate Eid at my grandmother Wadia's house in Damascus. My family's Eid routine has changed in the wake of Grandmother Tamra's passing. Alia and I no longer change into new clothes, scramble down the stairs, and cross the street to Tamra's apartment to spend the first day of the holiday with her and my uncles. Instead, we take the bus to Damascus to spend the holiday, as well as longer stretches of our summer and winter breaks, with our mother's mother. After years of associating Damascus and Grandmother Wadia's home with a period of my early childhood that I had no desire to revisit, these trips change our relationship for the better.

In the summer, we spend our days wandering through markets, the air smelling of incense and leather, men urging us to enter their stores. There, my mother teaches me the art of bargaining: She proposes a price to the seller and then starts walking away, and as if by magic, the seller chases after us, agreeing to my mother's initial offer.

Our winter visits always take place after our exams—first in grade school, then later in university. During these visits, the nights are so cold that the back of my nose stings whenever I take a deep breath. Every morning, I wake up and rush to the window, hoping that today will be the day I'll see my grandmother's lemon tree blanketed in white.

When we lived there as children, the tree and its fruit were off-limits—just like everything else in the house. But now, my grandmother seems to enjoy cooking for us, the house always smelling of fried garlic and ghee. It smells like a home, a home where I feel welcomed and that I eagerly seize every opportunity to visit.

DURING ONE OF MY TRIPS to Damascus, I decide to reach out to Walid, and he invites me over for tea. He lives in a small, beautiful house, the interior scented with woodsmoke from his living room fireplace.

DEFIANCE

Although he greets me warmly, I can tell that something is not right. We gaze into the flames as he finally confesses that he wants to spend the holiday with his family in Latakia, but he's terrified that he might disappear at one of the checkpoints because he is Sunni, and his village, marked on his ID card, has become a hotbed of protests. He tells me that the Mukhabarat showed up at the home of a family friend and shot him dead after someone reported that he had attended a protest, and two of his cousins got detained. Though he misses his mother, he can't risk imprisonment or death to see her. I listen quietly and nod, my head spinning. How is it possible that I have been so oblivious to this violence when all of this has taken place in Latakia, just a few minutes' drive from my university?

A few days later, I wake up late and sit drinking my coffee at my grandmother's kitchen table, waiting for the fog in my brain to lift. I find myself scrolling through Facebook, when I stumble upon an announcement for a protest scheduled for later that day.

The post announces the funeral of a young protester, Bassam Bara, who was shot in the head the day before. The protest will take place less than half an hour away in Barzeh, a neighborhood I have never visited. Damascus is a socioeconomically segregated city. Despite the time I've spent in the capital, I've never traveled outside of the few upscale neighborhoods within walking distance of my grandmother's house.

On impulse, I call Walid to ask if he wants to hang out, our conversation about his family and the checkpoints replaying in the back of my mind. I suggest Barzeh but don't mention the protest outright.

"Are you insane? Don't say this on the phone!" Walid shouts. He knows that there are daily protests in Damascus's outer suburbs, many of which begin with the funeral of a protester killed the day before.

"I just want to see it for myself," I say.

"Loubna, this is not some Father Frans hike!"

"Fine, I'll go alone!"

But Walid refuses to let me go alone. He meets me outside my grandmother's building, his face pale. Years later, Walid will tell me that he feared I had decided to go because of our conversation in his house and felt a responsibility to protect me. He flags a minibus, and I can see his hand trembling as he slides the door open for both of us to get in.

This moment would stay with me for years to come, as I came to reflect on the urgency I felt that day and that drove me to attend the protest, despite the risks. All my life, I had been taught to memorize, follow, and obey instructions, which was essential to being a good woman, daughter, and Syrian. I was never to raise my voice or disagree. My decision to attend was motivated not by politics, which were still largely opaque to me, but by a desire to challenge this ingrained obedience and gain a better understanding of myself. It was like disobeying my grandmother during our visit to the shrine and lifting the green cloth over the sheikh's tomb, risking being blinded and cast into oblivion, just to prove something to myself by glimpsing the bare stone. Or the high I got from cheating in school and challenging authority in a broken education system. I knew I needed to go, even if I couldn't articulate the reasons at the time.

However, going to the protest was not as harmless as lifting the green cloth. Despite Walid's warnings, I was still surrounded by such a facade of normalcy in my daily life that I could not anticipate the danger I was about to face; it was unthinkable. No one had questioned where I was going when I got dressed, said I was going out, and closed the door behind me.

TWENTY MINUTES LATER, Walid shouts to the minibus driver to pull over. He hands him a few coins and we jump out onto the street and into the fray. My eyes are immediately drawn to the green flags, each with three stars, waving over the crowd. This is the independence flag, the one that predated the Ba'athist coup. For the protesters, the current red Syrian flag is marred by its association with the Assad regime.

There must be hundreds of people in the crowd, possibly more; it's bigger than any video I have seen online or on TV. Women and men are clapping their hands in unison. "God, Syria, freedom, nothing else!" they chant in one loud voice. I feel my heart pounding. Above us, the bare mountain, Qasioun, radiates an orange glow in the afternoon sun. I hold Walid's hand as we make our way through the crowd. "Men to the front!" a woman shouts at him. He drops my hand and pushes his way forward, disappearing into the crowd.

I am alone with a group of women. One of them, to my left, wears a white scarf over half her face. Sweaty creases form on her forehead as she chants in a high-pitched tone, her voice joining the many others. The chants echo off the surrounding buildings, enveloping us all. "The people want the fall of the regime." I stay silent. "The people want the fall of the regime," they repeat. I feel a hand on my shoulder, squeezing and patting me the way one consoles or encourages a child. It is the woman in the white scarf. She is staring into my eyes. "The people want the fall of the regime." I hear her voice distinctly in the loud chanting of the crowd. I turn away.

"God curse your soul, Hafez!" one voice chants. The crowd repeats the words. I've heard this in videos before and read it in the comments sections on news pages, but hearing it aloud in real time is different. I stand on the sidewalk and look for Walid, but I can't find him. Hands over heads point cell phones toward the edge of the crowd. A wooden casket covered with a green shroud and flowers floats above the heads and shoulders of the protesters. It moves in circles as if the men carrying it are attempting to show off the body of the dead man, the martyr.

The crowd chants, "Bassam, Bassam," followed by "With our blood and soul, we sacrifice for you, our martyr." High-pitched ululations explode from deep within the women—the same sound women make to welcome brides and grooms at weddings, the same sound that used to send men off to battle from desert camps. Today, it is all for Bassam, the dead protester who lies in a coffin a few feet away. The men chant, "To heaven we are going, martyrs by the millions."

As I grab my phone to call Walid, I hear a loud sound, like a drum. I look toward the front of the crowd. The green wooden casket falls to the ground, and people run in my direction. Their eyes are wide with fear. I search the faces for Walid, but I can't see him, and I start running with the crowd. The gunshots get closer, becoming louder and louder. The people scream, "Allahu Akbar! Fuck your sister, Bashar!"

"I don't want to die, I don't want to die!" I hear myself screaming as I run with the sea of people flowing into narrow, unfamiliar alleys. I make a left turn and then freeze on a street corner between a parked car and a wall. My head spins as I try to locate myself and figure out where to go. I gasp for air, struggling to breathe through the fine, chalklike dust kicked up from the stampede. I look to my right and see a man running toward me. Our eyes meet and he slows down, then stumbles to the ground and rolls to his side to avoid the rush of the crowd, but when I see the blood tainting the ground underneath him, I understand he has been shot.

I take off running again. Someone pushes me from behind, and I fall to the ground. People step on my hands, pressing my palms into the pebbles. The weight grows stronger and stronger on my back and legs. I try to push myself back up again. Suddenly, two arms lift me under my armpits. "Are you okay? Were you shot?" The stranger sprints through the crowd with me in tow. I feel warmth trickling down my knee. Suddenly, he makes a turn, and I find myself at the entrance of a building. We climb the marble stairs.

He pushes a door open and lets me in. "Don't worry," he says, "this is my aunt's house." He disappears inside. Shoes are scattered at the entrance around the dark brown doormat. I untie my shoes with trembling hands and follow him. The house is oddly calm. I hear gasps and the soft sound of weeping coming from the women congregated around the windows. As I get closer to them, I move the white curtain, and I look down onto the street to see two men carrying the limp body of another man by his arms and feet. His torso is barely above the ground, and blood trails behind them.

The women mention the man's mother's name. He was one of the men carrying the casket of the dead protester, and tomorrow he will be carried in one himself. "May God curse your soul, Bashar . . . may God curse your soul," one of the women says as she wipes her tears. "This is the eighth person," she adds.

Minutes later, one of the women notices me struggling to roll up my jeans, stained with dried blood. "Come with me," she says, leading me to a chair in the corner. She is wearing an off-white prayer gown with a long hijab that covers her head and arms and flows to her waist, with a matching white skirt. She asks how I know Ziad, the man who brought me here. I tell her about the fall and his help. "Allah yerdha 'aleeh"—may God be pleased with him—she says as she sits cross-legged on the floor. She gently rolls up my jeans to examine the wound.

"Basita, basita," she repeats, bringing her eyes closer to my knee, scanning the dark red blood. "It's okay." She takes a cotton pad, soaks it in red liquid, and gently pats my knee. Then she rolls white gauze around it, which she tapes to my skin with Band-Aids.

"And here as well," I say, unfolding my scraped, raw palms. She holds my throbbing hand, wipes the palms with the same liquid, and then grabs a pair of silver tweezers to pick out the shards. I bite my lower lip hard and try not to cry.

"Do you live around here?" she asks.

"No, I came for the protest," I say.

"Do you know anyone in Barzeh?"

"No. I just saw the invitation on Facebook." As the words leave my mouth, I realize how foolish I sound. "I didn't expect it to be like this," I add, trying to justify my presence in her bedroom, lost and bloody.

She stops picking at my palms and looks at me.

"What did you expect to see?" Without waiting for an answer, she turns back to my hands. "You haven't seen anything yet," she whispers.

My phone rings. It's Walid. He's in a house nearby being served tea. He says he'll come find me as soon as he finishes. I try to give him directions to the building I'm in, but I really have no clue where I am. The lady takes the phone from me and tells him the name of an intersection where she will drive me. "No, please," I say. "I can go alone." I tell her how embarrassed I already am. She puts a finger to her lips, shushing me.

"Beware of the checkpoints that will be set up outside Barzeh," she says, sliding her arms into an ankle-length dark blue coat. "Especially the one on the Ish al-Warwar side."

"What about Ish al-Warwar?" I ask.

"The people there are monsters!" she exclaims. "They're often the ones shooting at the protesters, not the police. They even join the security forces when they raid houses. I can't believe we lived side by side with them all these years. They were always hiding all this anger and hatred toward us. May God take his revenge."

Although she doesn't say the words, I know she is referring to Alawites, the main residents of Ish al-Warwar. I know this neighborhood. I always thought the name was funny—it means "the bee eater's nest." It earned the name because of its high altitude, its alleys so steep and narrow that only motorcycles and small cars can reach its highest points. It's an odd slum in Damascus, often the first stop for young men from Jableh, as it's one of the few neighborhoods they can afford to live in. In fact, some streets in Ish al-Warwar are named after villages in the mountains of Jableh.

As I tie my shoes, I feel the urge to tell her that I am Alawite. That she shouldn't generalize, and that she doesn't understand the Alawites' fear of the president abandoning us. I want to tell her about the checkpoints across Jableh and the Alawite mountains and how, when Hafez passed away, hundreds of Alawite families fled their homes in big cities thinking the only reason they hadn't been killed by their Sunni neighbors was because the president had been protecting them. I want to tell her that they fled like their ancestors fled the Ottomans. But I stay silent. It does not matter. The men behind the guns now are monsters, and nothing can justify their brutality. I thank her again and go down the stairs.

We drive through the deserted neighborhood. It's almost impossible to believe that less than two hours before, these same streets and alleys were filled with protesters and chants, filled by a revolution. When she drops me off, I see Walid across the street. She waits for me to cross, I wave, and she drives away.

"Are you okay?" Walid asks. "Who is this woman?"

I start crying. I notice his red eyes and can tell that he has been crying, too. I try to apologize for dragging him along with me. I am responsible for the horror we've both experienced. But no words come out. I open my bloodstained palms to show him my wounds. He rolls his eyes and opens his hands as if he is thanking God.

"Al-hamdulillah. Now I don't need to worry about creating a Facebook page for your death. What would I even call it?" he says jokingly. "'We Are All the Martyr Loubna'? You wouldn't even be considered a martyr. You're an infidel!" We both burst into laughter as he tries to flag down another minibus.

On our way out of Barzeh, we pass through several checkpoints. Small groups of young soldiers are posted on every other street, their rifles held tight to their chests, poised to address any threat, believing they are the ones under attack.

Before too long, we find ourselves stuck in Eid traffic. Horns and music blast from cars around us. I look at the other passengers, searching for any signs of fear or anger about what happened earlier. Some are staring at their phones. Others look out the window, smiling at the radio program the driver has put on, interviewing people about what kind of sweets they made and which of their spouses' mothers they visited first for Eid. How can anyone keep going knowing that this level of injustice is taking place? It feels like an ordinary Eid, like every other Eid I've spent here. Do these people not care about what is happening? Maybe they've witnessed the violence but believe there's nothing they can do to stop it. Maybe they cope with the bloodshed and brutality by ignoring it.

I get home with the plan to go straight to my room, change clothes, and wash off the blood before anyone sees me. But as soon as I enter the apartment, I run into my grandmother. She smiles and asks me to grab a cup and have some coffee with her under the jasmine vine in the garden. I start to cry. She comes closer, concerned.

"What's wrong?" she asks. I hug her, pressing my face into her chest. "What happened? Tell me." She pushes me back to look at my face.

"They shot at the protesters. I saw dead men." Her eyes widen. She slaps her chest with one hand just like she does when she catches me eating from the pot while she is cooking or when I walk with my shoes on her carpet. "You were protesting?" she whispers so quietly I almost can't hear her.

"They killed people," I say. She looks into my eyes and squints. Lines deepen around her dark green eyelids. Her hand seems locked to her chest. "Allah yghdob aleke," she says. "May God curse your soul." Her lips tighten and she shakes her head. "Allah yghdob aleke."

I start rolling up my jeans to show her I'm not the one she should be angry with. "Look," I say, stretching my leg so she can see the white gauze, stained with blood. She covers her eyes with her hand. A horrible grimace takes over her face, and she looks away.

"Don't you know that if you curse the president you will go to hell?" She storms off, leaving me alone in the entryway.

I go to my room, lie down on my bed, and close my eyes. I'm not sure how long I've been asleep when I'm awakened by the sound of my mother shouting at me.

"Is my daughter without a brain or is she just extremely selfish?" She demands to know who took me there. I tell her Walid went with me, but before I can explain that I was the one wanting to go, and not the other way around, she asks how I can be so confident that Walid is not an informant.

But what she seems most angry about is that I told my grandmother. "I saw her on the phone. I'm sure she's already called half of Jableh. She might have even called your father. What am I going to tell him? You are my responsibility. I will be blamed," she says.

I bury my head under my pillow. She keeps shouting, demanding answers, but I can't describe what motivated me to go. She yells that I do not understand what I am getting myself into, what my father would do to me if he knew about this.

"Stop exaggerating! He doesn't have to know!" I shout back at her. She just shakes her head and leaves the room, slamming the door behind her.

When I finally push myself out of bed and walk into the living room, my mother is nowhere to be seen. My grandmother is sitting on the couch, legs crossed, staring at the television screen.

"Where is Mama?" I ask. She waves her hand toward the phone, her eyes still on the screen.

"Are you happy?" she asks. "Do you understand that your father is waiting for any mistake to blame your mother? Did you want to give her a heart attack?"

I roll my eyes. Every time she or my mother gets angry, heart attacks, the jalta, come up. They are certain that everyone in the family will eventually die from a heart attack, just like my grandfather. Any effort to disobey or anger them is a direct attempt to kill them. I sit on the couch next to my grandmother and I think of how stupid I am. I could have avoided this whole mess if I had just kept my mouth shut.

A news report on the state-run Addounia channel shows "the reality of Eid in Damascus." The broadcaster tells us how amazed he is by the courage of our people. He is proud that, despite all the lies of conspiracy channels such as Al Jazeera and Al Arabiya—all their lies to scare us—our streets are brimming in celebration of Eid. Behind him, a group of kids jump into the frame, making the two-fingered victory sign. "This is the real Syria of Bashar al-Assad," the broadcaster says. "If you watch the conspiracy channels, you won't see the truth of the streets of Damascus. You'll think that people are being killed left and right."

The broadcast shifts to a video showing the highway near the cemetery in Barzeh. I recognize the street; it's only a few steps away from where I saw people being shot.

"People died. I was there. I saw them," I hear myself say. My grandmother ignores me. I raise my voice. "I swear, people were killed there today!" She tells me to shut up and turns up the volume on the program, her eyes fixed on the screen, refusing to look at me.

TEN

At noon the next day, I'm sitting alone in the living room when Walid messages me a link to a video. I recognize the neighborhood as Barzeh. In the caption, there's a call for protesters to join the families to escort the bodies of the eight men who were killed yesterday to their final resting place, the local cemetery. It starts in two hours.

My breath quickens as I slip on my headphones and play the video. It is shot from a high point, possibly a balcony or a rooftop. As the camera shakes, it zooms in on a group of men. Some are dressed in army uniforms, while others are in plain clothes. Behind them, security force vehicles.

The men stand in the middle of the street, chatting and laughing casually with one another while holding their rifles. The sound of chants slowly gets louder. The men aim their rifles. From the upper left corner, protesters enter the frame carrying a casket. The men fire in the direction of the crowd. The body in the casket, wrapped in fabric, and the flowers are now on the ground while people run, stumbling around them. The men shoot again at the protesters. It terrifies me how easy it looks for them to fire at the crowd. At us. At me.

I take off my headphones. I feel grateful this was taped. These men will now be held accountable. They can't get away with this. No one should get away with this.

"Are you going to the funeral?" I type to Walid.

"Daymeh," he replies, which is what you say when someone offers you food, but you are full. He asks me if I am going.

"Of course not," I write. "I am not insane."

I shut my laptop, but I cannot get the video of the men firing at the crowd out of my mind. I could have been dead by now. What if I had been slower or had run in the wrong direction? It would have been my burial today. I would have been one of those eight people. A heavy sense of guilt washes over me. I go to my room, change my clothes, and sneak out of the house.

WHEN I ARRIVE AT THE MOSQUE, I see a dozen or so women gathered outside the closed door, waiting for it to open. I walk toward them but remain on the fringe.

A girl roughly my age approaches. She has a round face and is wearing a white headscarf and a dark blue coat. She presents her tight fist over my hand as if she is offering me something. I open my hand, and she places small swatches of soft white cloth. "Keep these with you," she says. "They are clean. If anything happens, just squeeze as hard as you can." She turns to the girl next to me and hands her white shreds of cloth as well. I press the cloth into my palm. I can feel the warmth of the girl still in it. I look at the women and girls around me. Some are laughing. I'm practically shaking with nerves, but they seem confident, as if they know what they're doing.

The wooden mosque door opens for the Islamic funeral prayer, the

Ṣalāt al-Janāzah. I remove my shoes, enter, and follow the women as they begin forming lines on the red and gray carpet. They all face one wall with big windows and white curtains.

I am the only one not wearing a long robe and headscarf. Glancing down, I notice my cleavage showing, so I quickly pull up my shirt to cover myself. My chipped dark nail polish catches my eye, reminding me that some Muslims believe one must conceal the body's shape and remove nail polish to meet God properly and have their prayers accepted.

Feeling self-conscious, I look around. Though I'm certain people are judging me for my appearance, no one seems to care. The prayer begins, and I focus on the girl ahead of me, mimicking her every movement. She stands with her hands crossed over her chest, then bends and kneels. The sequences continue, guided by the sheikh's voice reciting the prayer through the black loudspeakers. We can't see him; he's in the men's prayer room.

The girl places her face in her hands, and I follow, pressing my face into my palms. She starts to hum. Unsure, I move my lips, pretending to recite along. I sneak a glance around the room. Everyone's eyes are closed, their hands cover their faces. There are so few of us. The security forces could round us up and detain us in minutes. I scan for the nearest exit, my mind racing. Maybe it's better that I don't look like them. I could claim I'm not with them, that I ended up here by mistake.

The sheikh begins the Duaa'—a prayer pledging faith in God—in honor of the men who were killed. He tells us that martyrs can bring forty of their family members with them to heaven. Someone weeps behind him as he speaks. He concludes the Duaa', saying, "Please remember what happened yesterday. The graveyard is only a few blocks away. Carry the casket in silence so that these men may rest in peace. Let's not provoke anyone, for the sake of the martyrs."

Just then, the speaker blares: "Death over humiliation!" The crowd of men repeats the words over and over until the loudspeakers are turned off. We can still hear them in the women's section through the open windows. Everyone stands up and rushes to the door, some stumbling over the pile of shoes. I follow, and when I step outside, I can't believe my eyes. Hundreds of men and women are waiting for us. The ululations are so loud that I have to cover my ears.

The flagstones are cold beneath my bare feet. I quickly put on my shoes and follow the crowd. "Down with the regime!" the people chant. I open my mouth and repeat the words, softly at first, then louder. Hearing my own voice terrifies me, but I keep chanting. The more I chant, the louder I become.

A burning sensation in the back of my throat forces me to stop, catch my breath. I watch a line of older women leaning on each other as they march with the crowd, slowly, sobbing, wiping their eyes with the ends of the scarves covering half of their heads and faces.

"Mothers of the martyrs, we are all your children," we chant for these women. My heart aches, recalling the video of how indifferent the soldiers were when they fired at women and children. I wonder if they even paused for a second to consider the consequences of pulling the trigger. Did they think about the pain and agony they were inflicting?

I feel a tap on my shoulder and turn to see the woman who cleaned my wounds yesterday at her house and gave me a ride to Walid. She nudges the lady next to her and points at me. "This is the girl I told you about yesterday," she says. Then she opens her purse, takes out a scarf, and covers my nose and mouth with it. She ties it at the back of my head. "You should be more careful. They are monsters. You don't want to end up in their hands." She falls into step beside me, and we chant with the crowd until we reach the graveyard.

Up ahead, vehicles and armed soldiers stand in a semicircle, pointing at us. Despite their weapons, they look fearful and small compared to us. Still, I look over my shoulder, searching for a way to escape through the crowd. I take a few steps back and realize I'm the only one hesitating.

People continue marching forward, shouting, "To heaven we are going, millions of martyrs."

The woman from yesterday suddenly grabs my shoulder. "This way," she whispers in my ear. "Let's go."

The three of us break away from the crowd and head toward the same house as yesterday. I still don't know how many people live here, but the living room is full of women. I share a small couch with a woman about the same age as my mother. She removes the scarf covering her face, revealing short, light brown dyed hair.

The woman who brought me here goes into the kitchen, and a few minutes later appears holding a tray of oranges and barazek, round cookies covered with sesame served during Eid. She answers a question as she holds the handle of a doleh—coffeepot—and fills the cup of the woman next to me. "I am not trained. But we didn't have any choice. I had to do it."

"Tfadali," she says, holding the tray in front of me. "Help yourself."

"Thank you," I say and take a cup and a saucer.

She sits on the floor and crosses her legs.

"What do you mean you had no choice?" I ask.

"Protesters who are shot and taken to the hospital end up disappearing," she explains, taking a sip from the cup. "A friend of a friend who works in the hospital told us that staff members were ordered to inform security forces as soon as a person with a bullet wound is brought in. If the staff fail to do so, or if they treat the protesters—or 'terrorists,' as the government calls them—then they are considered traitors. Doctors often have no choice but to call the police. They know informants are everywhere, and there is no way to treat protesters in secret.

"It's silently agreed among us that we try to assist the wounded as much as we can. If we can't save their lives, it is better that they die here, with us. At least we can cleanse their bodies and bury them in peace. We can spare them being burned with cigarettes and raped with broomsticks.

"Medde aidek. Don't be shy. Help yourselves," she says to everyone, offering the plate of cookies as if this is a casual visit. She empties her coffee cup and flips it over onto the white saucer decorated with golden tree branches. "Let me see if I am going to find a husband soon," she says, turning the cup in circles to swish around the wet coffee grounds. They slide slowly down the sides of the upside-down cup.

"Perhaps he will be a doctor. A good doctor. One of the doctors who smuggles us medicines and medical supplies from the hospital." She lifts the cup and presses her thumb into the coffee grounds at the bottom of the cup. She then moves the cup in her hand and scans the rim.

"May God send a treasonous doctor your way," the woman next to me says, erupting in laughter. I force a nervous smile, hoping to rid my mind of the image of a broomstick being inserted into someone's body.

As the nurse stares at her cup, the woman next to me asks me if it's true that I was here yesterday and witnessed the killings. I nod. She introduces herself. When I tell her my name, she remarks that her daughter's name is Loubna, too, and that I remind her of her. "She is also an activist. She's been going to the protests every day," she says. I am too embarrassed to tell her that I'm not really an activist at all.

"Young people are always more courageous than the older ones," she sighs. She tells me that her husband left Syria during the first week of the uprising. He's a playwright, and Syrian state television had asked him, along with other artists and actors, to appear on a television show to speak about the conspiracy and pledge support to the government. I gasp when she tells me his name—I recognize it from the comedy shows I loved, mocking surveillance and Mukhabarat members.

Something about this connection makes her feel safe and familiar to me. I lean closer to her ear and tell her I am from Jableh. When she asks if I am Alawite, I nod.

"Where does your family stand in all of this?" I look around the room to see if any of the other women are listening, then quietly tell her my grandmother believes I am going to hell for protesting the president, and that people believe he is our only protection against radical Islamists and foreign powers.

There is a heavy pause before she exhales and says, "Government supporters don't trust an uprising that starts in mosques. But we're not allowed to gather in squares. It's the only way we can organize ourselves."

She tells me that young people have tried to organize protests around Damascus. There were a few attempts in Shaalan, an upscale market street next to my grandmother's house. The police rounded up the first activists the minute they started raising their voices. Then another group tried to demonstrate in silence by marching in matching white shirts. The police threw everyone in a white shirt into a minibus and took them to a government detention center. They were only released after signing papers that stated they would never protest again.

Another group that calls itself Days of Freedom scattered ping-pong balls bearing anti-government slogans across the streets of Muhajreen near the Presidential Palace. "You should have seen those government thugs running after tiny bouncing ping-pong balls with their rifles slung over their shoulders," she chuckled. Later, the same group poured red ink into the grand fountains at the heart of Damascus, a symbol of the bloodshed staining the country. They even installed hidden loudspeakers in busy streets, blasting revolutionary songs that had the security forces cursing as they hunted for the source of the music.

"We've tried everything, but the government will suppress any gathering against the president and the Ba'ath Party, no matter how peaceful or harmless it was."

She checks the time on her phone. "Do you want a ride home?" I thank her, say goodbye to the hostess, and promise to see her again.

ELEVEN

When I return home to Jableh after my time in Damascus, I begin noticing, as if for the first time, the propaganda that I had grown so accustomed to throughout my childhood. In our neighborhood and throughout the city, walls are plastered with pro-Assad slogans and photos of the president and his late father and brother. Some of the posters are so poorly enlarged and pixelated that their faces appear almost deformed. Around my university campus in Latakia, I notice young men and women my age wearing dark green pants tucked into military boots as if looking like Syrian army soldiers is a new fashion trend.

Songs praising the president are the background soundtrack of daily life, blending with the sounds of bubbling hookahs and laughter in coffee shops, and blaring incessantly from taxis and street vendors outside. "Bashar, there is none like you. We have pledged our allegiance in blood and declared our love for you. / May our souls and bodies be sacrificed for you, the guardian of Syria. / In your shadow, we unite, and in your glory, the country rises." These lines, a mix of different songs, worm their way into my mind. I catch myself unconsciously singing along, not even realizing when or how I memorized them.

Only at my laptop am I reminded of what is happening in other parts of the country. In the final weeks of 2011, social media is flooded with images of scenes similar to what I witnessed in Damascus. Across Syria, people are carrying caskets, burying their loved ones at the risk of being buried the next day. As the government intensifies its violence, more people join the demonstrations. They take to the streets, knowing they could die, but their anger outweighs their fear. It is a level of courage I hadn't known existed—like something out of a novel.

My mother often cries while watching the news. Though she is still angry with me for endangering myself by attending the protest, and terrified that my father will find out, she sometimes says that if her father were still alive, he would have condemned the government's reaction and sympathized with the protesters. "He would have been against this level of brutality. He was principled," she says.

EMAD IS THE ONLY ONE I feel comfortable speaking to about any of this. Despite his reservations, I know he can see through the propaganda being forced on us. During the long hikes we used to take together, he would often join other groups and engage in political conversations about things I didn't know much about: uprisings, revolutions, hunger strikes, imperialism. Although I often lagged behind, I admired his ability to talk to new people and the extent of his knowledge. Now, I finally feel that I have something to share, something to offer—knowledge gained from witnessing pivotal events firsthand.

I meet up with Emad one afternoon at one of our usual coffee shops in Latakia. In a low voice, I tell him about the protest in Damascus. I describe the blood on the pavement as men carried the bodies of the wounded and the heart-wrenching sight of women watching from their windows as their children and neighbors endured this collective agony. When I'm finished, I look at him expectantly.

"Loubna, this is not a revolution," Emad begins, crossing his legs and leaning back against the couch. Recognizing his tone as the one he uses to lecture me, I begin tuning him out. Behind him, the wall is adorned with photos of men and women known for their advocacy for freedom, dignity, and women's rights in decades past. Some of them are even former political prisoners. I know that many of these individuals are now vocal supporters of the government.

My gaze shifts between the photos and Emad, who is now recounting how his friend in Homs told him that the protests are led by people who forbid their sisters to receive an education. These same men and women are proponents of child marriage and honor killings. No freedom can come from the "Abo Shahata crowd" and the "slippered throng," he says, slang terms used to describe the lower class who wear slippers outside because they can't afford proper shoes.

Then Emad repeats something I've heard often in Jableh: "The president isn't doing enough." He worries that if the government doesn't act quickly to restore order, these slipper-clad, sectarian thugs will take over the country and kill us. For our safety, he argues, we must stand with the government. Not because the government is great—it is oppressive, he acknowledges—but because our safety is paramount. The government is protecting us. They are not perfect, but they keep us safe, and they're better than the alternative.

In all the years I've known Emad, whenever we've had disagreements, I've tended to stay silent because I lack the vocabulary to explain and defend my positions as eloquently as he can. I am intimidated by his ability to be a good medical school student, to read books and keep up with the news, and to absorb so much information that he can then wield in conversation.

Now, though, I am not silent from admiration, but from disgust at his prejudice. He is fascinated by the grand history of revolutions in Europe, yet he doesn't believe that his country's people have legitimate grievances and reasons to stand up for their rights; they are beneath him. He seems to be saying that if some of these backward people have to die to maintain order and keep us safe, then so be it.

But I know that nothing can justify the cold-blooded killings I have witnessed. How much ruthless repression can we ignore in the name of security? How can we trust a government that is constantly manipulating us into believing that oppression is an inevitability, and a necessary one?

LATER THAT WEEK, the phone rings, and I hear my mother's hurried footsteps approaching my bedroom. When I see her face, I know it must be my father calling because the news of me attending the protest finally reached him. My heart skips a beat.

As soon as she hands me the phone, he erupts in anger, threatening to cut off my allowance and the werteh. He warns that if I ever attend another protest, I will rot in jail, and he won't help me. No one has ever dared to humiliate him this way before, and now his own daughter is dragging his reputation through the mud.

"You're an ingrate," he screams. "After everything I've done, what everyone will say is that Doctor Jawdat's daughter is a traitor." He reminds me that, as his daughter, my actions impact him and his reputation, and my worth is measured by the honor or disgrace I bring upon his name. As punishment, he concludes, he will not pay my college tuition for the next year.

With that, I finally understand my mother's advice: I should never have depended on my father when it came to my education. She knew, long before I did, that he would use it as another way to control me. I feel trapped. If I had been killed that day, would my father have buried me in secret to avoid the shame of "Doctor Jawdat's daughter" being labeled a traitor? I could have died, and all my father cares about is what people might say about him.

In the silence that follows, I know what he is waiting for. I am one sentence away from appeasing him. All I have to say is, "I am sorry, you are right," and perhaps give him Walid's name to prove the sincerity of my apology—but I just can't do it. It is physically impossible.

"I will get a job," I hear myself whisper.

"What did you say?" my father asks.

"I will pay my own tuition," I repeat, a bit louder than the first time.

"Good luck finding anything better than cleaning houses," he spits and hangs up.

It takes me a few days to realize that my father is right. I lack the skills to get a job. I wonder if he has been preparing me all my life for this exact moment—the time when I think of breaking free from him, only to understand how desperately I need him; how helpless and worthless I am without him. I finally see why he was always happiest with me when I brought home poor school results, why he always reminded me that education was worthless. What mattered was his approval—men's approval—of my looks and my obedient behavior, not my knowledge or talent. If it weren't for my mother, Alia and I would never have even considered college. I wouldn't have attempted to learn English: It was my mother who always insisted that another language would "broaden our horizons," as she put it. My father called her crazy and wasteful, but she never wavered.

Walid is the only person I know who has a job and is financially independent from his parents. I call him and tell him my father has stopped supporting me because I went to the protest. Walid says it is his fault I ended up at the demonstration in the first place and offers to pay my tuition with the money he has been saving for his education abroad.

I object—I would have gone alone if he hadn't accompanied me. And I refuse to view going to the protest as a mistake, even in hindsight. The only help I need from him is in finding a job. Walid assures me that if I truly want to work, I can find something. "Do you think everyone in this country has a rich father? How do you think other people our age survive?" He offers to share his house with me and tells me that I can easily support myself by teaching Arabic, as he does. I'm too ashamed to admit that, unlike him, I'm not even qualified to teach my native language. I passed my Arabic grammar and poetry exams the same way I passed all my other subjects—by cheating.

After hours of scrolling, I stumble upon a job opening at a web design company in Damascus. The requirements are vague: computer skills, basic internet knowledge, and a "decent appearance." The phone interview focuses on my knowledge of the web and my ability to use a computer. A few days later, I'm offered the job. The salary isn't great, but it's enough to cover my share of rent and food. In a few months, I'll have saved enough to pay my tuition.

To my surprise, my mother is very supportive when I tell her about the job offer. She says it will be good for me to work and to understand the value of money. She has only one condition: My education must come first, and I must find time to study and return home to take my exams and graduate.

I am terrified at the thought of leaving home and being away from my mother and Alia. Walid is a man, and it is permissible for him to move to another city to work. He can move back to his family home and be celebrated for his return, but this isn't the case for women. Although Alawites are considered open-minded—women work alongside men and don't cover themselves, and family gatherings and weddings are never segregated, and men and women dance together holding hands—there is still a strong emphasis on reputation. I can name the girls from Jableh who left home. It doesn't matter that they left to study in Damascus and Aleppo and were living in dorms; they were stigmatized. A good woman only moves out of her father's home to move into her husband's. Many of these girls, knowing that people would look down on them, got jobs in Damascus or Aleppo and stayed there because they knew their reputation was ruined, ruling out good chances of marriage.

My mother's encouragement is reassuring, but I worry that, in ten years, I will look back at this moment and hate myself for a choice I knew would cost me the only thing that mattered—the reputation I had carefully guarded and maintained for so long. Still, I cannot bring myself to apologize to my father. That would mean betraying those whose deaths I witnessed. I cannot and will not bring myself to doing it.

But I suddenly see a third option, the route my mother often took when she couldn't rely on my father to send money: I could ask Uncle Jamal for help.

LIKE MY FATHER AND Uncle Wahib, Uncle Jamal is wealthy. A few years before, he and his family had moved into a mansion overlooking Jableh's corniche. "Our new living room is the size of your whole apartment!" my cousin said when she called to invite me over.

I never visited her; in fact, I never spoke to her again. Something in her tone made me feel small. Worthless. My father had disrespected us so much over the years in front of her and her family—I wondered if, growing up, she had internalized that it was okay for her to do the same.

Because my father had refused to give Aunt Samia one of Grandmother Tamra's houses she had spent years managing, she had moved in with Uncle Jamal after her husband's death and children's marriage. Though they had no formal agreement, I understood that she was allowed to live there in exchange for her assistance with housework and raising my uncle's six children. After I've knocked on the wooden door of their marble-faced home for the first time, my last exchange with my cousin still ringing in my ears, it is Aunt Samia who lets me in and leads me into the living room—which, I note, really is bigger than my mother's whole apartment. Uncle Jamal and his wife are seated on the couch.

Before I can say anything, he declares that I should be grateful that my father only cut off his money and not my tongue. He goes on, belittling me: I am a disgrace to the entire Mrie family, and I should be ashamed of myself. As he talks, his wife nods vigorously beside him.

I'm trying to find a way to interrupt Uncle Jamal and leave when Aunt Samia emerges from the kitchen, rag in hand, and begins scrubbing the dining table under the glittering chandelier.

"You should go tomorrow, first thing in the morning, to your father's house, kiss his feet, and apologize," she declares, cupping her hand beneath the table's edge to catch the stray crumbs. "There is no one like your father. Don't defy his word! Don't risk your werteh with your stubbornness!"

She is loud and insistent, but I can barely hear her. Sitting here in my uncle's opulent house, watching Aunt Samia behave like his servant, I am struck, finally, by total clarity.

I had often wondered how my aunt felt about the fact that my father had given his mistress one of Grandmother Tamra's houses instead of her. I had assumed she was furious—even I had felt righteous anger and shame on her behalf. She shouldn't be relegated to wiping crumbs from Uncle Jamal's table in her old age. She should be comfortable and secure in a home of her own. That she defends my father still—the very person responsible for her current circumstances—leaves me speechless. Despite everything, she accepts him as the family's guardian and won't say a word against him.

Nothing disgraces a man. For the first time, the implication of that phrase truly sinks in. Only a woman's actions can irreparably damage the family's reputation. A man's choices will never be deemed unacceptable—not my father denying his sister her inheritance; not my uncles' affairs, routinely humiliating their wives. These men hold the power and the purse strings. Everyone else exists to be controlled and play a supporting role.

It isn't just the government that is oppressive, I realize; oppression is deeply embedded in my own family. "Good" women, like all marginalized Syrians, must follow the rules and never question or challenge the powers that be. In return for total submission, we are led to believe that these authorities—fathers, husbands, dictators—will guarantee our safety. Anyone who refuses those terms and attempts to carve their own path is branded an outcast and made to suffer social, emotional, financial, and even physical consequences. I had watched my mother endure so much humiliation at the hands of my father over the years, only to ensure a future for Alia and me.

Though Aunt Samia has also suffered serious indignities, she doesn't retaliate against the family men in anger; instead, she is reinforcing the same misogyny, enabling them to threaten and manipulate everyone else, including me. She is complicit. But being an agent of their exploitation doesn't empower her—quite the opposite; she is still so obviously disrespected that my heart aches on her behalf. I wonder how much mistreatment she is willing to tolerate out of fear. I finally understand her bind, and I pity her.

In that moment, I realize that no stability could be worth this oppression, this degradation. I understand that our oppressors will never be our protectors. And, for the first time, I know I am not alone in this revelation. I show myself out of my uncle's house, never to return.

PART II

TWELVE

Right after I finish my exams, almost a month after my visit to Uncle Jamal's, I take Walid up on his offer and move into his apartment in Damascus. He gives me the bedroom and converts the couch in the living room into his bed. Every morning, I walk downhill to catch the minibus that takes me to my new job at the web design company.

Most days, as I wait for the bus, I call my mother. Between long sips of her morning coffee, she remarks that she never knew my obsession with my laptop would ever prove financially beneficial. "It seems like just yesterday that you were beginning first grade," she sighs, and then reminds me how proud she is of the woman I'm becoming.

I don't tell her that, although I do indeed work for a web design company, my daily responsibilities have nothing to do with web design. My only task is to go to the office every morning, open the catalog for businesses in Damascus, and search the internet to see if these companies have websites. If they don't, I call and introduce myself and my company in the nice, sweet voice my boss Muhammad asks me to use. He calls this "the art of marketing." I explain to the business owners what a website is and how hiring my company to design their first website could double—even triple—their profits. "Today, business is all about technology," I say, reading the sentences my boss wrote down for me during my first training. "Your website is your business's front window. Would you enter a shop if the front window was not enticing?"

At times, these opening words provoke yelling and cursing on the other end of the line. Sometimes they just hang up on me. But in most instances, the call lasts long enough for me to mention that we—my colleague and I—would like to pay him and his business a visit. And it's always a "him."

"You have nothing to lose except two cups of coffee for us!" I say, forcing the low-pitched laugh my boss taught me. This is another scripted line. I don't fully understand why it works, but it almost always does, and I find myself scheduling one free consultation after another. I write down the meeting times and addresses on a piece of paper and hand it to Muhammad.

Muhammad is in his mid-thirties and has been working for the same company for years. He comes in on time every single morning, after ironing his shirt and spreading a pound of gel on his greasy black hair. He constantly reminds me that he can't drink Arabic coffee because his stomach is "hypersensitive," which is really just his way to show off his sophisticated Western taste. The only coffee he can drink, he says, is hazelnut Nescafé.

Muhammad often insists that I accompany him to meet our potential clients. I resent this because I have to wake up early, wash my hair, and put on makeup. I have no interest in or knowledge of web design; my main task is to smile and compliment the owner on something in his office. It could be anything—the dusty plastic tropical plants, photos of his kids, the rug, the coffee, the metal cabinets. According to Muhammad, compliments make the client feel as though we have similar tastes and, therefore, would work well together. My other task is to nod along whenever Muhammad talks about our customers' businesses that are thriving thanks to the websites we designed. It's fascinating to see him explain the internet to old, balloon-bellied Syrian men. With a website, he tells one client, his small olive oil company could become internationally recognized. He might even be invited to food expos in Europe! Anything is possible—if you just sign the contract, he says. And whenever someone signs, I get a small cut.

BACK IN THE OFFICE, Muhammad always disappears into the big boss's room, and I make more calls. I never see the company's owner doing anything besides watching YouTube videos and yelling into the phone at our actual web designers, who are always behind on their schedules.

When I finish around 4:00 p.m. and walk to the minibus stop, I am met with the daily grind of Damascus rush hour. Now I understand what my mother endured every single day when we lived at her mother's house. For the first time, I truly appreciate how deft she was at concealing her exhaustion, making time to help with our homework and taking us out almost daily so we wouldn't feel trapped in that small room of ours.

I get off near the small bakery on my street. It sells fatayer—little pies stuffed with spinach, onions, sumac, and other fillings—the most satisfying food I can get for the lowest price. With fifteen liras, I can keep myself full until lunch the next day.

WALID ARRIVES HOME from work around the same time every evening. We keep the TV on, loud but ignored. I lie in bed in my work clothes, listening to Walid move about the house. The hiss of the stove's burners is soon followed by the familiar aroma of eggs frying in olive oil, Walid's daily dinner. We are both too exhausted to talk.

I scroll through Facebook, checking the news and updates on the recent protests. It's always depressing, but I only stop when my mother makes her evening call. She inevitably asks what I've eaten and curses every time I mention fatayer pies. She blames herself: "I ate too much bread and pastry when I was pregnant with you and that's why you eat so much bread!" She advises me to buy parsley and make myself a salad. She says she'll teach me an easy recipe for lentil soup. Or I can at least buy a can of sardines. "Eat it with lemon," she says. "Otherwise, you will deplete the iron in your blood. You need to eat more than just bread; this is why you have no energy!"

Her warnings start to make sense when I begin noticing the growing jumble of hair clogging the shower drain. No matter how much I sleep, I always feel tired and dizzy. Many nights, I just fall asleep in my clothes to the sound of Walid's Turkish language program alternating with *FarmVille*. Some nights, he comes into my room, angry about the mess I've left in the living room. "I am not your mother!" he shouts, throwing whatever he picked up in the common area on the bed: a jacket, a bag, food wrappers. It's embarrassing to admit, but over the last twenty years, I never learned to take care of myself—my mother was always there to clean up after me. Now, for the first time, I am on my own.

ON ONE OF THESE EVENINGS, scrolling through Facebook after work, I see a comment mentioning my street and a protest organized nearby. I send a private message asking one of the commenters for more details. We end up chatting for a few hours, and when he realizes that we live two blocks away from each other, he jokes that I could be an informant but says he is going to trust his gut this time and asks if I want to meet up with him.

The next day, after work, I get off the bus two stops before the usual one. A guy in a red flannel shirt with short, curly hair and glasses greets me. He introduces himself as Amer and leads me to the basement of a nearby building. As I step in, the pungent smell of Hamra—local Syrian cigarettes—hits me, and I wrinkle my nose. Noticing my reaction, Amer quickly reassures me that it's his friends who smoke, not him.

Amer is an art school graduate. "What the hell is scenography?" I ask. He tries to explain what he studied, showing me photographs from Syrian movies and theater sets. "I designed this," he says. "And this." He points at a photo of a big tree. Its branches are covered with old cassettes and strings.

"You're very talented," I tell him, not knowing what else to say. He pulls a small torn and wrinkled sketchbook from his back pocket. "Very nice," I say, flipping through pages filled with drawings of ugly, distorted human figures.

Truthfully, I can't tell whether Amer's work is good or not; I don't know much about art. But I like the idea of having met someone who calls himself an artist.

Amer tells me that he has been living in his studio since the beginning of the uprising to avoid his family, especially his father. Even though they are poor and have never received any privileges from the government, they oppose the change. Amer is Christian. Like Emad and my father, his family believes that if the president is overthrown, they might die at the hands of the Islamists.

I begin spending most of my evenings after work at Amer's studio. His friends remind me of the people I used to meet on the Maseer. They are all independent from their families, and their lives and futures don't revolve around marriage or their fathers' approval.

I come to understand that unlike in Jableh, a city divided between Sunnis and Alawites, no one judges people based on their sect in the secular, intellectual circles of Damascus. I am not the only minority. Naji, a journalist with long black hair who I come to realize is responsible for the studio reeking of Hamra cigarettes, is an Isma'ili from Salamiyah. The older girl with short hair who often accompanies him, and who uses phrases like "civil society," "secularism," and "transitional justice," is an Alawite who moved to Damascus years ago to study economics.

There is another short-haired girl, Walaa, which makes me wonder if women in this group cut their hair as an act of rebellion against societal expectations. I later learn that Walaa writes and records songs mocking the military and uploads them to YouTube, an incredibly risky—almost suicidal—thing to do.

We're all too broke to hang out in bars or coffee shops, so most nights, Amer's friends bring over cheap local wine. Sharing two large green armchairs and a few white plastic chairs, we sit around a wobbly table with pieces of paper folded under its legs to keep it balanced.

After I offer to buy Amer a new table when I get paid, he raises his eyebrows, almost in astonishment. "Are you insane? I made all of this on this table. All of this," he says, pointing at the off-white sheets nailed to the walls covered with large renditions of his ugly, distorted figures. "I might lose my talent if I get rid of the table!"

The table isn't the only thing in terrible condition in Amer's studio. His TV, which is often turned to the pro-opposition Orient News satellite channel, only works after he gives it a hard slam on the side. A rusty gray electric heater is the only source of warmth, blowing dry air that makes my face feel like chalk. When it's on, it shakes so hard that we often have to switch it off and put our jackets back on so we can hear each other.

Every day after work, I message Walid to assure him I am okay, then spend hours listening to Amer and his friends. Most are painters and writers. I am fascinated by how effortlessly they sprinkle big words into the conversation, and everyone nods as if they understand. I always feel out of place, out of sync. I don't speak because I feel too stupid to say anything. I take shelter in my silence and nod as they talk about a Syria I have never known.

From their conversations, I learn that most artists leave Syria after graduation. There are very few art galleries because, to obtain permission to open one, gallerists must know someone in the government. This connection is required as artists and intellectuals are known to oppose the government. The restrictions and surveillance are such that they move abroad.

Even Amer was planning to leave Syria; he wanted to pursue postgraduate education in Germany. But when the revolution started, he chose to stay. For the first time in his life, he said, he felt that the government could change and a decent and dignified future was possible.

I also learn that it's not only artists who are being monitored. The government controls most of the media; almost every news channel and website is state-owned. Before 2011, political journalists were forced to choose between writing uncontroversial pieces for these outlets or risking their lives by writing under pen names for Lebanese publications or websites, most of which were blocked by state-run internet providers. Naji tells me that many journalists refrained from reporting altogether at the start of the uprising, knowing that if they didn't toe the party line, they would be considered traitors or accused of collaborating with those conspiring against the president.

But now, with the advent of social media, Naji and others see an opportunity to subvert the government's censorship to an unprecedented degree. They feel it is their duty to document what is happening on the ground around the country, especially since the government makes it difficult for foreign journalists to enter and report freely. They believe every protester with a cell phone is a journalist. This is why, Naji explains, it became his passion to train protesters to record what they see. "This is not Hama, 1982," he says, referring to the largely undocumented massacre of more than thirty thousand civilians by the Syrian Arab Army and the Defense Companies who, under orders of President Hafez al-Assad, besieged the town of Hama for twenty-seven days to quell an uprising organized by the Muslim Brotherhood against the Ba'athist government. "We cannot let the government dictate our history."

Every time Naji speaks about journalism, I am riveted. The vast majority of the coverage on the uprising has been generated by regular people with cell phones and internet access. Documenting the government's brutality, Naji says, is the first step toward stopping it.

Naji's wife, Bushra, is pregnant. Although Amer will not leave Syria, he often advises Naji to move his family someplace safe. But Naji refuses.

"This is our moment. Bushra understands; she supports me. That's why she married me," he says. "She doesn't expect me to flee."

SOME EVENINGS, AMER'S PLACE hums quietly with the sound of voices counting money. The shaky table is covered with the face of the president's late father, printed on the national currency. Wealthy businessmen often donate money to people like Amer, claiming their hearts are with the revolution, though they can't afford to declare their support publicly. The money is used to feed the newly displaced people from other cities— cities that have been bombarded and besieged after soldiers defected from the army and fought back to protect the protesters.

In Amer's studio, I discover a very different version of the summer's events, when the dead soldiers were brought to Jableh and met with rice and ululations. State television had told us they had been killed in their sleep during an attack on their base in the Idlib governorate.

Now, I learn that the soldiers had been sent to the funeral of a young protester killed nearby the day before. The funeral had grown into a massive protest, with more than fifteen thousand people showing up. The soldiers prepared to fire at the protesters but were shot from behind by other soldiers from villages around the Idlib governorate who refused to see their friends and neighbors killed.

A few days later, a video circulated online of a lieutenant colonel in the Syrian army named Hussein Harmoush from Jisr al-Shughur, the town where the funeral had taken place. He announced his defection from the

DEFIANCE

military and the formation of a brigade to protect local protesters. Harmoush was believed to be responsible for the resistance in the town and the first army soldier to fire at government forces in defense of the locals that day. He soon became an icon of the resistance.

Many soldiers followed his lead, taking their ammunition and weapons with them, and forming small groups with other defectors. Civilians, ranging from doctors to construction workers, joined them, united in the belief that a peaceful uprising would never be powerful enough to overcome the government's brutality.

Between July and November of 2011, the armed rebels' primary mission was to protect protesters from security forces. For the first time, people could march without fear of being shot. Protesters chanted for the armed rebels. Before long, the rebels began fighting the Syrian army to liberate their towns from government control. These new rebel-held areas became subject to widespread collective punishment. Starting in 2012, the government deployed the air force to destroy these areas, bombing villages, schools, and hospitals. Anyone who lived in a place outside of government control became a legitimate target.

Meanwhile, cities like Damascus got flooded with displaced families, though the government offered no assistance to those who fled the bombardments. Activists reached out to Syrians living in exile to collect money to buy sugar, rice, wheat, and baby formula for besieged cities like Daraa. Security forces considered this an act of treason.

The refugees had to say they fled to escape the "terrorists"—the government's blanket term for anyone who dared to stand against the president. Those caught attributing their displacement to government bombardments were threatened with detention and even death.

The majority of the displaced fled to Turkey, which had opened its borders to allow their escape. Protest leaders and army defectors went with their families to Turkish border towns like Hatay—approximately a two-hour drive from Hussein Harmoush's hometown—where they could meet and organize safely. One colonel, in a written statement, made a plea for matériel support: "We ask the international community to provide us with weapons so that we, as an army—the Free Syrian Army—can protect the people of Syria. If the international community sends us weapons, we can topple the regime in a very, very short amount of time."

Although the Turkish government initially did not admit to providing the FSA with military support, it did offer a safe place for rebel commanders to meet with their donors.

Turkey also became an important conduit for financial aid from countries like Saudi Arabia and Qatar, despite the FSA's ideological disagreements with the Saudi or Qatari models of governance. Syrian rebels were so desperate that when Hussein Harmoush was later kidnapped in Turkey and resurfaced in Syria, leaders of the Free Syrian Army refrained from questioning whether Turkey had a role in his kidnapping, presumably out of fear that any criticism could jeopardize their only channel to foreign backers.

With money and support provided by other countries, they were able to cross back into Syria and take over their villages and cities. As border towns fell out of Syrian government control, many of those who had fled to Turkey returned to live in areas under Free Syrian Army control.

This exact topic often leads to heated debates among Amer's friends. "This is not an army!" is a recurring response when the term "army" is used in the conversation. As I understand it, the argument goes that an army implies structure, unity, and leadership, but the armed wing of the resistance is a group of people led and unified by anger and the conviction that a peaceful uprising cannot overthrow the government. Some are averse to the rebels because they believe that the rise of an armed opposition will only give the government further justification to escalate violence throughout the country. After all, countries like Saudi Arabia and Qatar are not supporting the rebels because they care about democracy and the ideals we are fighting for. These Gulf countries simply want a Sunni government to replace the Alawite one.

This argument is often met with the slam of a hand on the already-broken table. Someone shouts about the number of people killed and injured by government forces in the first months of the uprising—months before any government soldiers were killed. Or they shout about women being raped in front of their husbands during interrogations, just because they protested or wrote something on Facebook. The government doesn't need any excuse to kill or intimidate civilians. People are desperate for support to fight the government and willing to take what they can get, even if it's from the devil himself.

The disputes almost always end the same way. Amer shushes everyone, reminding them to keep their voices down. "My walls have actual ears," he says. His next-door neighbor, a single mother who shares a wall with us and often her weak Wi-Fi, might overhear us and feel obligated to write a security report.

SOME EVENINGS, THE STUDIO is empty. In February of 2012, there are nightly protests in neighborhoods outside the city center, masked, armed men protecting the demonstrations. They block the entrance to the neighborhood and ensure that government forces cannot attack. Amer and I travel together to the protests by minibus and meet up with our friends. I find it odd that the same friends who oppose the militarization of the revolution also hesitate to join if the protest is not protected by these armed men.

Almost every time, Amer argues when one of the protest leaders asks me to join the women's section. Just like in Barzeh, most of the protests here are segregated. They say women will be safer if they are behind the men, but here, I realize it's also because women and men shouldn't be touching shoulders. This enrages Amer, who insists that he and I are equals and should be able to march side by side. "The women here are more courageous than all of the men who are watching us from their windows!" he shouts.

It is only when I beg him to stop that he quiets down, and I go to the back to avoid conflict. I will only see him when he pushes his way through the women's section and extends his arm to me, asking to borrow my scarf, which he uses to cover his face before going back to the front of the crowd and taking the microphone. I slide my phone out from my pocket and film him shouting, "I am a Christian! I came here with my Alawite friend. We are here because we do not believe the government's narrative. They're portraying us all as Salafists and Al Qaeda, but we know the truth: This is a revolution for all Syrians. We are in this together. We are willing to die for one another." Amer then leads a chant: "One. One. One. The Syrian people are one!" The screaming and ululating around me become so loud that I need to cover my ears.

Many of Amer's friends are against him declaring his sect. "The government wants this to be sectarian! We are all Syrians. If we play the same game as them, it will only feed into their narrative!" I find it mind-blowing that, in the same country, some people cannot see past sectarian lines, while others don't see sect at all.

Amer believes that it is better to acknowledge our differences and prove that we are united despite them, rather than to pretend they don't exist.

AFTER THE PROTESTS, Amer walks me home and waits outside until I've closed the door behind me. Sometimes Walid is already asleep, but other times he is hunched over the table studying as the muted television casts its blue light. Without looking up, he asks me how my "Damascus Spring" meetings are going.

When I don't ignore him, I drop my bag on the floor and play him videos from the protests. "I don't want to see!" he shouts. Walid will not look or listen because, if he gets detained, he doesn't trust himself not to tell on us. He refuses to go to the protests. He only accompanied me to Barzeh because he felt responsible for my safety. He points out that Amer and I are minorities; the government trusts us and considers us innocent until proven guilty, just like in the classroom. He, on the other hand, is one of the kids forced to sit at the back, always blamed when chaos erupts.

Knowing all of that, I don't argue with him. Instead, I bring my printed lectures, which I pay the library in Latakia to ship to me weekly. I join him at the small, scratched wooden table in the living room, the air heavy with the aroma of the strong coffee he always makes in the evening to keep himself alert. We sit in companionable silence, interrupted only by the rustle of pages or the sound of Walid tapping his pen against the table when he's deep in thought. Eventually, our eyelids grow heavy, and the words on the pages start to blur. We head to sleep.

ONE DAY IN THE SPRING, when I'm visiting Amer as usual, two long white lilies stand in a glass jar on his table.

"These are for you," he says. "Today is your day."

I bend over the flowers to smell them. Nothing.

"Thank you!" I say, hiding my confusion. Today is March 8, the anniversary of the revolution we incessantly studied in school and had to celebrate every year: the day of the Ba'ath coup. It is the day when we would line up after the flag salute and sing anthems for the Ba'ath party until school was over.

"These aren't for the Ba'ath revolution," Amer says, sensing my misunderstanding. "We're reclaiming this date—today is International Women's Day!" I hold the two lilies and remain silent.

All my life up to this point, I had believed that the only way to be celebrated as a woman was to become a mother, because the only holiday dedicated to us is Mother's Day. I have always loved Mother's Day. It is on March 21, the beginning of spring.

Each year, we had the same routine at home. Alia and I would wake up, go to my mother's bed and hug her, then make her coffee and bring it to her bed as she talked to her mother in Damascus on the phone. Then Alia and I would walk to the flower shop a few blocks away and get my mother the only thing she requested every single year: red roses.

She often said that my sister and I were her gifts in this life. We were enough; she didn't need anything else except the flowers. For days, the house would be filled with the sweet scent of roses, which she always placed in a large vase on the dining table. As time passed, the flowers would die, their petals blackening before falling onto the tabletop.

My mother would collect them and make the same comment year after year: "This is what happens when you cut something off its roots. It cannot survive on its own."

I gaze at the lilies Amer brought me, admiring their green stems. I realize that, in two weeks, it will be Mother's Day. For the first time, I won't buy my mother red roses or be in the house with her to watch them die. I, like them, have been cut away from my roots. But being here, I wonder for the first time if my mother was mistaken. Moving away doesn't always result in wilting and death. She encouraged me to become independent so I could realize that I, too, deserve a day to be celebrated. My self-worth shouldn't be contingent solely on being a wife or a mother. My value shouldn't depend on a man's judgment of whether I am good enough to marry and bear his children. Nor should my mother's. If my mother had received the support she needed, she would have stayed in Damascus, and our lives would have been so different. My mother would have had a real, fulfilling life. She would not have been forced to live in Jableh, isolated just to raise us. She should not have had to choose between her life and our future. She should have been able to have both.

DEFIANCE

. . .

ONE EVENING, WHEN I get home, Walid tells me he needs to talk. His eyes avoid mine, focusing on the floor.

"The landlord came by," he says.

My heart drops. Walid and I have lied to the landlord, who lives on the top floor. We told him I was Walid's sister—the only way we could live together without raising questions.

"Did he find out that I'm not really your sister?" I ask.

"No," he replies. "But he says it's not acceptable for you to come home after midnight escorted by a stranger. He says your behavior might ruin the building's reputation."

Amer offers me his studio to stay in.

"I can crash at my parents' house," he says, brushing off my hesitation.

The studio isn't exactly suitable for living—there's no washing machine, no bed, just a mattress on the floor and a tiny desk covered in Amer's sketches and art supplies. I agree anyway; I don't want to deal with the landlord. I know I'm not going to stop attending the evening protests, and I can't risk Walid losing his home because of me.

It's temporary, I tell myself. The end of the government feels imminent. A few weeks, maybe a couple of months of discomfort, seems like a small price to pay for what we believe is just around the corner.

When I pack and say goodbye to Walid, he jokes that I should come study with him if I ever need a break from my sophisticated new friends. We hug and promise to stay in touch.

THIRTEEN

One afternoon, I walk into the studio and find Amer bent over a big white sheet on the table, dipping a brush into a can of bright red paint. In bold letters, he writes: "Stop the Killings. One Country for All Syrians."

"You have an exhibition coming up?" I ask, laughing.

"It's for a silent protest today near the old city market," he says without looking up from the table. "The plan is to hold up the sheets in front of cars and stop rush hour traffic."

"That's suicidal," I say.

This gives Amer a reason to spend the next twenty minutes explaining to me how assyan—peaceful acts of civil disobedience—are crucial, especially now, when the government is trying to portray the uprising as armed chaos.

"We need to show people that a peaceful movement is still in place, still the dominant effort," he says. Although I'm not fully convinced, I decide to come along.

A couple of hours later, we join others at the site of the demonstration. Once the traffic light changes from green to red, we are supposed to walk into the middle of the road. We split up and stand at the various corners of the intersection to avoid signaling a planned gathering, which could lead to preemptive arrests.

The green light turns to yellow. I clutch Amer's red plaid flannel shirt, and my legs begin to tremble. I keep my eyes on the traffic light. Then I notice a short man on the island between the intersections with a video camera, nervously positioning it on a tripod. This will be filmed. This could be aired later on news channels. And I can picture my father in his armchair, ashtray holding the last of his cigarette, half asleep, gazing at the screen. My father never misses the news; he watches both state TV and the pan-Arab channels. If anything, he watches the same reports over and over again. He might see this. My heart drops. Even though I sometimes feel that I've freed myself of his grip completely, the thought of him getting angry sends a shiver down my spine.

I cling harder to Amer's shirt. The light turns red. Amer breaks away from me and marches forward. I take a step back. Part of me wants to run, but I am rooted in place, perhaps out of shame or curiosity, with my eyes fixed on Amer. After a few seconds, there are fifteen or so people gathered under the traffic light. Amer takes one end of the sheet, and a girl takes the other. "Stop the Killings. One Country for All Syrians." They stand there, blocking the cars. Other demonstrators with banners surround them. I hear claps and whistles. Those who find themselves in the middle of all this start running away, terrified of being misidentified as participants.

The light turns green, and Amer and the others remain frozen in place, causing the traffic to come to a halt. The protesters lift their banners, forcing people to read their messages. The strategy behind the demonstration suddenly becomes clear to me. By disrupting the normal routine of life in Damascus, these people will go home and tell their families what they have seen. The people at the intersection are forced to look, read, and witness the courage of the few.

Suddenly, I hear a voice shouting from a distance, "Run!" The group starts rolling up their sheets, tucking them under their arms, and running in different directions. The flow of traffic returns to normal instantly. I walk down a side street, feeling ashamed. My phone rings, and I see that Amer is calling. I hesitate to answer but click the green button.

"Are you okay?" he asks, panting and running. "Where are you?" I give him my location, and minutes later, he arrives with the same young woman who was holding the sheet with him.

She turns to me. "Are you okay? Why are you crying?"

"I have been so worried about all of you," I say.

She rolls her eyes. "It was beautiful. No one got hurt. There's no need to cry." She slips her curls behind her ears and tucks her chin under the collar of her soft pink turtleneck sweater.

"I'll see you later," she says, hugging Amer goodbye. She waves at me and departs.

Amer tells me her name is Batool. She is Alawite as well. "She is as brave as ten men," he says, sliding his bag onto his shoulder. "And she's really smart. You two should be friends."

His words trigger pangs of shame and embarrassment in me. It feels like my smart and courageous facade has crumbled, revealing my true cowardice. They see me for who I really am. When they show up and commit, I stay behind. I feel lonely and weak.

I INTENTIONALLY DELAY returning to Amer's studio that evening, waiting until I'm certain he has left before I arrive. Instead of taking the minibus home, I walk along al-Hamra Street, famous for its mile-long strip of high-end shoes, handbags, jewelry, perfume, and clothing. Shop owners yell from their storefronts, swearing to God that all their items are from Turkey and Lebanon. Not a single item is made in Syria.

My mother, Grandmother Wadia, Alia, and I came here every summer we visited Damascus for back-to-school shopping. In elementary school, we were free to wear whatever we wanted underneath our brown aprons, and I was proud that my clothes came from this street; it made me feel special. Other kids showed up to class with their shoes reeking of gasoline, the most efficient way to kill germs from secondhand shops.

But what I really loved about al-Hamra Street were the bridal stores. I could spend hours staring at the white gowns covered with sequins that reflected the colored spotlights illuminating the window displays. My mother would pull me away, reminding me, as she always did, that I was too young to think about anything but my education. I'd look back, wondering when I would be old enough to get a gown myself. Old enough to marry. These memories make me feel even lonelier. Maybe I am too desperate to leave that version of myself behind and become someone I am not, and now I am just lost in between the two versions.

I walk toward Arnous Square, with its wooden benches and food carts selling fava beans and bright yellow ears of corn dusted with sumac. The air is rich with the smell of boiling lemon. In the windows of Maison de la Gaufre, waffles are smothered in hot dark chocolate and topped with vanilla ice cream.

My mother, grandmother, Alia, and I used to sit in the square after hours of strolling, window-shopping, and bargaining. Nothing has changed here. The benches are the same. The ugly palm trees with yellow trunks still look out of place. Families are scattered with their shopping bags and little plastic plates. I sit on a bench, fumble through my bag for my phone, and call my mother. The instant I hear her voice, I start to cry.

"What's wrong?" she asks, clearly concerned. "Tell me what's wrong."

"I'm fine. Don't worry. I just miss my bed, and I feel stupid. Leaving

Jableh has made me realize how little I know about everything, and work is exhausting."

She tells me not to worry. "This is how we grow. This is how we learn. Come home if you are tired."

"I am in Arnous Square," I say, changing the subject.

"Eat something! Sirop is only a few blocks away," she suggests cheerfully.

"I haven't been there since I moved here," I confess. "Can you believe it?"

Sirop is my favorite sandwich place, famous for its paninis stuffed with pickles and sujuk—Armenian sausage that is so spicy it is almost impossible to swallow unless followed with a gulp of ayran, a yogurt drink mixed with salt and garlic. I used to beg my mother to take me there.

"Go eat," she says. "It will make you feel better."

She's right. Just the thought of holding that toasted bun in my hands and inhaling the aroma of the sausage makes me happy. For a second, everything else—the street corner, the banners, the words, the courage, the pink sweater—seems so minor. My mother knows the real me, not just the person I am trying to become, the one Amer thinks belongs with him and his friends. In that moment, it is a relief to allow myself to be appeased by her. I thank her, and we say goodbye. I press the red button, wipe my tears with my sleeve, and set off toward Salhya Street.

A marble statue of Hafez al-Assad stands at the center of Arnous Square. I approach it and stop at his feet. I look up. The president's face is grim, lit by the orange glow of a streetlamp. His tie is tucked under his buttoned blazer. His right hand is raised slightly to the side as if to wave to the people and cars passing by. You can see the details of his outstretched hand, the lines in the palm that fortune tellers read. The other dangles at his side. His eyebrows curl neatly, casting a shadow over his eyes. His forehead is as big as it was in real life, as if his skull had been deformed in infancy. I wonder if the sculptor got in trouble for making his forehead too big. This is Hafez, after all; you cannot highlight his flaws.

DEFIANCE

I can't recall how many times I stood here as a child and jumped to touch the president's hand. I used to open my arms and hug his legs, and feel the cold marble against my belly, my face, the palms of my hands.

I wonder what the square would look like if Hafez's statue were finally removed, like in other countries whose governments collapsed, leaving their leaders, mythologies, and cults of personality drained of meaning. I take a few steps back. I squint and raise one hand, blocking the statue. Just like that, it's gone. Hafez is gone.

It's absurd to see Arnous Square without his pressed pants. Without the wave of his hand and the slope of his forehead. But way more jarring is the thought that the statue might remain for another twenty or forty years. What if the uprising fails? I picture my future children here on this square, playing in the shadow of their leader's grandfather, hugging his legs, jumping to kiss his permanently outstretched hand.

A few days after the protest, I message Naji. "Can you teach me?"

The shame I felt after the protest—the realization that I didn't have anything to offer—has crystallized into determination to do more, to do something that matters. Naji's words about broadcasting the brutality to help hold the government accountable have resonated with me. I want to help document the protests. I know that Naji is training amateur journalists and that taking videos isn't rocket science—anyone can do it, and I know I can, too. He messages back: "Come to my office tomorrow after work." He sends an address in Jaramana—a pro-government stronghold whose population consists mainly of religious minorities like Christians, Druze, and Alawites. It cannot be right.

"Your office is in Jaramana?" I type.

"That's right," he says.

WHEN I ARRIVE VIA MINIBUS, Jaramana feels familiar. It reminds me of Jableh; almost every wall has a poster of the president, and every balcony and window announces their loyalty to the government.

Naji opens the white wooden door and welcomes me inside. His office is a house so empty that my footsteps echo on the bare floor. There is a green futon, a gray desk, and a plastic map of Syria on the wall. Just like the ones we had in our geography textbooks in school, it still features the Sanjak of Alexandretta—a region Turkey has occupied since 1939. However, maps in Syria still include it within our borders because we believe we will liberate it one day, alongside the Golan.

"Aren't you scared here?" I ask.

"This is the safest place to be," Naji answers. "No one will suspect that the news footage of anti-government rallies in Damascus is edited here. They assume everyone here is ready to die for the president. There are no raids or checkpoints."

He lowers his voice and tells me the names of two men who hid in the house. They slept on the futon and bathed in the sink for days before fleeing to Lebanon. I don't recognize the names, but I can tell by Naji's tone that they are important.

I hand him a flash drive with some videos I took while protesting with Amer, the footage Walid refused to see. Naji opens my videos on his computer. He slides a chair next to him and asks me to sit down, putting on his headphones.

"Don't write anything down," he says. "Memorize what I am going to tell you."

Naji then begins, pausing every other second or so to make comments: Stop humming while filming. Keep your hands still. Why do you zoom in on the feet? Why do you keep zooming in and out? Count to six before moving to the next scene.

DEFIANCE

For every comment Naji makes, I have a justification. How can I not be shaking? It's a protest! How can I direct my phone at people's faces? People will think I'm a spy. What if someone sees these videos, recognizes the people, and takes them to prison? People have short attention spans, and six seconds might be too long, no?

Naji slides his headphones down, resting them on his neck, and squeezes the sides of his head with his fingertips. He takes breaths.

"Do you want to learn or not?" he asks.

"I do," I say. And then I shut up.

After nearly two hours of going through every clip and photo I took over the past few months, Naji says that none of my videos are usable, but I shouldn't be discouraged.

"You will learn!" he says. "Listen, if Abo Abboud from Hama learned to film and CNN uses his videos, you can do it, too. Just be patient."

NAJI IS RIGHT; I improve. I begin taping the protests, following his instructions, bringing the footage to Jaramana to be edited. Transferring the videos in person is safer and even faster than transmitting them over the internet. Afraid of the security services catching me with a hard drive, I keep the videos on my phone. When I'm stopped at a checkpoint, I use a hairpin to remove the memory card. I slide my hand through the minibus window, ready to drop the card if the soldiers decide to search me.

Following Naji's advice, I change my phone's screen saver to a picture of Bashar al-Assad with "We love you!" in bold red on a white background. But I am never searched.

At Naji's office, he slides his chair over, eyebrows furrowed in concentration, and watches my clips. More commentary follows, along with instructions to be memorized. As much as I try, I still can't overcome my fear and keep myself from shaking. It takes me a few tries to record a long, steady video of a nightly protest. The street's orange light reflects on clapping hands. Naji accepts the video and drops it in a Skype room, linking media activists and journalists inside Syria with news channels on the outside.

The government is trying to write off what is happening, but we prove otherwise. We are preserving history to say we, you, and I do exist, and we will always be here. Oppressive powers just wait for us to exhaust ourselves and give up. Cameras, pens, and journalists are the most powerful forces in this war. Naji tells me it is ironic that Bashar brought the internet to the country in 2000, thinking it would make him look progressive; he could not have suspected it would be our main channel to send videos to the world and organize. He did not know it would be the first nail in his coffin.

Naji and I become close. I feel comfortable around him, though I don't know exactly why. Maybe it's because he is the oldest of the people I've recently met in Damascus—we're fourteen years apart—I am twenty-one and he is thirty-five. Or maybe it's because he, too, moved to Damascus from a small town—Salamiyah, near Hama—that is home to the Arab world's largest concentration of Isma'ili Muslims, another minority sect like the Alawites. Naji is Isma'ili, and most of his extended family thinks that he has been brainwashed. Their judgment is familiar.

I tell Naji everything I cannot tell Amer. I tell him that I grew up worshipping the president. That I feel so embarrassed and inferior to everyone around me, like I've grown up in an entirely different country and will always be an outsider. I tell him about my father, my aunts, and my mother, and how, in a way, this political moment is what made me stand up for myself. If the uprising had never happened, I don't know if I would have had the courage to rebel, if I would have realized that I needed to break the cycle and that everything I grew up believing was wrong. And that at the same time, I feel guilty for standing against a system that has benefited me. It is like I am betraying both my future and my past. I always knew I was lucky, blessed to carry my last name and be my father's daughter and uncle's niece.

Naji is never judgmental. He listens and nods. He tells me to trust my instinct, to listen to what my heart tells me, and that I should be proud that I can see right from wrong at such a young age.

FOURTEEN

Following Naji's advice, I change my name on Facebook to Loubana al Ali—Facebook had yet to deactivate profiles with nicknames—and regularly post updates, which are often shared alongside posts by other citizen journalists. The Syrian conflict would later be named the most social-mediated conflict in history.

I create a new profile with my real name and set my profile picture to the president's photo. My timeline is filled with articles about the numerous conspiracies plotting to take down our government. We delete our chat histories, knowing that whenever someone gets detained, the first thing security forces do is open their social media accounts to read through their chats.

Everyone uses fake names. The only Syrians able to post their political opinions freely under their real names are those living in exile, in Europe, the United States, or the Gulf. They have left the country for better-paying jobs and new lives or to avoid getting dragged into some militia or the army. They are now glued to social media, sending friend requests to activists and following everything we post. We are their hope and their gateway. Some, to feel closer to us, send messages like "May God protect you!" or "Let me know if you need anything." I never respond.

One day, I get a message from a guy whose Facebook profile locates him in Egypt, asking me what kind of camera I use. When I tell him I use my phone camera, he offers to send me money to buy a real one, saying it's the least he can do to support those on the ground.

I could use a real camera, but it feels shameful to accept cash—like I am being paid to participate in the uprising, exactly what the government claims about us. I ask Amer what he thinks, certain he'll advise me against "selling out." But his reaction surprises me.

"I know many people living off the money sent by Syrians in exile, money they send out of guilt for being away," Amer says. "Some of the people asking for money say it's going toward aid for displaced families, but they use it to pay rent and buy expensive imported cigarettes. The real problem is that he might be an informant. Did you give him your full name?"

"No. I'm not stupid," I say. "The plan is to pick up the money from an address we'll agree on once I get back to him. He said his cousin lives here."

Amer slaps his forehead and pushes his glasses back up his nose. "This could be a trap! Are you really going to meet someone you don't know?"

"You and I met online! Stop being paranoid," I say.

After a long argument and an hour on Facebook making sure the person sending the money is real, with real friends who liked his photos and left real comments, Amer decides to go himself because, according to him, he is more likely to survive the interrogation if this is a trap.

When he returns, he tells me the guy who handed him the cash wore a scarf covering his entire face, except for his eyes, and never spoke. "He probably thought *you* were an informant!" he says, handing me the equivalent of $300.

"See?" I say, holding the cash. "I told you it would be fine!"

Most of my arguments with Amer revolve around what I perceive to be his paranoia and what he calls my "recklessness." Amer believes that we cannot trust our own shadows these days. Anyone could lay a trap and get us detained, and if one of us is detained, we could all disappear. Only the most reckless among us would take the bait, and Amer fears it will be me.

According to Amer, I often talk before I think. I've lost track of how many times he's kicked my foot under the table in a coffee shop or pinched my arm as we wait in line for a sandwich. But even if we lower our voices or don't speak at all, we should be wary of the "bait," as Amer calls it. The bait could be the taxi driver who complains about traffic and prices and the displaced people from across Syria overwhelming Damascus, or my boss at the web design company and the conversations he tries to have with me and Muhammad. He considers himself an intellectual elite for spending all day watching clips on YouTube from Syrian state TV about the conspiracies against our country.

Every morning, while pouring hot water from the water cooler into a cup for his tea, my boss narrates the recent updates from the news and often concludes that he doesn't understand what kind of freedom these people want.

"I don't watch the news! It gives me a headache," I tell my boss when he looks at me, waiting for my opinion. "It's all just so complicated." I thank him for helping me understand what's going on in the country.

Sometimes, though, it is impossibly difficult not to talk back. One time, he was ranting to us about the protesters' shamelessness. They were not even trying to hide their agenda. "'With blood and soul, we sacrifice everything for you, Israel' is their new chant across Syria," he said.

"That is a lie! That never happened!" I blurted out before I could stop myself. He lifted his head from his cup and looked past me at Muhammad, as if I didn't exist.

"It seems Miss Loubna hasn't been assigned enough tasks," the boss said. "She has time to argue about things she doesn't know anything about."

I could literally feel the anger hardening my limbs as my hands froze on the keyboard. "I go to protests. I've never once heard this chant," I heard myself declare, realizing too late how irresponsible it was of me to say. I kept my eyes on my screen, hoping that if I didn't look at him, he would ignore what I had just said.

I could see his silhouette still by the door. Then the office shook as he slammed the door to his room. Muhammad asked me to apologize, to tell the boss it was a joke and assure him that I would never say something stupid like that again. We both knew that would be my last day.

I was too ashamed to tell Amer why I stopped going to the office. I told him they had let me go because I was not bringing enough clients. I was embarrassed to admit that he was right. If one of us got everyone detained, it would be me.

I FEEL A SENSE of shame when I hand over the money to the guy at the electronics shop in exchange for a small black Sony camera. It was the first model he suggested for my budget for both video and photography. I decided to go for it, no questions asked. Around that time, electronics stores were advised to write security reports if they suspected the cameras, laptops, or hard drives were being used for anything related to the protests. I try my best to look relaxed. As Amer said, this is someone else's guilt, and I don't know what to do with the rest of the cash. Amer tells me to keep the money until I get another job.

"This is not mine alone," I say. "It's for all of us."

I decide to spend some of it on a nice dinner with Amer at a restaurant in the oldest quarter of Damascus. Since we met, our meals together have consisted of either sandwiches or fatayer. I cooked only once. Amer and our friends called it "your people's meal": the Alawite meal, bulgur with tomatoes and onions. After more than an hour and twenty phone calls with my mother to ensure I understood the instructions, dinner was served. There were smiles at the first spoonful, quickly followed by stones, about the size of rice grains, crunching under our teeth. I looked at them in horror. Amer slapped his forehead when he realized that I did not sift the stones from the bulgur. My people's meal went into the trash, and we walked to the fatayer place next door, the one that started giving us discounts on their stale, cold, end-of-the-day pies.

A marble fountain gurgles at the center of the restaurant. The walls are covered with jasmine. Old songs play from a ceiling speaker. The hum of conversation, the bubbling of hookahs, and the clinking of glasses in the background. Our table is covered with plates of raw meat soaked in olive oil and walnuts, plates of kibbeh bursting with ghee, and a tray of bloated bread that we deflate with a quick stab from a fork, releasing steam so hot it burns my fingers. The thought that this meal is paid for by someone else's guilt returns, but I force it away and take a spoonful of fresh, finely chopped parsley soaked in lemon. I'm not going to allow my feelings of shame to ruin the best meal I have had in months.

After dinner, we wander through the mazelike streets of old Damascus. On some walls, shiny posters of the president pledge him eternal loyalty and endless love; on others, fresh patches of white paint cover up spray-painted curses on Assad and his party. We slow down and try to read the words the white paint conceals. Then we give up and set off again.

The streetlamps tint the flagstones and the wooden window frames orange. The air here is always an unusual combination of scents: jasmine, lemon trees blooming from backyards, and grilled meat from the homes that have been turned into restaurants like the one we just left, so expensive that most people living next door to them cannot afford to eat there. It is strange to think of being unable to taste the meals whose aromas are pouring through your windows and into your home, being soaked up by the bedsheets, the curtains, and the laundry hanging on the rooftop.

Finally, the smell of bread reaches us from the ovens of Al Qaimarryeh bakery. A gray-haired man runs it. He once worked for a French baker and decided to open his own place in Damascus, where he stuffs traditional French butter pastries with Syrian white cheese and za'atar and sprinkles them with black caraway seeds. The smell is so hypnotizing that, no matter how full we are, we always stop by its large window just to gaze at the copper trays stacked with fresh croissants. That night, we can't resist buying dessert there, then we walk to Al Nawfara, a small coffee shop with low wooden chairs and cheap tea. There we stay, talking and laughing until the workers start flipping the chairs onto the tabletops, signaling that it's finally time for us to go home.

My former boss at the web design company was right about one thing: The slogan "With our blood and soul" is indeed the most popular chant during the protests across Syria. But it is not, as he claimed, followed by "we sacrifice it for you, Israel." No, the slogan is followed by names of neighborhoods in Damascus under siege, and towns—Jarabulus, Manbij, Saraqib, and other hot spots—that I and many other people had never heard of.

I am going to the demonstrations every other day now to record. Naji offers to pay for my videos. At first, I refuse. But Naji argues that I have become a journalist, and journalism is a profession like any other. For the first time in my life, earning money isn't synonymous with mindless obedience. It seems surreal; only a few months earlier, I was hunched over my laptop in Jableh, watching the same kinds of videos I am now shooting myself.

I struggle to keep myself from reading the comments and arguing with people. Commenters often debate whether the demonstration leaders are paid by the West. It is incredibly difficult to refrain from explaining that the protests are so chaotic that anyone, even I, could chant something, and the crowd would repeat it.

The people watching safely behind their computer screens and judging the protesters are missing the point of what is going on entirely: For the first time, people are risking their lives to speak out publicly in support of cities and towns they have never heard of before, places never mentioned in our geography textbooks. Now we feel united in a common cause—a phenomenon that I've never witnessed in Syria before in my lifetime.

I do not yet understand that coming together and chanting in unison does not mean that everyone participating in the protests shares the same vision of Syria's future. We are against the killing and detention of people; pondering the finer points of politics seems like a luxury. Defending ourselves against the government's brutality leaves us no time to think any further about what we want. The future is something we assume we will have time to discuss after the wanton death and destruction has ended.

A POPULAR CHANT around this time is for a city called Amuda, an iconic village in the Kurdish areas, but a town so isolated that most people have to spend some time searching for it on a map when they first hear the chant. Its protesters are famous for their signs that carry quotes and poems from the Spanish Civil War. However, I knew of Amuda long before the uprising.

Years earlier, under the blazing late summer sun in Latakia, I had helped a student who seemed lost submit his registration papers for the upcoming semester. I wouldn't typically go out of my way to help a man I didn't know—it could be read as flirtation—but I took pity on this guy.

He introduced himself as Masoud and thanked me for helping him elbow his way through the crowd; he was due to catch an eight-hour bus ride later that day. I remember struggling to draw a mental map of Syria, the borders of which ended around the four-hour mark, to figure out where he was from—the longest bus ride I had ever taken was to my grandmother's house in Damascus.

"I am from Amuda," he said, sensing my confusion.

"Where is that?" I asked.

"Near Qamishli."

I paused. "Are you Kurdish?" I uttered the words before thinking them through. He nodded, and I reflexively stepped back.

Growing up, I understood that many of the dark-skinned delivery boys in Damascus were Kurds. My grandmother used to order a week's supply of groceries from the supermarket, and when she opened the door to the delivery boy, I would notice a strange accent offering to bring the bags inside.

"No! Thank you! I still have my strength!" my grandmother would say, grabbing the heavy bags with blue veins popping from her hands. She did let delivery boys place the groceries inside the house—just never the ones with the accent. I knew she didn't have the strength she claimed; she complained about her aching hands every night before bed and massaged them with lavender-scented oil to ease the pain. But perhaps it was better to endure pain than to let a Kurd step into your home.

More than a decade before, my mother's sister had fallen in love with a Kurdish man and eloped with him before having her first son with him. My grandmother didn't speak to my aunt for a few years until she, as my grandmother would put it, "returned to her senses," left the Kurdish husband, abandoned her son, and redeemed her sin by marrying her Alawite cousin. Grandmother was so happy—especially after my aunt delivered a second son, who got named Ali, after our imam and my dead grandfather.

I didn't hear this story from my grandmother. After my aunt's return, Evan and his father vanished from the family's collective consciousness, as if they had never existed. It was my father who told me about the Kurdish husband, using the story to remind me of the importance of marrying a decent man, meaning a man who is "one of us."

"Do you want to be like your mother's sister?" he often asked when the topic of marriage came up. "She married a boyaji."

"Boyaji," shoeshine boy, is the pejorative word most people I grew up with used for Kurds. Boyaji rhymes with apoji, a term for followers of Apo, the nationalist Kurdish rebel leader, Abdullah Öcalan, who was imprisoned in Turkey. Many Kurds fleeing the poverty of northeastern Syria would come to Damascus and find work as shoe shiners. It meant nothing to my father that my aunt's husband was an artist, a painter. My father simply dismissed him as a boyaji. Someone unworthy of marriage. A Kurd. Low-class—dangerous, even.

I was in eighth grade in 2004 when one day, after the flag salute, the principal told us that our spring trip had been canceled. My friends and I looked at each other in horror. It couldn't be—the spring trip was the highlight of the school year. We would travel by bus into the highlands to one of the big restaurants in the mountains near Tartus or Baniyas, where we would eat grilled chicken and dance until our feet ached. Often, on the way back, we would stop by Qurdaha, only half an hour from Jableh, to visit President Hafez al-Assad's grave and read Al-Fatiha, the first of the Holy Quran's surahs, or chapters.

Reverence for the president, however, was not the reason we demanded the bus driver stop at the grave—what we really ached for were the pies with red pepper, onion, olive oil, and black sesame seeds from the many tannour sellers along the road. We dreamed of the trip the entire school year. Before then, it had never been canceled.

"No, please! Don't cancel the trip!" we shouted until the school principal shook the bell to silence us.

"It is not safe!" she said. "This is for your protection."

Other students—those who were the daughters of teachers—knew why the trip was canceled. They had heard from their mothers that Kurds in Qamishli, a town near the border with Turkey, had been rioting and burning shops and police stations. They were armed and attacking police officers. They wanted to separate Qamishli from the rest of Syria just as the Kurds had done in Iraq. Police officers got killed defending Syria's unity and territorial integrity, they told us. They even took down a marble statue of the president, an act as sinful as treason. We heard that one police officer from Jableh was tied to a car and dragged along the streets of Qamishli until his flesh was all scraped off.

Even though no one knew the name of the police officer or anyone who actually died in these riots, we were scared. Even though Qamishli was an eight-hour drive from Jableh, the trip had to be canceled because the Kurds could be hiding in the mountains and waiting to ambush and kill anyone who passed through—and as was the case with every single historical event in Syria, we, Alawites, would naturally be the first target. Everyone resented us. Everyone wanted us dead.

For years, I thought back to that spring day in eighth grade and felt angry. We did not get a school trip because of the goddamned Kurds and their problems. But now, I can still feel the sense of shame that overcame me when I reflexively moved away from Masoud the second I realized he was a Kurd. I remember how I rushed to conceal my repulsion.

"Just let me know if you need help with anything else!" I said. "Here!

Please take my number!" We exchanged our information, but I never answered the messages he sent me a few days later asking something about one of the textbooks assigned for the coming year.

I think of Masoud again when I hear the Amuda chants. I wonder what he thinks of all these demonstrations and whether he is taking part in them. I spend long minutes on Facebook's search bar, trying to figure out the right spelling of Masoud's full name. After running a few variations, I find him. The same face that was pouring sweat under the humid Latakia sun is now smiling in a picture with snow. I scroll through his timeline and see photos of green meadows, grazing sheep, and so many siblings.

"Your town is famous now," I type, reminding him of who I was.

He responds a few hours later. "Yes! Amuda is the capital of everything beautiful."

Without saying much, we both know exactly what we are referring to. Only anti-government channels are mentioning Amuda. My heart aches when Masoud tells me he missed the last exams and is likely to fail and be suspended. And he won't be able to make them up before graduation. It is no longer safe for him to travel to Latakia, even for university exams, with an identification card that mentions Amuda.

I change the subject, writing how surprised I am to see that Amuda is green and grassy. "I always thought that region of Syria was dry! Does it really snow there?"

"April is the best month! You should come. My family would love to host you!"

Although it is common for people to extend invitations like this just to be polite, I want to go. I could shoot a short documentary, I think, showing how a small Kurdish town is teaching us, through their signs, about world history and the revolutions and poets of generations past.

Later that evening, I message Masoud again. "If you are serious about the invitation, I will come as soon as possible! I would love to see that part of Syria," I write. I should have known that Kurdish communities are traditional, and when a Kurd from Qamishli offers their hospitality, it is always sincere.

A FEW DAYS LATER, I spend eight hours on the bus—the longest trip I have ever endured in Syria. It feels as if I am traveling to a different country. We pass through many checkpoints. Most are routine. But at one of them, the soldiers drag out a man and handcuff him. The bus is silent, and everyone is keeping a blank face, as if knowing something bad just happened but trying to pretend otherwise.

The bus grinds ahead to the Euphrates River and beyond, and finally, we reach the station of Qamishli. Masoud is there waiting with four of his sisters. I sit in the back of a truck as we travel to Masoud's family farm. The beauty of the photographs was no exaggeration. Rolling hills, a big sky, and to the west, the glowing hills of Mardin, across the border in Turkey.

For my first lunch, they slaughter an animal. I take a photo and send it to Amer. I assume that it is an elaborate welcome lunch, but I am wrong. Every meal at Masoud's family farm is a feast. Masoud's mother teaches me a few words over the next days, and the most helpful phrase by far is "Na khwazim"—"I don't want [it]."

The house smells of baking bread and the heavy cigarettes Masoud's father rolls, smokes, and offers me nonstop. Masoud's sisters work on the farm, and I try helping them a few times, but I struggle to wake up early enough. They teach me how to milk a goat.

It is not entirely my fault that I am sleeping late; almost every night, Masoud's younger sister, who is around my age, keeps me up as she whispers on the phone, late into the night, with the man who will later become her husband. As I lie there, listening to her hushed voice, it reminds me of Alia, and how she used to do the same—burying her head under the comforter, the phone cord stretching as she whispered into the receiver. I would pretend to be asleep and strain to hear whatever she was talking about.

I meet the rest of the family, including Masoud's uncle, who is an author and a well-known political figure in Amuda. Several days into my stay, we go to a house where signs are being prepared for a protest the following day. One sign reads:

> **What is a human without freedom, Mariana! Tell me?**
> **How can I love you if I'm not free?**
> **Can I give you my heart if it is not mine?**

THE SIGN REMINDS ME of Amer and how he often says that political freedom is intertwined with every facet of life, from love to personal freedom. During our long conversations in his studio, when I would often find myself nodding along and pretending to understand, Amer would argue that the revolution wasn't just political; it was personal, too—a rebellion against the outdated societal ideals we'd normalized. That he believed we couldn't truly be ourselves in a repressive political climate. When the painter notices me staring at the sign, he tells me these are lines by Federico García Lorca, a poet assassinated during the Spanish Civil War.

Sitting on a rug that evening, I hide behind my camera and ask questions I had never dared ask before—questions about 2004, the year etched into my memory, the year my eighth-grade trip was canceled. I learn that there was an uprising that began during a football match between a local Kurdish team and an Arab team. Arab fans reportedly chanted slogans mocking Kurdish figures. Fighting broke out in the stadium, and Syrian security forces intervened—brutally and one-sidedly—killing many Kurds. People were angry, not just about the dozens of deaths but about the long years of discrimination and injustice they symbolized. More than three hundred thousand Kurds had been denied Syrian citizenship by that point.

A person in Syria with no identification card is a person with no access to education, no career, nothing except the slim hope that a food market might pay them to deliver groceries, or that they might be able to collect tips from women kinder than my grandmother, or that they might be able to get away with shining shoes without being harassed by the police. Tailors risk jail for sewing traditional Kurdish clothes. Even speaking Kurdish is considered a crime, and officers have been known to attack the bonfire gatherings that mark their new year's celebrations, Newroz.

In many border areas like Amuda, the Ba'ath Party installed hundreds of Arab families along the Syrian border with Turkey to create an Arab Belt. This, it was assumed, would more effectively separate the Syrian Kurds from relatives in Turkey than the border that the British and French had drawn after World War I.

"My aunt's ex-husband is Kurdish!" I say, but I don't elaborate on the full story.

LATER THAT EVENING, I write my sign for the protest: "Love from the Coast to the Brilliant Minds of Amuda." The next day, we march, chanting for Barzeh, Douma, and other areas in and around Damascus. Just like people do in Damascus, young men and women here chant for places they have never seen.

When Masoud's mother learns that I live alone in Damascus, her first question, like any mother's, is whether I know how to cook. When I tell her I rely on cheap fast food, she insists on making me cheese from their farm to take back. On my last night in Amuda, we salt the cheese together before sealing it in a jar, and she carefully packs grains into small plastic bags. I feel a wave of sadness as I realize just how much I've missed being looked after, how deeply I've missed my own mother, and how I've taken her love and care for granted throughout my childhood.

The day of my departure, the painter I met comes to Masoud's house and presents me with a gift—the sign bearing Lorca's words.

"This is now your second home! Visit us again," he says.

I tear up when I hug Masoud's mother and sister. I truly feel this is, indeed, my second home. I place the sign in my bag and, for once, I do not think of prying men in uniforms at checkpoints. When I arrive in Damascus, I tape the sign on the wall in Amer's studio.

"I hope that by next International Women's Day, we will all be free!" I say.

FIFTEEN

After returning from Amuda, I realize how easy it has been for me to travel across Syria without undergoing even routine questioning at the checkpoints along the road. The soldiers there were mostly, if not all, Alawite; they would see my hair, glance at my ID, and hand it back the instant they saw that I was a resident of Jableh. Sometimes they would ask the name of my village.

"Al Qala'a," I'd answer. And they would mention the names of theirs: Bet Yashout and Harf Al Msetra and Al Boudi, places in close proximity to my village that I knew by name. This prompted a feeling of camaraderie, of sharing more than geographic familiarity, something like a secret bond that connected all Alawites. Perhaps our ancestors drank from the same source. We might even be relatives. When one soldier told me he was a distant cousin of mine, I wasn't surprised.

I never thought much of these encounters, but I felt self-conscious whenever they occurred in front of others. Amer once joked that I came from a celebrity family. Though he had always known that my family was well-connected, he gradually came to realize that my father's family was even more powerful than he had originally estimated. For me, it was no laughing matter. If anything, Amer's jokes reminded me that however hard I tried to distance myself from my father and the shadow of his family, even my new friends in Damascus would always associate me with them.

Amer never implied that he thought I was a poser; my inner shame about how different our backgrounds were made me feel the need to prove myself to him and others further, and to take more risks. I decided to put my ID to use and become a courier. I would deliver any supplies our group collected: gauze, rubbing alcohol, aspirin, and medical items I couldn't even name—items that could save the life of a wounded demonstrator who would be detained or even killed if they went to a hospital. Medical supplies were contraband. Anyone caught delivering them risked being tortured or executed.

The main item I carried, however, was cash, bundles of it, that we collected from businessmen or doctors who supported the uprising but wanted to stay off the government's radar. We used it to buy sugar, baby formula, lentils, cooking oil, and other basic necessities, then dropped them off at the doorsteps of displaced families.

This was long before the Syrian government realized that the increasing number of internally displaced people could prompt substantial aid from the United Nations World Food Programme and other international organizations. For the time being, it was up to us to secure the funds and distribute food to people in need.

I learned at one point that in many instances, for security reasons, the senders and receivers of the cash I was carrying were not in touch with one another. In fact, the amounts of money in the envelopes I was delivering were often unknown until the receiver counted it out. This made me realize how easy it would be to slip some of the bills into my pocket, and I did, remembering what Amer had told me: Some activists used the aid money to buy things for themselves. I was risking my life, so why not take a cut as compensation for the peril I was facing? I always found a way to rationalize purchases like new shoes (I was, after all, walking around all the time) or eating out at a fancy restaurant (I needed sustenance).

The sweet scent of cash in my hand reminded me of the rush I would feel when my father reached into his pocket to reward me for doing something that pleased him or to make amends for some horrible thing he had said or done to me, Alia, or our mother. When I realized this, I was shaken, and I decided I couldn't trust myself with money deliveries anymore. It held too much power over me, and I refused to let it continue to dominate my life. I decided to only handle supplies.

My original plan had been to go home in June of 2012, when my fourth-year exams were scheduled. But by late May, I couldn't wait any longer. I missed my mother. I missed her so much that I started to feel the same angst I had felt in my childhood when she would leave Alia and me alone in the apartment to visit one of my aunts. The separation anxiety stayed with me until my teenage years, when it became embarrassing to be seen in public with her, as it was for most of my friends and their parents. Alia and I had reached an age where we only wanted to be with our friends, eager to assert our independence, and we took our mother for granted, assuming she would live forever.

I text Naji and Amer to tell them I'm going home earlier than planned. When Naji asks why, I tell him my mother is sick.

Naji calls me right away. I hesitate to pick up, fearing that he will sense that I am lying. I reject the call. He sends a message: "I just wanted to say that if you never come back, I won't judge you."

"I'm coming back after my exams!" I reply. But I can't say the thought of leaving Damascus and moving back to Jableh has never crossed my mind. Many people I met through Amer have left. We know they are safe, that they aren't in jail. When they realized that the revolution would not take three weeks, like the overthrow of Mubarak in Egypt, they simply decided that staying involved in politics was too risky.

However, this is not what would keep me in Jableh. I worry that I will simply be overwhelmed by how comfortable life is back home. When I pack my bags, I consciously leave most of my belongings behind in Damascus so that I will have something to return to.

◆◆

As I climb the stairway to my mother's apartment, I can tell our door is open. There is a wisp of cool air from the air conditioner carrying a familiar aroma of dolma cooked with lemon and garlic. When my mother had asked me what I wanted to eat, dolma had been the first thing to spring to mind.

"You've lost so much weight!" my mother exclaims the moment I come into view. I fight back tears as she hugs me tightly. She lists the dishes she will prepare for us during my stay and asks me to keep my promises to study hard and pass my exams.

So much has changed since I left. There's so much my mother doesn't know about my new life. For the next few days, I am struck by how different I see my home, and my mother, and what I took for granted for so long: the clean floor beneath my feet, the comfort, the orderliness of everything. I realize I've never thanked her enough.

We fall back into our familiar routine, but our conversations are new. They are mostly about Damascus: how, despite the difficult adjustment period, working has not turned out to be as hard as I assumed, and life out there is not as scary as my father always led us to believe. Alia tells me she is trying to get a summer job as a translator in Istanbul. My mother approves—she has always wanted to take us to Istanbul—but jokes that Alia is too messy to live alone. I tell my mother bits and pieces of my involvement in the uprising and the protests, and, as always, she reminds me to be cautious. She warns that if my father knew, he would punish me. But in my mind, the only punishment I fear from him is the withdrawal of his money, a consequence I've grown accustomed to. At this point, I am still unaware of the full extent of the criminality he is capable of. But once again, my mother refuses to let this fear of him take root or make me question the path I'm on. She tells me she is proud, never doubting my ability to distinguish right from wrong. She follows the news and knows how badly the government and the army are responding to the protests.

I HAVE MISSED JABLEH with its familiar sounds wafting through our open window—the fishmonger's call, mothers shouting for their children to come home, the approaching rumble of the fumigating truck and our rush to slam every window shut before the gas invades the apartment. The corniche is exactly as I left it. Evening waves lap along the shore. Music blasts from cars filled with attention-seeking boys. The air is still heavy with the same humidity that carries the scents of boiled fava beans and toasted nuts.

But when I look closer, I do notice one difference: Missing are the tough young men from the mountains who perched on benches and the stone parapet along the edge of the corniche to watch the promenading young women. They didn't have cars, and we did not dare to glance at them twice: These were the men my father would have disowned me for marrying.

There are so few of these guys now because so many are off fighting for the Assad regime. They don't have money or university registration papers or any other means of avoiding mandatory military service. These are the Alawites I have "bonded" with at checkpoints in Damascus and elsewhere. Meanwhile, the sons of ranking officials, riding in their cars with tinted windows, are here as if nothing has changed. They cruise the corniche looking for girls. They will later travel to Lebanon and Dubai to invest the money they have obtained through their government connections. The regime considers their lives precious.

In the first eight years of the uprising that became a war of many factions and proxies, Alawite villages were emptied of their young men. More than forty thousand were killed fighting for the regime. And the regime would laud Jableh as the "Capital City of Martyrs." The faces of the dead would cover our street walls. And the young women of Jableh and its surrounding villages would despair at not finding a husband from our Alawi sect.

When army defectors first started firing back at government soldiers, the martyr posters were larger and glossier. People would slow down to read the names of the martyrs; some pedestrians would stop, and with their eyes closed and the palms of their hands turned toward the sky, they would recite the Fatiha, the verse of the Quran used to bless the souls of the departed. They would wipe the tears on their faces before walking away. Every death was graced with a funeral, which Syrian state television broadcasted live, always showing nearly identical scenes: an ambulance driving up a winding road into the crags of the Alawite mountains to return the dead young man for burial in his village of origin.

Now, a year into the war, the posters have faded to the point where I cannot make out the faces. The words "hero" and "martyr," however, shine in clear, bold, red font. Death has become commonplace, and few people stop to pay their respects. In Damascus, I would often come across news of young Alawite men from Jableh dying while fighting for the government. Facebook pages dedicated to Jableh's martyrs would list new names—often several each day. From afar, it felt like justice; these men were the backbone of the government's army. But seeing the faded and torn faces plastered across Jableh felt nothing like justice. It was a reminder that those too poor to avoid military service were the ones being thrown into this war to protect a system that had never benefited them—had never even glanced their way.

SIXTEEN

The exams take nearly ten days to complete, and over time, I find myself growing less irritated by the constant presence of the president's photos, the students, and the strange fashion choices, like the military pants. It's as if part of me has given up on this place, resigned to the fact that the only thing I can do now is get through these exams. My focus is singular now—just to finish, get it over with, and ensure I can leave as soon as possible.

A few days before I return to Damascus, I call up an old friend of mine, Ghaith, one of the people I met at the coffee shop where I used to study, and we decide to spend the day at the beach in Wadi Qandil. Its light brown sand, gently lining the water's edge, surrounded by white cliffs and the evergreen slopes of the coastal mountains, makes it one of the most beautiful beaches in Syria. It's less than an hour's drive from both Latakia and the Turkish border.

Ghaith and I lie on the sand, and when the sun is too strong, we sit at a table under a straw umbrella. We sip Barada, a local beer, and gorge ourselves on slices of salted fried potatoes smothered in ketchup. Droplets of sweat trickle down my arms. To cool off, I rush across the blistering sand into the cold turquoise water. I float on my back with my eyes closed, feeling a mild beer buzz as I bob in the waves. Slowly, I lift my arms, legs, and torso, just to see how high above the water I can get them, before exhaling and sinking into the Mediterranean, rooting my feet in the sand. Being pulled out to sea while floating on my back is one of my most persistent nightmares. For all the days I've spent at the beach, I've never swum out past where I can stand. I would never trust myself in deeper waters.

Despite this fear, I love the sea. I can spend hours in the water, holding my nose and diving beneath the surface, eyes wide open, feeling the warm burn of salt on them. The Mediterranean, especially in the morning, is so clear that you can see the wavy lines of sand, dotted with big shells, from the water's surface.

"Seashells bring bad luck; we don't need any more of that," my mother used to shout from her white chair whenever she saw me collecting shells to take home, forcing me to throw them back in the water.

I return to shore feeling high, dizzy, and refreshed, my skin rubbery from the salt. I lie on the edge of the beach and feel the slow, gentle waves sweep sand over my feet. Then I walk back to Ghaith and the Baradas on the table. The air smells acidic from the ketchup baking in the sun. We order more food.

Later in the day, a friend of Ghaith's joins us. His name is George. I have seen him around before and always admired him from a distance. He has a piercing in his tongue and cool tattoos on his arms. George works on American Street in a Christian neighborhood in Latakia, in one of the overpriced cafés that serve milkshakes and lattes and play American MTV on mute.

Around sunset, an artillery round echoes off the mountainside like a thunderclap, reminding us that the front lines in the Latakia mountains are less than ten miles away. It's impossible to believe that, somewhere among these beautiful green mountains and the outcroppings of sharp white rock, men are killing one another. As I gaze at the pink clouds toward the end of the blue sea, George cuts through the silence. I can't recall exactly what he says—something about how, if the rebels take over, this will all be history. He draws a circle with his finger between us and our beers. He says that we will have to show our children photos of days like these. If the rebels take over, our children won't believe that we were able to sit here, half naked, consuming alcohol. I nod.

"I am not a government supporter," George says immediately, as if he knows he sounds like one and wants to defend his position. "Both sides are terrible." He says that he doesn't feel like he belongs in this country. The two sides should kill each other off and let the rest of us be rid of them.

"They're not against the government because it's corrupt," he says, "but because the president is Alawite."

"What about Bassel Shehadeh?" I ask.

It was mid-May, less than a month ago, that I met Bassel. I was walking in Damascus with my friend Walaa when we ran into him on the street, and she introduced us.

"This is Bassel, Syria's greatest filmmaker," Walaa told me, laughing.

"I'm not. Don't listen to her," Bassel replied, extending his hand.

Walaa asked him if he was working on anything new. He said something about buying a new hard drive and editing.

"She looks like a boy now," he said, smiling and running his hand through Walaa's short hair.

I scanned his face, his Metallica T-shirt, and his curly hair. I noticed the fine lines forming around his eyes.

DEFIANCE

After a few minutes of conversation, he told us he had to go to Bahsa, a computer market in Damascus near Shaalan, to buy the new hard drive. As soon as he was out of earshot, I turned to Walaa.

"He's so handsome. How do you know him?" I asked her. Walaa told me it was one of those friendships that started after 2011, a time when having similar politics was enough to form a bond.

"He's insane," she said. "Last year, he took my red lipstick and wrote 'hurria'—freedom—on a police station. He ruined the lipstick and never paid me back for it."

She told me that Bassel had been detained in the first months of the uprising but was ultimately released. "They can't keep a Christian in jail for too long," Walaa said. "That would make the government look bad."

After his release, he went to the United States to study filmmaking on a Fulbright scholarship. But he quit because he found it immoral to stay away from Syria in this political moment. "I told you!" she said. "He's insane!"

I glanced back in Bassel's direction and caught a glimpse of his torn backpack. I would never have guessed that he was paid to study in the US—and it was even more unbelievable that he had left to come back and film the uprising.

I felt a surge of both jealousy and admiration. I, too, wanted to study filmmaking. The thought that what Naji was teaching me in his empty office could actually be something I could study in college instead of memorizing English literature lectures was almost unfathomable to me.

Later that month, Walaa called me. When I picked up, she was sobbing. "Bassel was killed in Homs," she said.

I can still recall the numbness that spread through my body when I heard the news. It was impossible to believe that Bassel's curls and smile could be wrapped in a white, bloodstained cloth and buried in the dirt. That he left his studies to return to Syria, only for Syria to kill him, was almost too painful to process. I was in shock.

Later, I learned the details: A mortar bomb fired by government forces had exploded near Bassel and three other young filmmakers in the old, rebel-held city. He was dead by the time the ambulance reached the hospital.

Bassel, like most of the deceased at this time, was buried where he was killed, in Homs. No one dared risk transporting the dead to be buried in their hometown, as once was common. The rebels—the ones who were being called Wahhabis and Salafis by state media and people like George—gathered around his lifeless body, singing, "Heaven open your gates. Your seeker is coming soon."

Meanwhile, in Damascus, Bassel's mother and friends were trying to get permission to have a funeral in a church in Bab Touma, the Christian neighborhood where he was born and raised, but security forces threatened to detain anyone who dared attend any service or gathering honoring him. Commemorating the life of a Syrian Christian who was killed by government security forces would be a threat to government propaganda that insisted the opposition was purely Islamist, the battle between conservative radical Sunnis and the Alawites and secular Ba'athists.

Ultimately, no funeral was held for Bassel in Damascus; his friends came to console his mother in her home instead. But he did become an icon of the Syrian uprising. For days, his face was all over my Facebook feed. His death was covered by every opposition newspaper and even by international outlets like NPR and *The New York Times*. He was a young, talented man with a bright future and opportunities abroad who had decided to fight for the future of his country—a country that most men his age dreamed of leaving behind.

"He must have been promised something," George mumbles when I mention Bassel. He licks and seals the edge of a cigarette paper, rolling it into a cylinder.

"Promised?" I ask. "Promised what?"

"Do you believe that he would have left America if he hadn't been promised something?" George asks. He puts the cigarette in his mouth. "And why did he go to Homs? He was probably working for someone and getting paid a lot for it." George lights his cigarette and gazes out to the sea.

My hands shake. I tighten my grip on the cold beer bottle to hide my fury. The frosty surface bites into my skin. This is the exact same thing people say when a girl decides to leave her parents' home and walk her own path. They cannot fathom that someone might stray because they envision a better future for themselves. Someone must have brainwashed them; they must have been misled by some nefarious actor.

I want to scream, but I hold my tongue as Amer has told me to do countless times to avoid taking the bait. But even if George isn't trying to trick me, nothing I could say would matter, I realize. No argument in favor of the uprising would make any sense to him—just as none ever made sense to me in the past. Honestly, I might have said the same things myself.

Part of me wonders if George would have been less skeptical of Bassel's story if it hadn't involved America. I understand his thought process— Bassel didn't just leave any country to come back to Syria; he left America.

Our generation of Syrians measured how cool, educated, and informed you were by how many American shows like *Friends* and *How I Met Your Mother* you could download illegally, or how many American bands you knew and CDs you collected. If you could breakdance, you could probably count on an invitation to a DJ Steve party (his real name was Mustafa, but no one wanted to go to a party hosted by DJ Mustafa, so he became DJ Steve). I was not yet eighteen when we crowded these parties every other weekend, drinking Absolut Vodka mixed with Red Bull and downing B-52 shots.

One summer, while visiting my grandmother, I spent all my money on a ticket to see the band Gorillaz, even though I had never listened to their music. I couldn't even see the stage until the last song, but I didn't care—I was able to post a few photos on Facebook and show that I had been there, blessed to attend a Western band's concert. In Latakia, people I knew would save for a year or more and cross the border to Lebanon to see American and European rock bands that no one had ever heard of, take photos, and brag on social media. For my fifteenth birthday, during a visit to Damascus, my gift was a meal at KFC, Syria's only American fast-food chain. It was the coolest place to dine. Any encounter with Western culture was a reason to show off and signal elitism—even though, when it came to politics, we were taught to hate America.

When news of the September 11 attacks reached us, I was ten years old; I had never heard of Al Qaeda before. "Those who raise wolves end up eaten by wolves," the pundits on Al Jazeera repeated over and over. The TV showed footage of men carrying plates stacked with kunafeh—a doughy dessert with cheese and honey—through traffic, serving passing drivers. The imperialists have collapsed, they said, and it was cause for celebration.

Hassan Nasrallah, the leader of Hezbollah, would call for "Death to America," a phrase we were then taught to repeat because he and our government shared a common enemy. In 2006, the year Israel bombed Lebanon, his face was plastered all over Latakia and Jableh. That summer, hundreds if not thousands of households along Syria's coastline hosted displaced Lebanese families fleeing Israeli air raids.

In school, on TV, in state print media, America was trying to destroy every Arab country, not just ours. The idea that America hated the Arab world and feared our power and our principles was impressively pervasive; it explains why, when the uprising started, we were told it was a plot by the West to destroy Assad, the last titan to resist American imperialism. Any attempt to change Syria that didn't originate from Assad's regime was portrayed as driven by the imperialist West, its advocates no more than Western puppets.

But somehow this hatred never affected the hopes of most young men and women to see their applications for entry visas to the United States approved by the consular section of the US embassy in Damascus after graduating. They remained fascinated by life in a country where, as the received wisdom went, if you worked hard, your work paid you back—unlike Syria, where it was common knowledge that only one's connections, or what we refer to as wasta, can bring success and stability. It didn't matter that some of those who obtained visas and booked one-way tickets to the US couldn't use their college degrees when they arrived and ended up working in gas stations or delivering food. They were considered the luckiest among us.

For this reason, I know it will be incredibly difficult, impossible even, to convince George that Bassel, who received a Fulbright to study in the United States, had purely noble reasons for leaving Syracuse University after one semester and returning to Syria to participate in an uprising—something that George doesn't believe exists.

Words can't convey how a revolution transforms you; you have to live it. No matter how many books you read, nothing compares to the first chant you hear emanating from the depths of your heart. Nothing compares to the sound of the first explosion or the sight of the first death. For George, accusing Bassel of being paid is easier than believing that there is a real, grassroots revolution in Syria. It's easier than believing that people are dreaming of something greater than an American visa.

I watch the sun spill its yolk into the clouds, staining them dark pink and orange. Fishing boats emerge, black dots with lamps glimmering at the water's edge. It's a scene that has captivated me since the summer we moved to Jableh. I remember how happy I was to be closer to the sea. I never would have thought that a day might come when I would willingly leave all of this behind.

Amer once told me that he had never been to the coast, though he lived only four hours away. Summer beach trips were a luxury his family couldn't afford. He had never felt seawater, soft as tissue paper, or the rush of the ground disappearing beneath his feet.

A round of bombardment echoes through the mountains, piercing my reverie. There is no way this brutality can last for another year. Maybe by next summer, the government will be overthrown. Amer might be running his gallery or working with Naji on his dream project, a newspaper. Maybe they will come to Jableh, and my mother will cook for them and hear the embarrassing stories of my attempts to do the same, once again blaming herself for not forcing me to become more capable and independent at a younger age. Soon, I think, things will change for the better.

My bus to Damascus is scheduled to leave at noon. The night before, I promised my mother I would have coffee and breakfast with her in the morning, but by the time I'm finished packing, there's no time.

My fears were unnecessary; in the end, I don't even entertain the idea of staying in Jableh. Visiting makes me realize that my future is not here. The comfort of Jableh seems negligible compared to what I've found in the wider world. It is impossible to go back to a smaller life, one built around obedience and fear. It is perhaps the same revelation people around the country are having about their lives before the uprising.

I try to wake Alia to say goodbye, but she puts her head under a pillow and shouts at me to close the door.

When my mother hears the wheels of my bag on the tile floor, she calls out from the kitchen, "Wait! Let me finish this and wash my hands."

"Mama, my car is downstairs! I have to leave."

My mother rushes in, drying her hands on the sides of her pants before reaching for me.

"Come! Hug me!" she shouts.

"I'm so late—I have to go," I say, barreling down the stairs. "I'll come back soon, I promise!"

My mother stands in the doorway as she always would, murmuring pleas to God to protect me. As I climb into the car, deep regret washes over me for not hugging her goodbye. I had no way of knowing that this would be the last time I would ever see her.

SEVENTEEN

A few days after I return to Damascus, there is an assault on the government leadership's inner sanctum. Four high-ranking government officials, including a top Mukhabarat officer—who also happens to be President Assad's brother-in-law—are killed. The state media say the attack was a suicide bombing by an armed rebel, but media outlets outside Syria report that President Assad and his brother, Maher, poisoned the four dead officials.

The motive for the poisoning—if that is indeed what happened—would have been to create a pretext to escalate military attacks on the anti-government forces. Per this version of the event, the officials and officers who died had been arguing for a political solution that included a proposal for President Assad to step down. No one outside of Assad's close circle knows the truth of what really happened. All that is apparent to us is that the gates of hell have opened, and we are right in the middle.

DEFIANCE

In the aftermath of the killings, Damascus undergoes a drastic change. Every night, we hear distant bombs going off and gunshots that sound like firecrackers. Mount Qasioun, towering over Damascus with its coffee shops, hookah bars, and panoramic city views, is now a military no-go zone. The protests, once a daily occurrence, skid to a halt after security forces fire a mortar round into a demonstration in Barzeh, killing four people.

Before this, we knew the locations of the checkpoints we had to pass through, which roads to avoid, and which branch of the security police was manning each checkpoint. But after the officials' deaths, checkpoints start to appear at every intersection, even in areas we'd considered safe. If security officers notice people walking away after spotting the checkpoint, they shout at them to come back, assuming they have something to hide. People start disappearing. Some leave the country intentionally while others simply vanish without a trace. Security forces begin arresting people en masse and executing some of them on the spot, resulting in horror stories that quickly spread throughout the city.

Limb amputations become commonplace because injuries from the bombings are treated in living rooms turned into makeshift field hospitals. Shrapnel is removed from oozing wounds without anesthetics. In July, instead of being filled with water and fruit, Amer's fridge becomes a storage cooler for vials of tetanus vaccine.

I don't know—and I don't ask—how we obtained the vials. Part of me doesn't want to know. They may have come from the same hospitals where the stories originate—stories so horrible I can't tell if they're real or imaginary: stories that prompt people to have a limb sawed off in a field hospital rather than face the alternative; stories about injured people chained to hospital beds while doctors, accompanied by security forces, pour rubbing alcohol into their open wounds; stories about doctors burning the genitals of detainees. Whichever doctor smuggled the vials for us might have also engaged in some form of torture to prove their loyalty to the government and protect their access to the vaccine.

I take the needles out of the fridge and wrap them in a towel that I left in the freezer overnight. In the minibus, I stash my bag under my seat, knowing how aggressive the police are at the checkpoints and that I can be searched at any moment. However, I know that even if the bag with the tetanus shots is found under the seat, I can simply say it's not mine, and the person next to me or behind me will be blamed. I am trustworthy. With "Jableh" and my family's name on my ID, my loyalty is still considered unquestionable.

For weeks, I deposit the hypodermics at a specific location: a small shop at the entrance to Barzeh. The shop is owned by a middle-aged man people refer to as Al Hakeem.

"I am returning this," I say, placing the bag into an ice cream freezer decorated with a grinning snowman wearing a red neck scarf. I meet his little son in the shop one day. I ask the boy for his name, but he just hugs his dad's leg and hides behind it.

"I am doing this for him," Al Hakeem says. These six words are the only ones he will ever utter to me. He vanishes soon after, and before my heart can ache for the little boy and his loss, I feel relieved that I managed to stay quiet around him. I am proud of myself for not giving him any indication of who I am and for not being as reckless as I once was. I know by then that detention is often a death sentence that means torture and an unmarked grave somewhere. And for me, an Alawite, the punishment would be doubled.

During a protest in early summer, I overheard a thick Alawite accent from the guy standing in front of me in the crowd. I tapped him on the shoulder, and when he turned, I saw that he was strangely handsome, with glasses and a large mole on his cheek. We exchanged a few words, and he told me he was from Tartus, only half an hour's drive from Jableh.

DEFIANCE

We connected on Facebook, and later in the summer, he went back to visit his family. While there, he was forced into a car, beaten, driven to a remote village, and dumped on the side of the road. They shot at him, hitting him in one leg, but he managed to crawl for help. When he was found, he was taken to a hospital, where the doctors and nurses notified the police, as they were required to do if they encountered a patient with a bullet wound.

The security forces showed up and detained him. When he begged for medical help because his leg was still bleeding, they told him, "Good. You won't be able to go to protests again," and stomped on his leg. For weeks, they told him that his sister was being raped in the cell next door, and he could hear her screams through the wall. The security police said they would release her only after he gave them every name he knew. He eventually gave them a few names, and he was released. Later, he learned that his sister had never been in jail, though he swore that it was her voice he had heard pleading for help. He ultimately left Syria with no intention of ever returning. He was in Lebanon when he Skyped with me a few days after crossing the border.

"You don't understand," he said. "If an Alawite gets caught, they make sure to make an example of you. Our disloyalty to them is not just political. It is considered a deep betrayal of their trust in us. Our betrayal is equivalent to a thousand betrayals."

◆◆

Two miles separate the Damascus outer neighborhoods, with their field hospitals and amputated limbs, from Bab Sharqi, the city's ancient core. Just two miles from those narrow cobblestone streets; from the fragrance of flavored tobacco wafting from hookah bars; from the boutique hotels in buildings that, in a better world, would speak of love and intrigue;

from the murmur of fountains splashing onto the leaves of jasmine in bloom; and from the bars, of course, and the art galleries that become after-hours speakeasies where the upper class of Damascus dances and sips martinis and wine, wondering what kind of "freedom" the discontented are demanding for Syria.

One of the bars in Bab Sharqi is a rustic place called Abo Elia, named after its white-haired owner who spends his evenings preparing meze platters and mixing drinks. After strolling through the maze of old streets and the cramped marketplace, my friends and I frequently end up here. Abo Elia's drinks are the cheapest in the area, and you can easily get a free one—or five. Abo Elia says he's keeping his bar open despite the conflict, as an act of love for his country. He refuses to close, no matter how intense or frightening the sound of explosions coming from outer Damascus may become.

"The terrorists want normal life to end," Abo Elia laments as he lays slices of cucumber and carrot onto our meze plates. "I won't give them that satisfaction. May God bless our army!"

"God bless our army!" we repeat in unison, clinking our glasses and watching Abo Elia top them up for free. He refers to us as his rifaaq, his comrades, and sees our drinking together as another act of courage. Unity against whatever the West is plotting against our leader. We play along, drinking for hours. The bill is always a small fraction of the alcohol we've downed, and we always leave Abo Elia giggling and buzzed, God-blessing the army and swearing to each other never to tell anyone how we compromised our morals and hailed our oppressors, just to get free splashes of vodka with grapefruit.

One morning, after a night out, I wake up in bed fully clothed. I find my phone under my pillow. The battery is dead. I plug it into a charger and see a message from Walaa asking me to call her immediately.

I ignore the text. My phone rings.

"Sorry, I just woke up," I say.

"I'm outside," she says. "Open the door." Seconds later, I hear a loud knock and drag myself up to answer it. Walaa pushes her way into the house.

"Are you stupid?" she barks, and I'm too ashamed to ask her what she's talking about. The last thing I remember is drinking at Abo Elia when the bombing intensified so much that our glasses were shaking on the wooden tables. "You don't remember?" she asks, and I try to come up with a lie, but I can't. My brain throbs with the pain of the hangover. "You should stop drinking. You are putting yourself and everyone around you in danger," she says.

ALCOHOL CONSUMPTION has been part of my identity as an Alawite since childhood. Drinking alcohol and walking around without a headscarf were ways of blending in with Christians in past centuries of Ottoman oppression. We Alawites raise our glasses and say "bi sahtak"—cheers to your health—to demonstrate that we love life. The local beverage, arak—a powerful brandy made from figs—is distilled all over the high Alawite mountains. Arak featured at every dinner and barbecue throughout my childhood, even those we would have in the shade of pine trees around Alawite shrines, where we would feast on the grilled meat from the sheep Aunt Samia sacrificed as a kafara after breaking one of her many promises.

"Sip a little!" my aunt would say, placing a glass filled with milky white liquid under my nose. A sip of arak is said to kill the bacteria in the raw meat of kibbeh nayeh or on the unwashed parsley of our tabbouleh. Children down the stuff, most with grimaces, as their parents and older relatives watch and laugh and joke about how a true Alawite child can handle arak. It is in our blood from birth.

Arak is for private family gatherings. For weddings and other public events, whiskey—Black Label in particular—is served because it is another way of flaunting one's wealth. Champagne and whiskey bottles mark a class divide between the Alawites who "made it" and those who did not.

I was fifteen when I got drunk for the first time. I was with the daughters of my father's cousin, Hikmat, who ran the Mukhabarat branch in As Suwayda. One night—I can't remember the occasion—the girls placed a bottle of Black Label on the table, probably the most common bribe for army commanders and intelligence officers. It is an expensive gift and an intentional sign from the giver that he is as open-minded and liberal as the recipient. We took turns sipping the throat-warming whiskey. It never occurred to me that this bottle might have come from a parent who was desperate for information about a detained child.

The last thing I remember is lying on the couch, my head on one of the girls' laps, as we were making prank phone calls from their no-caller-ID phone line—something only available to people with a security clearance. We laughed and drank until the night faded into nothingness.

When I started university in Latakia, cocktail bars were the cool, Western places to be seen. I loved cocktails and how relaxed and happy they made me feel. Thanks to my father's large allowance, I would use cocktails and their implied sophistication to distinguish myself from other people my age who could only afford arak and canned mixed drinks.

My mother would always be furious when I came home reeking of alcohol. She would admonish me for not prioritizing my health and remind me that her own mother was still beautiful because she never drank, even at the embassy parties she attended with my grandfather.

Later, when I no longer had the money to go to bars, alcohol was still always around, in the form of the bottles of local wine on Amer's table. Lebanese and Syrian wines were the cheap social lubricant for broke writers and intellectuals, just like bitter coffee. We would drink and talk, talk and drink. Often, as the last drops were being poured, Amer would say something about everyone drinking too much and call it a problem.

DEFIANCE

I never agreed with him. In my mind, alcohol was only a problem for people who started drinking in the morning or couldn't hold their liquor—those who ended up puking all over themselves. But it wasn't a problem for me. I could drink, and my ability to consume alcohol was, as people often said, impressive.

It felt as though I had been taught how to drink but never taught how to stop.

WALAA'S PALE FACE tells me I did something bad. It is excruciating to sit still as she fills in the blanks of what happened last night. She recounts how, at some point, the shelling grew so intense that I started crying. Abo Elia told me not to be afraid. "Syria Alla Hamiha," he said—Syria is protected by God. It was the phrase people in Jableh repeated when the uprising first started, refusing to acknowledge what was going on in the rest of the country.

"If a limb has cancer, we remove the limb to keep the rest of the body alive," Abo Elia said. "This bombing is necessary to rescue the country."

"You started arguing with him and you wouldn't shut up! I kept pinching you under the table," Walaa says, "but you didn't stop!"

I don't ask her what I said, exactly—I don't want to know. But when she tells me we cannot set foot in Abo Elia's bar again, I know that I am lucky to be waking up at home and not at the police station. I am so ashamed I can't look Walaa in the eye. I almost got both of us detained, all because I couldn't control myself around alcohol.

"I'm sorry," I say. "I will never drink again."

This is a lie, of course. I drink again, just not with Walaa. Alcohol is my only reliable source of comfort as the situation worsens. A cloud of sadness has been hovering over us and it is only growing heavier. There is no end in sight. I feel trapped.

LOUBNA MRIE

My mother has been following the news closely, and every day she calls to check on me. She tells me that when I don't answer, she is terrified that I've been arrested. My father found out about what I have been doing in Damascus, and he declared that if I end up in jail, he will make sure she never sees me again. It was all her fault, he told her; she had failed to raise me properly.

If my mother had her way, I would leave Syria in the footsteps of Alia, who is working as a translator in Istanbul for the summer, just as she had planned. My mother repeats what she always told us growing up: If anything ever happened to her, she was confident that we would take care of each other. I know my mother is struggling financially. My father stopped sending money. Since Alia and I are both working, he said, he won't be responsible for anything to do with us anymore.

My mother sells a few pieces of gold—her last, pieces she had saved for Alia and me on our wedding days. She will support herself until we can send her money, she says. In my fantasies, the three of us are reunited, but freed of my father's shadow. Alia and I take care of our mother the same way she looked after us. But I cannot find a job. Businesses are closing, roads are dangerous, and I find myself stuck.

"We don't need him," my mother assures me before she starts crying. "I'm just worried I will never see you again." She tells me the house feels so empty, and that she doesn't want to cook if Alia and I are not there to eat.

"Mama! Don't be dramatic! We're coming back—please don't make me any more stressed than I already am," I say. I start avoiding her calls.

I am twenty-one, and I am trying to stay alive in what the United Nations would later call the worst man-made disaster the world has seen since World War II. I do not want to assume the burden of my mother's fear on top of my own. I refuse to see what she does: that I should fear my father. I resent her for reminding me of the consequences of defying him.

The escalation of violence and the armed rebels' declaration of their intention to seize Damascus have given the government the justification it needed to redouble their efforts and arrest every activist they possibly can. Checkpoints grind traffic to a stop. The whole city begins to feel like one big, awful trap. "Death under torture" becomes the common cause of death for those who disappear at checkpoints.

By July of 2012, several of my friends have left or are making plans to leave the country. Walaa is in Lebanon. Naji is in hiding; he might have fled to Jordan. Most of the people I've met in protests or at Amer's studio are scattered across these two countries. And those of us who have yet to find a feasible exit strategy hide out in various houses and apartments, always moving from place to place, crashing on couches in living rooms where we drink throughout the day and night.

Amer and I never discuss the departures until one day later that month when we meet up with one of his friends, a young woman named Samar, who is about to leave Syria. Amer wants to see her one last time.

She walks into the old coffee shop, her curly raven hair lifted and secured with a wooden paintbrush, revealing thick eyebrows and a dimple on one of her cheeks. She is engaged to a journalist and former detainee who, after his release, received an arts scholarship to study in Germany in a program that has provided asylum for artists from Palestine, Iraq, and other conflict zones for decades.

After dropping a few sugar cubes into her dark red tea, Samar describes the torturously complicated process of joining her fiancé in Germany, though she also received a scholarship from a similar program. I see Amer glancing at her pack of Marlboros, the expensive cigarette of choice in Syria, where what you smoke is as much a status symbol as your brand of mobile phone or car. So much cash turning into ashes. Amer opens Samar's pack without asking and takes two cigarettes.

"What is keeping you here?" Samar asks, knowing that Amer has no plans to apply for a scholarship himself.

"You want me to be another exiled artist who writes about Syria from Berlin?" Amer asks. He says that people who are leaving Syria now will never return.

Samar becomes visibly irritated, aware that Amer is referring to her partner, who used to post updates from Damascus—as if he were still there—on social media but was routinely mocked by friends, asking him how the "revolution in Berlin" was going. Eventually, he stopped posting on social media altogether.

"You can help more from outside the country than if you stay here. You can meet with donors and businessmen and send money to people like you who cannot find jobs," she says, taking a long drag from her cigarette.

My throat tightens. I grip my teacup and avoid looking at Amer. For Arab men, no matter how progressive, money is always a sensitive topic. It's as if not having money is somehow akin to being impotent.

I know that Amer hasn't worked in weeks. He can't admit how broke he's become. He's even resorted to smoking the cheap local cigarettes, which is why he's always taking cigarettes from his friends' packs without asking permission.

I haven't dared to ask him how he is paying rent. I assume he is getting money from friends or from someone outside the country—either that or allowing himself some cuts from the donated money circulating around. The money I was distributing. Regardless, it would be a betrayal to point out the fact that he is not working the way Samar has just done—I would never do that to him.

"Where are the Syrians who left in the eighties assuming they would be back after just a few months? They are online! Friending us on Facebook just so we can mock them," Amer says angrily.

"Being locked inside a house isn't really helping anyone," Samar replies, pushing her chair back to stand. "I'm sure I'll be seeing you in Germany." She takes another cigarette from her pack and places it on the table for Amer. Perhaps she sincerely wants him to have one; perhaps she wants to remind him that he needs handouts just to smoke. Whatever her intention, I can feel Amer's leg violently shaking under the table. Samar slides the strap of her bag over her shoulder and walks out.

"These people want to leave, and they want everyone else to leave, too, just so they don't feel guilty!" Amer says, taking off his glasses and throwing them onto the table. "Countries bring in people like her to show that they support Syrians in their struggle. But they are only willing to help the educated ones. The ones who make them feel and look good."

Amer picks up the cigarette Samar left and slips it behind his ear. We head out and stroll silently through the alleys until Amer cuts the silence to complain that we paid for Samar's tea because she assumes all of us live off European Union scholarship money. I distract myself by inhaling the atmosphere of the old city, trying to detect the comforting smell of jasmine and lemon trees blooming nearby, but it is the peak of summer, and the alleys stink of rotting food and the vapors rising from the Barada River.

Anti-government slogans have vanished here. Now, on narrow street after narrow street, the walls are lined with glossy posters of the president, as if the revolution had never existed.

Those who painted anti-government graffiti or posted anti-Assad leaflets are by now detained in dungeons, or have joined the rebel militias—or, in the best-case scenario, are living abroad.

"Samar is right," I whisper to Amer. "You should leave."

"I would rather die of hunger here," he replies without even glancing my way.

"Why? What are you doing here?" I ask. "Outside you can at least find work. Being away for a few months is better than being dead."

"Do you want me to leave and send money back so people here can buy Marlboros and live off my guilt?"

"Aren't you living off the guilt of other people? You can't even work!" I freeze, knowing I've crossed a line.

Amer turns toward me and explodes. I've blocked out most of what he said. He calls me naive and materialistic. "I don't expect you to understand, because you will always care about money more than anything else, just like everyone who grows up rich," he says.

I blink. Amer has never said anything like this to me before. He knows the material comfort I've left behind. I feel betrayed that he's using what I have shared with him to hurt me. Rage unleashes inside me, and I hear myself begin to shout words I never thought I would utter.

I tell Amer he is poor because he is a failure. He is afraid of leaving Syria because here, he can blame his lack of work on the government. Abroad, he will have to face the fact that he is not getting a job because he has no talent, and his incompetence is his alone. Amer's eyes well up. His lower lip quivers.

"Admit it!" I yell. "You will always be a loser living off of other people's charity."

The next thing I see is blinding light. My head swims. Amer slapped me so hard that I nearly lost my balance. Heat rises from my left cheek and travels down my neck. People walking by slow for a second, but no one stops. They probably assume that Amer is my husband or my brother and that I deserved it.

I start to run. The lipstick and pens and coins inside my bag rustle and jingle as it swings from my shoulder and bounces off my left side. I hear Amer panting behind me and shouting, "Coward! Coward! Jbaneh!" I'm not sure if he considers me a coward for admitting that leaving is a good choice or because I don't fight him back.

My breath is heavy and wet. My eye burns and won't open. I hail a taxi and jump in.

"Are you okay?" the taxi driver asks. He turns around in the front seat. "Do you need me to stop at a checkpoint and ask them to help you?"

"NO! I'm fine. Just go!" I give him a friend's address.

At my friend's, I ask if I can sleep over. She wonders what happened to my eye. I tell her I fell, and we laugh. I once read that the trouble with letting people see you at your weakest is not that they will remember, but that you will remember. I don't allow myself to cry because I don't want anyone to suspect that Amer hit me. In that moment, I am alone in my shame. It was my fault. And the fact that I couldn't fight back is a further embarrassment to me.

I look into the mirror and see a red blotch on the white of my left eye. I start drinking to calm the anger and shame. I wake up the next morning with a sour taste in my mouth, knowing I vomited in the night in the pink plastic bucket by my bed.

I pull my phone from underneath the pillow. Amer hasn't called. I think of reaching out to my mother. I feel so isolated in this moment. The person who was my dearest friend, who had always protected me, has left me with a black eye. Amer was the reason I wouldn't leave Damascus, though I was scared for him and for myself. I wanted him to respect me. I wanted to be one of the real ones who stayed until the end, who fought, who was not harassed and intimidated into fleeing.

It would take me years to understand that, under pressure, under the fear of death by execution, by torture, by bombing, people can release the monster they've spent most of their lives repressing. I didn't know then that almost every marriage, every friendship that I saw blooming around us in Damascus during this time would die. The two couples that went to jail together and married right after they were released. The girl who was so scared her partner would be taken away by the police that she got pregnant just to preserve something of his smell. Or the girl whose boyfriend's family rejected her because she was not Sunni, and who agreed to elope with him because the whole country was revolting against injustice, so why couldn't they? Even Samar and her partner's relationship would eventually collapse under the strain of exile and the guilt Amer was talking about. So many love stories. All of them decimated, just like our hopes of what Syria would become.

LATER THAT DAY, I go to Amer's studio to pack my belongings. I find him sitting in an armchair with the lights off. A thin wisp of cigarette smoke hangs in the stale air. Avoiding eye contact, I start putting my books, laptop, clothes, and everything I own into one bag. When I am done, I stand in front of him, unsure of what to say.

I can't believe Amer could hurt me the way he did, and the confusion is overwhelming. Should I apologize for what I said? Should I yell at him? Or should I pretend that everything is okay and let it rest as our secret?

As I search his face for some acknowledgment of what happened, I hope for an apology that would allow us to move forward. But he remains silent, still as the smoke hanging in the air. His glasses are on the table, and he bites his thumbnail while holding the cigarette. As the tip glows orange, reflecting off his eyes, he gazes into space, as if I weren't even there.

On the wall is the sign from Amuda that I risked my life to bring because I knew Amer would appreciate it. It was my gift to him.

Beneath the sign, above the table where Amer threw his keys, is one of the white lilies he gave me months ago on International Women's Day. He hung it upside down, and it blackened over time, but still, there it remains: his gift to me.

"You can keep the flower. I'm taking the sign," I say, stepping around

Amer's chair. I read Lorca's poem again as I tear the clear tape from the edges.

> **What is a human without freedom, Mariana! Tell me?**
> **How can I love you if I'm not free?**
> **Can I give you my heart if it is not mine?**

I tuck the sign under my arm, grab my bags, and walk out of the studio for the last time.

EIGHTEEN

Damascus, which once helped me find my voice and sense of self, has become suffocating. I've never felt such a drastic shift in emotions toward a place—or anything else, for that matter. I know I need to leave.

Lately, I've been sleeping at a friend's apartment—not a close friend, but at this point, closeness isn't a prerequisite for crashing on couches—in Jaramana, the neighborhood where Naji had his office and where I received my first journalism lessons. Every day for the past week, I've heard helicopters churning the air overhead, followed by shelling and sirens screaming through the night.

Every time we speak, my mother urges me to find a way to join Alia in Istanbul. My father has been calling frequently, asking about us, and this worries her. She fears he's realized he's lost control over us completely and she is anxious about what he might do next to regain power over our lives. She insists it would only be temporary and that it would reassure her to know I'm safe.

Adding to my concerns, I've heard from a friend of a friend that my name has been added to the checkpoint lists at the Lebanese and Turkish borders. I'm unsure if my father is responsible for this, or if someone else informed on me. Despite being unable to verify this rumor, I can't afford the risk of being caught, though I know my mother is right; I can't stay in Syria. I'm left with two options to get across the border: I can either cross illegally through one of the rebel-controlled areas or bribe government officials. Unfortunately, without money, the latter option isn't available to me.

IN EARLY AUGUST, after a week of quietly asking around, I finally have a breakthrough. A trusted friend gives me the number of a rebel commander named Abo Ammar who's known for helping protesters cross into Turkey.

When I call, he meets my nervous, low voice with a confident tone that reassures me: He has done this many times before. He tells me that the second I get to his village, Salma, I can consider myself in Turkey already.

"It will be a long walk. Pack as little as possible," he says.

"Can I bring my camera and take some videos?"

"Fine. Just make sure to hide it. They're ruthless at the checkpoints along the road here."

He asks me to write down a number that belongs to a woman named Raneem. Since I am traveling alone, I will stay with a family in the village rather than at the rebel base, where the men sleep.

I roll my eyes. I want to tell him that women and men are equals and I'll be fine; I can take care of myself. Amer would have said something like that if he were on the call. But it's just me, so I stay quiet. I need this man's help.

After we hang up, I take a deep breath and all I can think of is Walid. I know this village—it's his.

I want to call him and joke that his presence is inevitable, that I haven't been able to shake him since that first protest. Maybe this is a sign from God that I'm supposed to talk with him before I leave Damascus. Maybe he'll laugh and forget that we haven't spoken in months; he'll suggest we meet and walk for hours and talk about everything—everything except the last time I saw him, standing silently by my room in our house, watching me pack after I decided to move into Amer's studio.

We won't talk about how, the last time we hugged, he asked me not to replace him with my new "intellectual friend."

"Of course not!" I assured him, though I never saw him again after that.

Deep down, I don't know if I have the courage to tell Walid that my "intellectual friend" hit me in the street. But maybe that's something else we can joke about and push aside, the same way we've dealt with every other painful thing.

I dial Walid's number, but the call won't go through. I try a few more times that night and send some text messages, too, all to no response. I curse him under my breath for being dramatic.

It isn't until a year later that I find out that Walid didn't answer because he was being held in one of the most notorious prisons, where he was subjected to torture for months. All he wanted was to study and get away, but he was taken off a bus on his way to university because his ID showed that he was from the village of Salma. By that time, Salma was no longer under government control, so Walid was deemed a terrorist by default.

FOLLOWING ABO AMMAR'S ADVICE, I try to pack as little as possible. I sit on the floor and dig through a pile of clothes. I make one pile to send home to my mother and another, roughly the size of my backpack, to bring to Turkey.

This is not an exile; this is temporary, I tell myself. So I don't walk my favorite streets one last time. I don't inhale the scent of jasmine or the smell of the Barada to imprint them in my memory. I don't go to Jableh to hug my mother and kiss her hand and tell her how much I love her.

This is nothing like the departure I imagined or saw portrayed in movies. There is nothing remarkable about my last night in Damascus, only the usual street bustle, the ordinary faces reflecting off shop windows, the sound of casual conversation mixing with the music blaring from passing cars. There are some explosions in the distance, but it's warm enough that many people leave their windows open in hopes that the breeze will offer easier sleep. I close my eyes and try to rest, knowing tomorrow will be a long day.

In the morning, I drop the bag I'm sending to my mother in the mail and board the bus for the four-hour-long ride to Latakia. When we finally arrive, I find myself enveloped by the familiar humidity of the coast. It doesn't take long to find Raneem, a tall young woman in blue jeans and a sleeveless shirt with hair so long that it brushes her hips. She makes a joke about how I'm so short that the guys at the checkpoint might believe I'm her daughter.

"Are you hungry?" she asks.

I shake my head no.

"Great!" she says. "You'll need your energy. We won't reach my family's home before sunset."

IN DAMASCUS, I HAD only had a few short, cryptic telephone conversations with Abo Ammar to coordinate my arrival. From his deep voice, I expected him to be older, so when Raneem and I arrive at the first rebel checkpoint in the mountains, I am surprised to meet a young man. He seems even younger than Amer and is only a few inches taller than me, with slight jowls lightly concealed by a trim beard. Once we get to Raneem's family home, her mother cooks us a meal.

Over dinner, I tell Abo Ammar that I have never been in a rebel-held area before and want to take some videos before crossing into Turkey. He offers to drive me around so I can film and speak with people. Aside from the money I desperately need and can make by selling the footage, I am excited to be in a part of Syria where I don't have to worry about checkpoints or my chat history. Here, our political allegiance doesn't need to be kept secret; it is evident from the green flags paraded on cars.

When I ask Abo Ammar how he became a brigade commander, he tells me he'd never touched a gun before 2011. After the protests, the government's security forces raided the area and arrested both men and women, detaining anyone with an ID card bearing the village's name.

People had no choice but to protect themselves, fighting back with weapons supplied by army defectors or smuggled over the nearby border from Turkey. They formed brigades across the mountains, and Abo Ammar, along with some of his cousins, created their own.

The next day, I ride behind Abo Ammar on a motorcycle, clutching his shoulders. His AK-47 hangs across his back and sways with us as we take the sharp curves, winding through the serpentine roads in the cooler air of Latakia's highlands, which is misty and smells of the sea. We bolt across hills covered in conifers, houses scattered on the hillsides. Smoke rises. Wildfires from the fighting have charred these forests and, from afar, the patches of ash resemble snowdrifts.

We are less than thirty miles from Wadi Qandil, the beach where I went swimming on my last visit home—where I sat in the sun and listened to the distant fighting between the rebels and the government forces that eventually turned this into a rebel-held area. Exploding artillery has cratered the asphalt. Abo Ammar avoids these rough sections by swerving to the edge of the road. I look down and see the rocky cliff drop into nothing but an ashen and evergreen abyss.

Abo Ammar slows his motorcycle as we drive up a steep hill and enter a bombed-out village.

We navigate between scarred stucco walls, shattered white tiles, and bent steel. Faded writing on one wall welcomes people home from the Hajj, Islam's obligatory pilgrimage to Mecca. I snap a photo. Gusts of wind are flinging the ends of curtains through shattered windows. A few miles down the road, one home has lost its entire facade. I see a green couch and a ceiling fan in a room with three damaged walls, a few gilded picture frames still hanging. As we drive slowly, I notice clothes hanging on some balconies, indicating that, despite the destruction, the village is still partially inhabited. I adjust my camera and start taking a video.

Abo Ammar turns his head. "I'll stop for you."

"That's okay," I say politely, wary of bothering him when so much of my future depends on remaining in his favor. But the motorcycle slows.

"This mountain needs more media coverage. Look," Abo Ammar says, pointing toward a pile of rocks. "This was once a house with three floors." He comes to a stop beside more destruction. The stench of what I realize is decomposing flesh taints the air. I cover my nose with my collar and step off the bike, broken tiles and shards of glass crunching underfoot. I struggle to find the right angle to capture the entirety of the rubble. The smell coats the inside of my mouth and the back of my throat.

"This is a problem in summertime," Abo Ammar says, referring to the air. He keeps talking, but I barely pay attention to what he's saying; I'm focused on determining the correct exposure so I can finish as quickly as possible and escape the stench. I hear fragments of sentences about how, after the air strike, they were only able to extract parts of the bodies of the dead. "We only had field shovels and sledgehammers. It took days to break through the mounds of bricks."

I pay full attention now. I lower the camera and look at what I am standing on. A yellow curtain with green and white dots. Perhaps a kitchen curtain. A white sink. Green plastic flowers. Part of a wooden door. I check the soles of my brown leather sandals, the shoes I bought with a few bills slipped away from the stash allocated toward rice for displaced families in Damascus. There are parts of rotting bodies underneath my feet, the rotting bodies of real people who were killed while I was on the beach and heard the thud of bombs exploding. My stomach tightens and I feel as if I might sink into the rubble.

It is not as if I didn't know that houses and apartment buildings were being destroyed in rebel-held areas. I understood that, in many parts of Syria, the government was using its firepower to force the armed rebels to withdraw, sometimes destroying entire neighborhoods. Any rebel foothold has become a target. Streets. Schools. Hospitals. Whole neighborhoods. Everyone is considered a potential traitor, and the government rains down death from the skies.

On Facebook, hundreds of news pages post videos and images of destruction hourly. Arabic-language news channels overflow with footage, and some even appear on English-speaking channels. After a while, scrolling through the images barely registered for me. They were all more or less the same. Most of them began with a shaky frame and a group of people hunched over a pile of rocks. Then the voice of the videographer would shout the date and the place, as other voices around him screamed things like "May God curse your soul, Bashar," or "Where are the Arabs? Where are the Muslims?" and with one simple scroll, I could make it vanish from my screen. But here, I can't make this disappear. I feel trapped. My head spins and my legs shake as I try to make my way back to Abo Ammar. The sun is blazing. Rubble gives way under my feet. I struggle to walk faster.

I see a large piece of marble, remnants of a kitchen counter, light brown with beige splotches, much like our kitchen counter in Jableh, and think of home. My bed. My vanity. The smell of our house. Our floor. I never want to see it like this. If I had to choose between the rebels taking over and keeping my home safe under the government's control, I know I would choose the latter, though I feel like a hypocrite to admit it.

Perhaps that's why some people decide to stay in their partially destroyed buildings, hanging on to what remains of their home rather than abandoning it entirely. It suddenly dawns on me that many oppose the uprising not out of love for the government but because the pain of having to dig through the rubble of your house in search of the bodies of your family members is more real than abstract ideals like democracy or freedom.

I raise the camera to my eye and try to snap one last picture, but I can't press the shutter. No photograph can do justice to this scene. No image can capture the smell of death and how it leaves you confused and helpless, like a wounded, wide-eyed animal trapped in a corner with nowhere to run, breathless, with that taste of death inside your mouth. I put my camera into my shoulder bag, then make my way back to the motorcycle and climb on, still shaking.

"Did you get the footage you wanted?" Abo Ammar asks.

"Yes," I say quietly.

Abo Ammar drives me to the home of a mother whose son, who is around my age, was arrested at a checkpoint solely on the basis of his village of origin, which was known for its frequent protests. Before his detention, he'd been on track to attend college, and his mother had planned to add a floor to their house for him and whomever he chose to marry. Now, he can no longer speak and is incontinent.

After talking with them, all I can think about is Walid. He knew the punishment that awaited anyone with his village listed on their ID. In Damascus, high on courage and the sense of power I felt after every protest, I saw his caution as cowardice. I thought he was favoring himself and his degree over the collective good of Syria. But now, I understand what he feared.

Abo Ammar has also been detained. "To this day, whenever I think about it, I smell rust. The soldiers kept beating me in the mouth. And every time I wanted to spit out the blood, a soldier put a gun to my head and forced me to swallow it."

After that, we ride to the village's mosque. Outside, I take photos of the minaret still standing despite two large, round blast holes. Abo Ammar points at it and says something about God's protection before walking in through a large wooden door. I follow him. Dust-covered rubber slippers are lined up in pairs in front of the entrance. The mosque must have been bombed while people were praying. Inside, the carpets are barely visible under a thick layer of white dust, shattered stone, and broken pieces of chandeliers.

"The army installed military posts in most nearby Alawite villages. They want to take revenge on us by destroying our mosques. They are pigs. Alawite pigs."

"Not all Alawites side with the government," I say, asking Abo Ammar not to generalize. "Many Alawites are supportive of the uprising. And many Alawites support the government not because they condone the violence but because they're scared of being exiled again to the mountains. They fear that if the president steps down, we will all be killed. The government is preying on that fear," I say.

"We? You are Alawite?" Abo Ammar asks, eyebrows raised. "The guy who asked for my help told me you were from Damascus."

"I moved there recently," I say, "but I am from Jableh." The mosque caretaker, who is standing nearby, senses the tension in our voices, and says he agrees with me. When I turn my camera on to interview him, he states that their problem is with the government soldiers, not with any other civilian sect. He asks me to post this publicly so people can hear that they should not be scared. Alawites should not see their fate tied to this government's.

That evening, Abo Ammar drops me off at Raneem's house and darts away. I lie on the couch. My body throbs in pain and I feel dizzy.

Raneem's mother places a glass of water near my head. "You must be dehydrated. Drink some water."

I take a sip. The water is warm. I frown and put the cup down.

"The fridge isn't working. The electricity barely came on today. But we had some spare fuel to heat up water in the bathroom. It's your turn if you want to wash."

She gives me a saucer with two candles sticking out of it so I don't have to shower in the dark. In the bathroom, the air is still and humid and smells of bay leaf soap. I light the candles and place the saucer on the sink. The flames move and light flickers on the sweating tiles. The smell of the dead lingers in my hair. I take off my shirt and hang it on the sink edge, unzip my pants and lower them to my knees. Then I raise them again.

How am I going to soap up, rinse off, dry, put my clothes back on, and rush out if the planes come back? There won't be enough time. I will either have to run out naked or die right there, amid the rubble. I stand, immobile, for a few long seconds. I feel the tile on the floor beneath my feet, cold and wet. When I move to get my shirt and the candles from the sink, I notice the black muddy footprints my feet left on the floor. I have to shower. At least I can die clean. I fill a plastic bottle and slowly start splashing water onto my body. I pause every minute or so to listen for screaming outside.

That night, lying in bed, I feel the urge to cry and call my mother. But the only way to get a signal is to go upstairs to the roof. I try to close my eyes, hoping for sleep and for the next day to come quickly, so I can leave as soon as possible.

In Damascus, we could move between the areas that were getting bombed and those that were safe. We could leave the danger and cross back to the neighborhoods loyal to the president. There we could drink and forget about everything else. The sound of the distant bombardment was the only reminder of reality. But here, there is no place to take shelter if we need a break from the relentless danger. Being completely outside the government's control means no one is ever safe, not naked in a shower or asleep in bed. Here, in a split second, everything around me can be transformed into flying madness that can kill me: shards of glass, hunks of stone and brick, splinters of wooden doors. I stare at the blades of the fan hanging on the ceiling, the white cup filled with water on the nightstand. I reach over into the darkness, grasp the cup, and place it under the bed.

NINETEEN

I wake up the next morning in an altered state. I grab my backpack from beneath the bed and gather my things near the door. All through the day, I am ready to spring up at the sound of Abo Ammar's motorcycle, signaling that it is time for us to cross into Turkey. I feel pain in my chest as if something is pressing on my ribs and preventing me from breathing.

Raneem's mother says it must be the smoke from the fires. But there is something else—uneasiness, anxiety, irritation. I think of the young man I met in the village, the torture he came back atrophied from, and try to push his memory aside. I'm grateful to be able to flee, that I have, thus far, evaded detention.

I go to the roof to see whether Abo Ammar has messaged me to get ready. Nothing. I go up and down the stairs so many times to check my phone I lose count. I go once more, nearly choking with frustration, and I stay to watch the sun set behind the green mountains.

A layer of creamy fog rises rapidly like a body of water. It occurs to me that my village is on the other side of this mountain. Just a year ago I was on the other side of this war.

I try to stifle a horrifying thought that dawns on me: What if I am never going to see that side of the mountain again? What if crossing here means I can never cross back? Now, so much stands between me and that place: military brigades and armed men and boys of different armies, all sworn to uphold different flags and different ideas about what Syria is and what it is supposed to be.

Instinctively, I call my mother. Perhaps I want some reassurance that the other side is still within reach. My mother's voice breaks as she tells me how empty the house is without my sister and me. How she has no money left, but she doesn't mind. She wants us to work and be independent. What pains her is the crippling fear that she might not see us again.

"We're coming back!" I shout when I hear her low weeping, irritated that the call fails to comfort me as I'd hoped it would, only compounding my worry. Instead, I tell her I have to go. I might have even yelled that I did not need more stress before I hung up, not knowing that, for years, I would replay the phone call in my head and wonder what would have happened if I had turned back. If I had understood that she had seen my exile before I did.

A FEW HOURS LATER, back in the living room, I finally hear the engine approaching. We are gathered around the wooden table peeling and slicing potatoes, then placing the cut pieces in a bowl of water to soak. Raneem's mother is planning to fry them for dinner. The engine cuts off and Abo Ammar steps into the room. His grim face is barely visible in the flickering battery-operated light.

"She has been waiting all day!" Raneem's mother says. "Where have you been?"

"Give me your camera," Abo Ammar demands, his tone so dry and sharp that it's almost unrecognizable.

"Why?" I ask, my voice shaking.

"Did you hear what I said? Give me your camera," he repeats more forcefully.

Raneem's mother stands up and asks him what's going on. He gestures with one hand for her to step aside.

I freeze, unsure of what to say; the glint of light off his rifle's gray barrel reminds me that he has the authority. I find myself reverting to the tactics I know best. I unplug my camera from its charger and hand it to him. He walks out.

I sit back at the table. Raneem's mother mumbles that I should not have let him take my camera because it's expensive. I stay silent.

In my head, I go through what I've photographed, what Abo Ammar might be looking for—what I might have done wrong. By now, he has probably seen the last images, the photos of the sun setting behind the smoky mountain. And before that, the girl on the swing. The road. The mosque. The minaret. The rooftop of the family whose child was detained and tortured. The video of the destroyed houses and, further back in time, photos of a protest in Damascus, the green flag with three stars and kids filling the frame with their tiny fingers making victory signs.

I feel a sudden sense of relief. These photos of the protest are proof that I am no threat. We are on the same side. It must be some misunderstanding or an abundance of caution.

"It's okay. This is normal. He has the right to make sure I didn't record anything that might help locate him or other rebels," I tell Raneem's mother. I know that government forces often examine videos and photos from the areas they attack to see if they successfully hit their targets or killed the people they wanted to kill. "I have nothing to hide."

Minutes later, Abo Ammar walks back inside holding my camera. "Come with me," he says.

I stand up and step behind Raneem's mother. "I didn't do anything wrong."

"Come with me right now," Abo Ammar says. "I brought you here. You follow my orders. You have to come with me."

I start to cry. I grab Raneem's mother's robe. "Please, tell him I don't want to go."

"Don't scare her," Raneem's mother says. "You brought her here, but now she is under my protection. If she doesn't want to go, she won't go. At least not this late. We can talk in the morning. Tonight, she is sleeping here with us."

Abo Ammar pushes the door open and disappears.

"I didn't do anything wrong, I swear," I tell her.

"Are you sure? What's in your camera?"

"Ask him. Let him show you. Ask him what I did wrong."

"I don't want to get involved," she says. "He has power I do not have."

I can hear Abo Ammar's voice outside. He didn't come alone; there is at least one other person with him. I want to go out and ask him why he is angry with me. If I stay inside, he might suspect I am hiding something. I want to say that he should trust me. That my life is in danger here just like his and everyone else's. There must be some misunderstanding. I'm trying to organize my thoughts when I hear a car pull up. The door swings open.

"Loubna! It's you! I knew it was you!" a man at the threshold shouts, turning to the man standing behind him. "It's her!"

The voice steps into the light. I recognize this face. I have seen it hundreds of times on news stations, Skyping from nearby villages, especially a few months back when battles for these mountains intensified. His name is Omar, and he is one of the main media activists in this area. Even when I was still in Jableh, he was among the people I followed closely to understand what was happening on the other side of Jableh, the Sunni side. When I moved to Damascus, I connected with him on Facebook and told him I was from Jableh. At first, he was skeptical because he knew my father's family's reputation. But as time passed, he came to see that my opposition to the government was genuine; we began talking and sharing videos and photos.

A few weeks ago, when I was searching for a way to cross the border, I asked him about the road to Turkey through the rebel-held areas, but he never responded. Days later, after I was in touch with Abo Ammar, he posted that he had been wounded in a bombing.

The man behind Omar is holding a rifle across his chest. He introduces himself as Saeed and says he is the leader of another brigade in the mountain.

"How did you know I was here?" I ask Omar.

Raneem's mother stands up and places herself between Omar and me. "Who are you?" she demands.

"I'm here for Loubna," Omar replies. "I know her. She's coming with me." He turns to me and tells me to gather my things.

"Why?" I ask.

"Loubna, trust me. You have to come with us right now. We drove all the way here, risking the government checkpoints, to pick you up." I am skeptical; I stay silent for a few seconds, trying to decide what to do or say. But Omar is the only person here I have known for more than two days, and he knows I'm on his side.

"I know Omar," I tell Raneem's mother. "I trust him."

I walk straight to the bedroom; Omar follows me. I pick up my bag.

"Tell me what is going on," I whisper.

"Is this everything?" Omar asks, taking the bag from my hand.

"Yes, but Abo Ammar has my camera."

"I'll get it," Saeed says. I hug Raneem's mother. She makes me promise to call her when I reach Turkey.

We drive away with the headlights off—Omar explains that, at night, government forces have been known to fire at any moving light. I watch Abo Ammar become smaller and smaller until he is nothing more than a black ellipse against the orange glow of the living room.

"Do you think he'll follow us?" I ask.

"Of course not," Omar says. "He's nobody compared to Saeed. Did you see how quiet he became? Not a single word!" We take a turn and the house disappears.

As we settle in for the drive, Omar explains what happened. A few hours earlier, someone from the group of rebel commanders he was with mentioned that Abo Ammar had captured an Alawite spy in the village.

"I didn't pay much attention at first," he says. "I assumed it was actually someone from the government. But he mentioned that the spy was a girl from Jableh who lived in Damascus, that she came with a camera and claimed she was here to cross to Turkey. Then I remembered that you messaged me a few weeks ago asking about the road to Turkey. My instinct said it might be you and I had to do something.

"I asked how they were so sure the girl was a spy. No one could provide an answer; they simply ignored the question, placing their trust in Abo Ammar because they knew him well.

"I tried calling you, but it didn't go through. I was horrified. I thought Abo Ammar had already killed you. That's when I told everyone that I knew you and that you were one of us. I asked who wanted to come with me to try and help you, and only Saeed stood up. No one else wanted to get involved. It took us hours to find out where you were staying. When we finally did, Saeed loaded up his rifle, and we drove to rescue you," he says.

"That can't be true," I say. "You must have misheard. He wouldn't just kill me without evidence!"

"Do you think we would risk our lives on these exposed roads if this hadn't been serious?" Omar retorts, irritated that I don't believe him, that I don't appreciate the danger he faced to help me.

"He was planning to kill you tomorrow," Omar says. "They even told me exactly where he was going to do it—in a partially destroyed building outside of Salma. We honor the dead by burying them, but an Alawite spy wouldn't be honored. He had to find a place to kill you where the smell wouldn't be a problem."

I rest my heels on the edge of the car seat, wrap my arms around my shins, and press my forehead to my knees. I want it all to pause for a moment to allow time for me to absorb what Omar said. It feels like fiction; it can't be real. It's as if events are unfolding at lightning speed, pulling me into their wake, and I have no say in any of it. No power.

I feel my heartbeat throbbing in my head. Every few minutes, the car pitches forward in a pothole, and I am certain we're about to plummet into the valley below.

"Omar," I whisper, looking up. "I swear I didn't do anything wrong."

"I know," he sighs, exasperated, fiddling with his phone and shielding the light from his screen with his open jacket. "But you were stupid. You can't just show up in a place like this and tell everyone you're Alawite."

"But in Damascus . . ." Omar cuts me off by holding his hand before my face without looking at me. He doesn't give me the chance to explain that, in the circles I had been a part of, Alawites and Christians like me and Amer declared our sects outright to challenge the government's narrative of a purely Sunni resistance.

Through Omar's account of the brigades, I begin to understand why some people at Amer's studio objected to using the word "army." Here, any small group with weapons or external funding could form a brigade, each with its own agenda. That didn't make it an army. An army implies structure and leadership. An army implies unified principles. But that isn't the case—the reality is far more fragmented, and far more dangerous.

And Omar is right. I am stupid for assuming that the only threat I might encounter would be from the government, the military, or Mukhabarat. I cannot completely fathom how I have found myself fleeing from someone who is fighting for the same cause I am. Why do I have to prove myself to Abo Ammar and people like him if we are both participating in this uprising?

I am as Syrian as they are. I am as sincere in my opposition to the government as they are. It is not their movement alone; it is ours. And what is "liberation" if the liberator is going to assume I am a traitor simply because I am an Alawite—and then, at his sole discretion, with no trial, take me away and execute me somewhere where the smell of my rotting body will not disturb anyone? And who were these rebel commanders who did nothing when they heard him brag about killing an Alawite woman? How is Abo Ammar any different from the checkpoint soldier who detained the young man we saw two days ago solely based on the village listed on his identification card?

Yet part of me knows that I can't entirely blame Abo Ammar for not trusting me. In almost every torture video from Syria posted online, amid the sounds of blows and the victims' screams, the soldiers can be heard shouting curses and insults in thick Alawite accents—as if flaunting their loyalty to the sect, their obligation to their protector. It's an accent I never had, because my mother had lived in Damascus, and I never inherited the tongue that could reveal my sect.

Almost all the videos of regime soldiers celebrating after blowing up Sunni mosques show them dancing to traditional Alawite songs. And the majority of Syrian army soldiers killed by armed rebels such as Abo Ammar will be buried in the Alawite mountains—my village mountains—

the site of the Alawite shrines where I have worshipped and cried, the launching ground of missiles, artillery shells, and mortar rounds aimed at houses and villages like Abo Ammar's. But I am proof that Alawites who oppose Assad do exist—no matter how many government officials or rebels try to deny it.

"Please don't let his prejudices change your mind about this mountain and its fighters," Omar says. "Yes, it's true: Many rebels are anti-Assad because they are sectarians who feel that they, as Sunnah, deserve a Sunni president. But you must understand that our fight is not only against the government; it is against these people, too. Do not let them erase you. That's what the regime wants."

After an hour, Omar parks the car outside a one-story house. A loud electric generator on the front porch fills the air with exhaust fumes. I see shapes moving inside the house. I can't tell how many men are there.

"Do you have anything to cover your hair?" Omar whispers. "They haven't seen a woman in months."

I take out a white scarf with black squares and throw it over my head before stepping out of the car. I keep my eyes lowered as we enter a dimly lit living room with a few scattered couches. Cameras, phones, and batteries are piled up in a corner.

"Hamdullah al Salameh!" someone says to me—thank God you are well.

I follow Omar to one of the rooms, where he puts down my bag. "Sleep here. The rest of us will sleep outside on the porch. Tomorrow, we will take you to Turkey."

Although I am the only woman in the house, I feel safe. I am one step closer to Turkey and many dark and targeted roads away from Abo Ammar. It would be too dangerous for him to try and follow us.

For most of the next day, I feel nothing but anger—the same searing anger that consumed me when Amer slapped me, the same anger I've swallowed for years, choking it down each time my father humiliated me.

Each act of obedience feels like a betrayal of the progress I thought I had made. I wonder if I will ever truly escape the patterns of submission ingrained in me since childhood. I'm scared that my father took away my voice, and now, even though I've made so much progress in gaining it back, in moments of danger—in moments when men hold the power and the gun—it vanishes. I refuse to let Abo Ammar have the final word.

Blinded by anger, I suggest filming a small video to speak about being an Alawite here, in the rebel-held area, and how so many Alawites like me exist in the uprising.

Omar agrees. I sit on a green armchair in the living room facing his Sony Handycam on a silver tripod.

"Are you ready?" Omar asks me.

"Give me a second," I say, trying to tie the revolutionary flag across my face to protect my identity.

"Okay, I'm ready," I announce. Omar signals me to begin.

It is a short clip. I explain that this is a revolution for all Syrians, including Alawites, and that I am here, on this side of the mountain, with the rebels. When the camera stops filming, I feel powerful. Abo Ammar and the government say that I don't exist, but I do. The battle isn't just with the government. The battle is with anyone who tries to capitalize on sectarian divisions, anyone who tries to tell me who I am.

IN THE CAR THE NEXT DAY, I call my mother and stay silent on the line while she prays for my protection. We drive a short way in the dark until we are told to get out and start walking. The night smells sharp and is tangled with pine trees. I step into the unknown, relying on the kindness of strangers and the thin thread of hope that I will make it to the other side. In the dim light, I can detect other people on the trail walking in the opposite direction, toward Syria. I try to glimpse their faces, but all I see are flickering shadows.

A few cigarette packs are passed to a young man wearing a military uniform with a Turkish flag emblazoned on his chest. He orders us to unzip our bags. I hold my breath as I watch him rummage through my belongings—everything I have left from my old life. He zips the bag closed; we are free to go. I grab my things and walk forward. I am free, I tell myself. I survived.

PART III

TWENTY

A couple of days after the video is uploaded, I am in Hatay, the southernmost province of Turkey, staying with a family Omar had asked to host me. I'm waiting for Alia to arrange my flight to Istanbul, where I'll stay with her while I look for a job. I call my mother, but she doesn't respond. I assume she's sleeping. The next day, I call again, both on the landline and her cell phone, but no one answers. Worried, I call Alia to ask if she has been in touch with our mother. She tells me she's been trying to reach her, too, and the fear in her tone unsettles me. My mother hardly ever leaves the house, and she would never keep her phone turned off. I think of all the times my mother warned us about the heart attack—the jalta—she might have, just like her father. I imagine her inside, needing help.

As the days pass, my concern escalates into panic. Alia and I call her nonstop, until we decide to call my mother's uncle—the one who had been to jail—since he lives close by, and ask him to check on her. A few hours later, he calls me back, his voice tense with alarm. He tells me that when he showed up and knocked on the door, someone must have seen him. My father appeared out of nowhere with a few of his men. They pushed him to the floor and took away his phone to check his recent calls. My uncle demanded they break down the door; he demanded to see if my mother was inside, needing help. When they busted their way in, he sensed she had been taken by force because he noticed that the television was on, and there was a half-drunk mug of tea, a napkin with grapes and seeds piled next to them. Nothing was packed. She had been taken by force by someone she trusted enough to open the door for. Weeping, he asks me not to put him in this position. He cannot afford to risk what my father might do to him, he says; he cannot be locked up again. I try to convince myself that my mother might have gone somewhere of her own volition. She has nothing to do with any of this. I call Alia to tell her what our uncle said.

Years later, when I try to recall these days, or how Alia reacted, or what was said on the call, it all seems like a blur. I remember how my brain tried to piece together who she might have opened the door to, or if my father had told her he was sending money and she opened the door for that reason. If only I had found a way to send her money, or had found a way to get her out of Jableh when I left, or had forced her to move to Damascus to be with me. Then came the denial.

I cling to the hope that maybe, just maybe, my mother is giving herself some time away. She has always been so dedicated to Alia and me that it feels almost logical to think she has simply decided to take a break. Perhaps she believes that, with Alia and me finding our footing, she can finally take some much-needed time for herself.

I see Alia's room. A temporary summer sublet, a bag packed for when she goes back to Syria. A blue scarf, folded neatly with a hay thread, sits on the table. Without her telling me, I know it is for my mother.

That first night together in Istanbul is quiet. We barely speak. It is also a blur. Alia's room is in a shared apartment with Erasmus students. We walk around aimlessly, neither of us knowing what to say or how to bridge the unspoken chasm between us. The weight of our shared loss hangs in the air, but we can't yet find the words to address it. Istanbul—a city my mother had dreamt of taking us to. A city we had a photo of on our wall. A city that came to light in my imagination through my mother's stories about her time here with her father. Now, it is a city that will forever be associated with her absence and the pain I've endured.

I am in Istanbul with Alia when my phone rings. My mother's cell phone number appears on the screen. I answer immediately.

"Mama? Can you hear me?" I ask. Her voice comes through, trembling. Something isn't right. I fear the worst has occurred—the very real danger of my father and what he might do if I did anything public against the government under my real identity. I hadn't listened to her. I had done what she warned me against and left her to deal with the consequences alone—consequences she had seen coming long before me.

"Mama, are you okay? I've been so worried about you—please tell me you're okay," I beg. It seems as if she isn't able to hear what I'm saying. Later, I would wonder if she could even hear my voice, or if she had been forced to speak without hearing me on the other end.

"Loubna, please come back. I need to have surgery, and I want you to come home," she says. I hear the pain in her sobs, and it makes me wish for my own death, knowing that I am responsible for what is happening to her. If my father ordered men to detain her, I should be there instead. Before I can say anything else, the line cuts.

In the following days, I spend everything I have on SIM cards for making phone calls, convincing myself that if I can just reach her once more, I can find a way to fix this. What I did wasn't that wrong. The severity of this punishment doesn't match my actions. I hadn't harmed anyone.

I call my father close to a hundred times, and when he doesn't answer,

I try reaching out to everyone I know who has worked for him, even the maids whose numbers I can find. I call my aunts, my uncles, their children—anyone whose number I can track down. The silence—the lines that cut off when they hear my voice, or after I introduce myself as Loubna. The blocking of my numbers. The social media accounts that shut me out. It all feels like a collective agreement to erase me, to uproot me from the family.

The rejection I face makes me hate myself for my recklessness—for leaving my mother alone with them, for filming the clip while she was vulnerable, fragile, surrounded by my father's side of the family. A side that would do anything to prove their loyalty to the government, to my father, and to whoever held the power.

I find myself overtaken not only by the pain of not knowing what happened or what to do but also by a consuming rage. I fantasize about the harm I will inflict on them if I ever have the chance. My anger transforms me into a version of myself I barely recognize. I think about going back, about giving myself up just to allow her to go free. But what guarantees are there that they won't keep us both? Who would fight for us? Who would speak up, especially when not a single family member is willing to even acknowledge what happened?

My mother's family can't do anything. My grandmother does not even pick up the phone, too terrified perhaps, seemingly afraid of what even the simplest action might bring down on her. My mother's uncle doesn't respond when I try to contact him to tell him that my mother called and that she has been abducted. I feel the suffocating weight of isolation—so much isolation. An isolation that makes me spiral and start to blame her.

It's an isolation my mother perhaps agreed to early on, a compromise she made to keep me and my sister under my father's wing, under his protection. Isolation she chose because her own family refused to help her when we were children, and she desperately needed their support. I wonder if this isolation was entirely her choice, or if it was imposed on her by others—by my father, who knew how to control and isolate, and by her own family, who turned their backs on her when she needed them most.

It wasn't just isolation—it was abandonment. The kind that slowly erodes any hope of escape. Did my grandmother's silence, her refusal to help, teach my mother that she had no one but my father to depend on? Did her own family's apathy push her deeper into a life where she had to rely on the very person who kept her trapped?

And now, the isolation has consumed her completely, swallowing her whole, leaving her with no one to turn to and no way out. I can't help but wonder if my mother resigned herself to this long ago—if she saw this moment coming and accepted it as inevitable, just as she had accepted so many other sacrifices to protect us.

As time passes and we fail to reach anyone back in Syria who might know anything about what happened to our mother, we find ourselves unable to talk about it. At the ages of twenty-one and twenty-three, in a foreign city hundreds of miles from home, avoidance seems to be our only tool for dealing with the shock. Maybe if we don't acknowledge the abduction, we can convince ourselves it isn't real. If we can just keep moving normally through life—whatever "normal" means at this stage—we can minimize our mother's absence and our helplessness.

I feel a strong urge to get away from Alia. I obsess over the blue scarf she bought, and all I can feel is that I'm responsible. She came here assuming she would be going back, buying a gift for my mother, only to have that stripped away because of me, because of my recklessness.

"It was for Mama," she says softly. But my guilt is so overwhelming that, for some reason, I hear it as an accusation. The scarf won't make it to my mother, and in my mind, it is because of me. I am the reason. My actions are the reason Alia no longer has a mother.

Though I don't have the words for it, I know deep down that my life will forever be fractured into two parts: before my mother's disappearance and after.

LOUBNA MRIE

. . .

TO TAKE MY MIND off Alia and get away from her, I accept an invitation to a "civil society workshop." These workshops have become commonplace in Istanbul and Egypt, funded by the US and members of the European Union. The workshop is held in a fancy hotel in downtown Istanbul, and I am given an incredibly spacious room with the biggest showerhead I have ever seen.

When the sessions begin, I realize why I was invited: I'm Alawite. The participants, who come from different parts of Syria, seem to check all the demographic boxes: the woman wearing a headscarf, the man with a beard, the Christian, the Isma'ili, the Kurd. It feels so transparently curated, nothing like the organic diversity of the Maseer. We are here to spend the next three days listening to academics who studied Bosnia and peaceful resistance movements worldwide explain the concept of civil disobedience to us in broken Arabic.

One session is led by an Egyptian activist. She connects her iPad to the screen and shows us how to create a YouTube account and upload a video. She speaks slowly and in painstaking detail, as if we have never heard of the internet before. In another session, which is even more bizarre, I am seated across from a Kurdish man, and we are given an orange. Our task is to find a way to split it equally without arguing. I assume the orange represents Syria, and we're meant to demonstrate that, as an Alawite and a Kurd, we can engage in conversation and share the fruit equally between us.

I wonder why they believe Syrians need education on civil disobedience, as if we haven't already executed countless tactics on the ground. If anyone should be teaching these workshops, it's us. As the Kurdish man and I consume the orange and whisper about how ridiculous this is, the woman leading the session observes us from a distance, smiling and content, occasionally snapping photos that, I assume, are intended to reassure donors that their quest to save Syria is going well. It all feels so performative. Contrary to my nature, I sit silently, observing rather than engaging, and imagining what each participant's life was like at home.

I would later learn that my skepticism was shared by many. Almost everyone spent these sessions on their laptops, chatting or watching YouTube videos. Some, even, who had fled Syria and had nowhere to stay, lived in hotels, moving from one workshop to the next. For a broke, exiled Syrian, a luxury room with three free meals and a seventy-five-dollar stipend per day was a great deal, when all you had to do in return was sit, nod, and pretend that you needed to be taught about political resistance.

In the final session, a young woman with short, curly black hair and round green eyes enters the room. As she connects her laptop to the projector, she introduces herself as Laila. She explains that she recently fled Homs and, with the help of international donors, is currently building an organization that will support media activists across Syria by providing them with training, equipment, and pathways to publication. "What we need now is documentation," Laila says, and a stab of fear hits me as I realize that I haven't heard from Naji in a while.

She presses play to show us a video she filmed and edited. For the next five minutes, the room is silent. All eyes, bathed in the projector's light, are wide open. It is a report from a field hospital in Ar Rastan, located in the Homs governorate, after an air strike. The footage of bloodied, screaming children and the red hospital floor is so nauseating and graphic that the woman who led the "split the orange" exercise has to step out.

When the video ends, I think of Amer blocking traffic with his banner, forcibly interrupting whatever reality the commuters were living in to confront them with the truth of what was happening in their country. Laila's video has the same impact. It makes all these "Have you ever considered peace?" academics remember that the level of brutality in Syria is unlike anything they've seen before. The silence lingers for a few minutes until one participant raises his hand and shares that his cousin died in that very same air strike.

During the lunch that follows at the hotel restaurant, I find Laila and ask to sit with her. I tell her how much I admire her for showing us the video and place my memory card on the white tablecloth between us.

"I shot some videos on my way here," I say. "But I have no access to news outlets or editors. Please make sure they get out."

When she asks what led me here, I find myself sobbing, trying to hide my tears from the other participants. I explain that I ended up in this workshop because I needed an escape; I am responsible for my mother's disappearance, and I can't face her absence or the pain I have caused my sister. She shares that her father was detained throughout her childhood, and her earliest memories of him were in the visitation room, behind a barrier.

When the uprising started, despite being married and the mother of a four-year-old daughter, she couldn't stay silent. She was angry at the government that had taken her father away from her family. She led protests in Homs and recorded videos. Her English skills allowed her to send footage to international outlets and translate for journalists covering the siege of Homs, the city that would later become known worldwide as the place where the American journalist Marie Colvin was killed.

Her husband, perhaps out of fear or loyalty to the government, warned that he would tell the police if she didn't stop; to him, politics was not for women. She eventually left him and fled to Istanbul with her daughter, where she taught English to rich Arab expats. One day, she was invited to one of these workshops, just as I had been.

She knows from experience that Syrians do not need lectures on the art of peaceful protest. Like Naji, she believes that the only way to truly make a difference is to document what is happening on the ground. "Bearing witness will ensure justice for our dead in the future," she says.

While helping photographers and local journalists inside Homs disseminate their work from Istanbul, she proposed a plan to one of the workshop organizers that was then implemented. Because of the semi-open borders between rebel-held areas and Turkey, she requested funding to bring activists to Turkey. Here, they are professionally trained to take videos that can be used as evidence of war crimes and that news channels would buy. They are given laptops, audio recorders, cameras, hard drives, and even equipment for pirate radio stations and local internet connections. Once back inside Syria, they send their materials to be edited in Istanbul and then delivered to news media around the world.

"Would you be interested in joining our team?" Laila asks. "I need more women. You speak English and you can film. That's exactly what I'm looking for."

I stab the soggy green beans with my fork, trying to suppress the guilt that surfaces whenever I think of Naji offering me money for my videos. It feels wrong to accept payment for what I once did purely out of love for the country—what ultimately led to my exile. I remember the rumors about Bassel, and the supposed financial incentive he received to return to Syria. Remuneration aligns with the government's narrative, painting us as mercenaries driven by Western funds.

I know that the nobility of my work, which I am using to numb my pain about my mother, will be diminished if I accept Laila's offer. But I also recognize that working a random, low-paying job that has nothing to do with Syria or the uprising is not a better option. I am a twenty-one-year-old unexpectedly exiled in a foreign country with no safety net; I cannot say no to an employment offer, especially one that will allow me to use the few skills I've developed. I accept.

At that point, I had yet to understand that millions of dollars had already been sent to Syria to study the war and support civil society activism—or, as it was referred to by the West, the "spread of democracy." I will always wonder how much being an Alawite factored into Laila's decision to offer me the job; it was exactly what the international donors wanted to see.

Laila lends me money to rent my own place, a room near her office in Cihangir, which is not far from Alia's—a hip neighborhood where exchange students like to spend their summers, and rooms are often readily available. My room isn't much—a brown desk with pamphlets of must-see attractions in the city and a twin-size bed—and the landlord admits that the heating is not great, but that's fine by me. I'm convinced I won't be here by the time it gets colder. All of this is temporary.

A FEW DAYS AFTER moving in, I receive a call from one of my father's associates. I hold my breath as he whispers on the other end of the line. Even though I had all but confirmed the truth to myself, it is still shocking to hear him say it out loud: My mother is dead. He explains that he is telling me this out of kindness, to give me closure so I can move on with my life. Now I can stop calling. Stop demanding information.

I don't say anything back to him. I can't. My mouth feels dry, and everything in my brain empties. I try to remember if I know this voice—if I should believe him, or if I should ask him for evidence. My heart races, and I can feel the blood pounding in my ears. Should I demand proof that she is dead? How did she die? Who killed her? Who should I be angry with? Who should I kill if I ever get the chance in the future?

I feel small, exposed, as though the world has peeled back every layer of me, leaving nothing but raw loss. The questions swirl in my mind. My body feels frozen in place, incapable of action or thought.

And later, I would wonder if it was a mistake to believe him. If, by telling me she had died, he was really just telling me to move on. To let it go. What if she was still there, alive, waiting for some miracle? Does it make me selfish that I chose to believe him—that I just wanted this to be over with? Because I didn't know what the alternative was. What was the alternative? To demand answers and closure?

How do you even ask for answers in this country? How do you force someone to give you a piece of someone's body to bury?

What had I done that was so horrible, so unforgivable, that I deserved this punishment? That she deserved this for simply being my mother?

When I hang up, I sit there, frozen, unable to move or speak. But then the silence becomes unbearable. I call Alia, though my voice is so unsteady that she knows something is wrong the second she picks up.

"What happened?" she asks, her voice laced with panic.

I try to tell her, but the words get stuck. I finally manage to say, "He said she's gone. He said she's dead."

There's a pause, the kind that stretches so long it feels like the air has been sucked out of the room.

"How do you know he's telling the truth?" she asks.

I don't have an answer for her. I tell her I don't know. I tell her I don't even know if I believe him, but what else can I do? Her silence feels like judgment, like she's blaming me for accepting what he said without a fight.

As soon as we hang up, I message my father: "I know you killed her." Then I call him, and for the first time since my mother's disappearance, he answers.

His voice is disturbingly calm, as if his words are a simple statement of fact.

"You don't care about her. If you cared, you would have come back."

TWENTY-ONE

The days following the news of my mother's death are a blur. All I remember is overwhelming anger. I want the whole world to know what my father and his men have done to her. Yet I feel silenced again, as though I'm howling into the void. Sometimes the weight of this knowledge completely immobilizes me, and I find temporary refuge in numbness and dissociation. But it never lasts long. Reality pierces through again—I can't escape what happened, and I am powerless to change it.

IT FEELS LIKE everyone around me has normalized the cruelty so much that the commonsense response is to blame me. I am to blame. It isn't the government's violence. It isn't that my mother vanished, with no one daring to ask or answer. It's me. I invited this punishment. I deserve it.

For months, my social media feed has chronicled others' tragedies—snipers at funerals, detainees killed under torture. I have always been the storyteller, the witness to their pain. Now, the narrative has shifted. The loss is mine.

I open a Facebook tab on my computer. I change my fake name back to my real one. The cursor blinks for a moment as I pause, and then I begin typing a post: I want everyone to read what my father did. It feels surreal, almost out-of-body, to see my own story unfold in the same space where I have shared the suffering of countless others. I publish it to my feed, hoping in that moment that this might mitigate the pain, hold someone accountable, bring my mother some measure of justice. I still believe that speaking out about atrocities can stop them, can change something.

WITHIN HOURS, MY POST goes viral, and I receive interview requests from the Syrian and international press. The most popular Facebook news page for Jableh, which posts daily about local soldiers who died fighting for the government, shares one of my interviews. Hundreds of comments appear, but I hesitate to read them. My heart races. These people know me. We grew up on the same streets. We sat at the same school desks. I am one of them. Eventually, my curiosity prevails, and I click.

> If I ever see her again, I will drag her by her hair across Jableh.
>
> She wants freedom. Well, if I see her again, I am free to do to her whatever I want.
>
> She is stupid and young. She doesn't know what she is doing.

I scroll down. People are saying horrible things about me and my mother. A few write that they were once my friends but stopped talking to me years ago because I am a whore like the mother who raised me.

Other comments are less aggressive. They say that maybe everyone should reserve judgment until they know the entire story; I might have been abducted and forced to write what I did. They say they feel bad for me. It may only be a matter of days before I'm killed, now that I've served my purpose.

One comment stands out. It is by someone who claims to know me and my mother very well. The commenter says he's not surprised we have turned out to be traitors. The traitors among us Alawites, he believes, are far more dangerous than those sent by Qatar and America. For this reason, once I am caught, I should be hanged in the public square near my house as an example to the other traitors hiding among their fellow Alawites who dare to participate in the destruction of our country.

When I read the name again, I recognize it: This is the owner of the supermarket where, for years, my mother bought our groceries. I don't understand how he can bear such hatred toward us. How is it possible for my world to turn against me like this just because I had the audacity to call for change and say that the government is corrupt?

I am reminded of a video a friend showed me when I was sixteen. It featured a Yazidi girl in Iraq who had disobeyed her family and community by running away with a man from another sect. Months later, her family told her they forgave her and asked her to come home. When she did, the entire village, hundreds of people, gathered in the main square to welcome her. At first, there were cheers. People held up their phones to record her arrival. The video showed a girl with long black hair and an orange sweater. Then, suddenly, the crowd turned vicious. She collapsed to the ground, covering her face with her hands as villagers kicked her mercilessly. She had been tricked into believing she was welcomed back—only to become a vessel for their irrational revenge.

The person shooting the video knelt down and placed his phone inches from the girl's face. I was certain that, at any second, someone would step in to shield her and say "enough," but no one did. Instead, legs approached from the corner of the screen, and someone threw a big white brick at the girl's head. Blood streamed onto the dry ground. A hand appeared in the frame to cover her exposed black underwear. More people stepped closer and continued to throw rocks and stones at the girl's body until she stopped writhing and lay motionless. Men dragged her away by her arms, leaving a streak of red in their wake. Then the video cut off.

This footage haunted me for days. Her own family set her up. I could never fathom how not a single person would stand up for her—not her childhood friends, or her relatives, or the kids with whom she had shared a classroom. I couldn't believe that every person in her life had either participated in her stoning or stood by and filmed her public execution, all because she had dared to break the taboos of her society and religion. It went beyond individual punishment; it was as if the community believed they were purifying themselves by killing her. The hunger to inflict such misery, and how quickly everyone adjusted to it, terrified me. Even sharing the video and watching it was a form of participation.

Now I am the traitor. I continue to scroll through the comments, desperate for someone to say that I am not a bad person and that, no matter what I have done, my mother did not deserve to die. But seemingly no one considers that detaining my mother to force me to come back is wrong—or no one has the courage to dissent. They are like the people in that Iraqi village, sacrificing their humanity to reinforce the status quo. And with this, I realize I have lost not only my mother but everyone.

Another comment stands out:

> Before you rebel against the government, go hold your own father and your uncles accountable. You lived off what they stole from our country.

Without thinking, I type a reply, an attempt to perhaps reclaim some control over the narrative about me, to remind them that I am a human being who can read what they say.

> If you acknowledge that the government is allowing my father and my uncles to steal, then you agree that the government is corrupt. This is exactly what we have been saying when we ask people to join us.

The guy counters:

> Are you stupid? This is not a revolution. Alawite soldiers are being slaughtered just because they are Alawites. Imagine a mother who has worked so hard to raise her child, to see him grow up, only for him to come back to her in pieces because he was butchered by a Salafist Saudi. This is the revolution you are calling for.

He says he knows me very well, and he is surprised that I would even try to pretend that I am political. He knows people like me, who read a few articles by Karl Marx and act like they're smart and know all about revolutions.

I google Karl Marx. I have never heard of him before. The internet says he was German. I don't respond. I still don't understand why every time we talk about change, government supporters claim that some foreign influence drives our movement. They can't imagine—or don't want to admit—that we witnessed real injustice and are demanding change of our own volition. It's as if change and equality are Western concepts that do not apply to us.

As I continue to scroll, two categories of comments by those who knew my family emerge. The first group isn't surprised that my mother was killed. It is my fault for assuming my actions would go unpunished; how childish of me. I have killed my own mother. The members of the second group insist that they know my family very well and I can't be trusted. One commenter claims my uncle Wahib converted the basement of his steel factory in Tartus into a detention center, and that my father and uncle sent me to infiltrate the revolution. They call me a liar and claim that my mother must be hiding somewhere.

DEFIANCE

Many agree that the story isn't credible. No family would do this to their daughter. And why does the Western media love her so much? they ask. Why was I given a platform to talk rather than the thousands of others who also lost their relatives? Some say the British intelligence service fabricated the story. Others suggest that I made it up for fame or political asylum. Even in the revolution, Alawites have to be the center of attention.

I receive direct messages that add to my pain, like the neighbor who casually writes one night to tell me that our apartment is now occupied by strangers. He saw people on the balcony and at first thought it was me, but then realized it wasn't; my father must have rented it. I try not to picture our home, the place my mother had fought so hard to obtain and poured so much love into, and everything in it exposed and discarded—our photos, my clothes, my books, my mother's jewelry. The portrait of Grandfather Ali on the wall, the albums tucked deep in her closet that attest to a time before she met Jawdat. She always took such care to preserve those images in honor of her father's memory. Now it is all gone, replaced by newcomers who will never understand what any of it meant to us.

I don't hear from a single member of my family on either side. No one. Their absence, again, inflames my anger and, below that, reinforces my guilt. It is all my fault. It is all my fault. The video I recorded at the border, crossing into Turkey, was my public declaration. I made a choice, a stance that aligned me with the "bad side." It was my decision, my mistake. If everyone collectively agreed that I don't deserve even a phone call, I must indeed be the only one to blame.

※

In the weeks and months that follow, I often regret having spoken out about my loss. In doing so, I gave others the power to scrape at the coagulated blood and enlarge a wound that will probably never heal. I also unintentionally opened the floodgates to strangers who, in the aftermath of a loved one's death, are seeking an interlocutor for their agony and grief. It's as if they see an invisible bond between us.

One guy I vaguely know from Damascus, whose father was questioned and killed by security forces, even calls me on Skype. He is so drunk that I can barely understand his slurred words, as he curses God for how unfair this pain is, for how much he misses his father, and rambles about how he hopes his father forgave him for fleeing to Lebanon. I end the call abruptly and message him later to apologize with the excuse that my internet cut out.

Though I try, I am totally unequipped to comfort him or anyone else. I stop responding to these calls and messages, not out of bad faith but because nothing can lessen my pain. If anything, these interactions only exacerbate my misery, preventing me from finding my own way to cope with my loss.

The only person who could possibly understand what I'm feeling is Alia. She knows that our mother was so much more than that—she was our one true parent, our everything, the guiding force that allowed us to pursue our own destinies. And we meant everything to her; she would often say that seeing us happy was all she wanted. No one outside of the three of us can truly comprehend the depth of my mother's devotion to us and the devastation of losing her.

Alia is also the only person who fully measures the extent of my father's cruelty and depravity. She knows firsthand that he never treated us like daughters; she experienced the pain and humiliation he put us through for years. Without saying so directly, our mother always warned us that he was capable of great brutality; Alia heard these same warnings and probed the depth of our mother's fear.

Although part of me desperately wants to, I cannot bring myself to talk to Alia about this ever again. Even years later, once this moment in our lives has become a more distant memory, bringing up our mother's death between us is too painful, too real and horrifying. Avoiding the subject and pushing our feelings aside is easier than speaking about the unfathomable truth that our mother is gone.

NOT KNOWING WHAT ELSE to do with myself, I go to work. Though I'm half dead, it gives me a sense of purpose. If I'm occupied—if I can focus on what I have instead of what I've lost—I can go on. Laila doesn't press me to share how I'm feeling. Like most Syrian activists, she follows the unwritten rule that it's best not to dwell on our losses. If we do, the pain is so immense that it might consume us. And we are not the only ones who have suffered. We owe it to the uprising to remain strong and hopeful about the greater future that awaits all of us.

Even though we don't talk about it, I know Alia shares my instinct to throw herself into work. I'm not surprised when, less than a month after I speak to our father, Alia tells me she found a job at a human rights organization in Cairo, where she'll be able to use her law degree. Egypt and Syria have very similar legal systems, and since returning to Syria is no longer an option, she explains that she needs to jump at the opportunity of a job more directly related to her field of expertise. Though she doesn't say so, I'm aware that distancing herself from me is another factor in her decision. My presence in her life is a reminder of the loss and pain she is trying to ignore. I don't blame her; she is grieving and exiled because of my actions. Living in different countries might help both of us retain our sanity.

I once heard that, in times of conflict, people have no time to count their losses. It's like being shot while running for your life: You don't notice the pain until you stop, catch your breath, and begin to feel the warmth of the blood trickling down your skin. Grieving consumes time and energy that I don't have; survival is my priority. Alia and I—like so many other Syrians—are still running for our lives. We need to keep moving forward. We cannot afford to be vulnerable, sad, or incapacitated. We need to feed ourselves, put a roof over our heads. We cannot afford to grieve.

Years later, I would be told that guilt walks hand in hand with trauma. But my guilt is more than a symptom of the trauma of losing my mother. Part of me will always believe that I am indeed guilty. I am guilty of underestimating my mother's fear of my father; of assuming she was overreacting; of failing to measure the severity of the shame I was bringing upon my family; of not realizing that taking a stand against the system that had lifted my family out of extreme poverty, making them one of the wealthiest Alawite families in Syria, would be considered a mortal sin. I am guilty of failing to understand that my father would do anything to prove his loyalty to the government.

I am guilty of not remembering that, throughout my life, whenever my father was angry about something I had said or done, he would blame my mother, claiming she didn't know how to raise me properly. I am guilty of not hugging her goodbye when she ran behind me as I rolled my bag out the door for the last time, worried about missing my bus. I wish I had stayed. I wish I had emptied my bag on the bed, put it away in the closet, and forgotten about Damascus. I wish that, when Naji called to ask if I was coming back, I had said, "No, I'm staying home. My mother is more important than everything we're fighting for."

I try to find comfort by reminding myself that this is not unique. Everyone has experienced loss. I repeat the mantras I've learned from other people: Nothing is too difficult for us to tolerate; this is war; this is the price of liberation; nothing comes for free. I try to act normal and pretend this is not a big deal, that I can overcome this. I just want to be normal, even though I don't know what normal truly means.

At first, I feel grateful that I don't know the details of my mother's death—they would only be more traumatizing. But random cell phone videos leaked by soldiers and Mukhabarat torturers give my brain enough fuel for seemingly infinite possibilities. In one video, a government soldier, his face unmasked, pours gasoline over the heads of two women and lights them on fire. The women scream and run wildly around the chamber, slapping their heads with their hands, desperate to extinguish the flames. The soldiers laugh. Later, I learn that the two women were the wife and daughter of a soldier who had defected from the army and fled to Turkey. In another video, a group of prisoners sits on the floor of a white cell with their eyes covered and hands tied behind their backs. Soldiers, their identity exposed for all to see, kick them in the face with their jackboots. The prisoners crawl to the walls. They reach out with trembling hands, pressing their palms against the white surface, leaving behind crimson imprints. The handprints streak down as their strength gives way.

Government soldiers leak these videos on purpose. They want to instill fear by showing us what awaits us inside detention centers if we dare to challenge the government. Before my mother died, I found these videos empowering: Almost every time one leaked, I watched it and thought about how stupid the soldiers were to document their barbarity with their faces completely exposed. I was certain they were digging their own graves. I was certain that, one day, the International Criminal Court or whoever was in charge would use these videos to prosecute the soldiers and the government they were serving. The videos worked in our favor, I told myself—an interpretation I hung on to because I wanted it to be true, and because I did not know these victims.

But after my mother's disappearance, the torture, flames, and blood all become possible indications of the fate she suffered. All because of me. The images flash into my mind out of nowhere, dissociating me from my surroundings, leaving me shaking and breathless. "They cannot do this to women," I try to convince myself, even though I know they can and do.

The websites of human rights organizations are full of similar testimonies from women who have been released from jails. I avoid them to the best of my ability, swiftly scrolling up and down the page. No matter how determined I am to remain ignorant, these stories and images still manage to seep into my mind: women stripped naked, lashed with metal cables, their wounds oozing blood and pus; women yanked and hurled by their long hair until interrogation rooms are covered in blood, strewn with clumps of hair and shattered teeth.

A ROUND THIS TIME, one of the Syrians I have met in Turkey loses his mother in a bombing by the government forces in the town of Manbij, near Aleppo. Though we are not close—perhaps his knowing that I, too, lost my mother led him to share—he tells me how he crossed back to Syria from Turkey, went to the hospital, and slowly pulled the white sheet back to see his mother one last time. He says he wished he hadn't done it. Her body was gone from the waist down. I say nothing. I watch as he brings his hands to his eyes and exhales loudly, as if trying to purge the image from his memory.

I would like to comfort him but I can't. I resent him for forcing me to think about my mother's death, but even more so I resent him for not realizing how lucky he is to have seen his mother one last time, to have had the opportunity to wash what remained of her body, to wrap it in a white cotton shroud, and to lay her to rest under a gravestone marked with the dates of her birth and death. How fortunate he is to have a place where he can grieve. To have had a chance to say goodbye.

When I was a child, my mother made Alia and I promise that she would be buried alongside Grandfather Ali, whose grave we visited every year on the first day of Eid. Talking to this man, I think back to those Eid days, and I wonder if I will ever be able to fulfill my promise. A tombstone for my mother: a place to mourn and talk to her and tell her how much I love and miss her. When I was in Damascus, I never understood why families would pay large sums of money to collect their children's lifeless bodies from detention centers. To do so, they had to sign papers claiming that their child was killed by terrorists; this felt like a betrayal, just to retrieve what was left of a body and bury it. Now I fully grasp their need. I would settle for just a piece of my mother's body. Anything to lay her to rest.

I open my mouth. I think to pat his shoulder as he holds his head in his palms. But I can't. A heavy wave of sadness debilitates me. The sadness of realizing that I never imagined experiencing a war where I would be overwhelmed with uncontrollable jealousy toward someone because he was able to bury the upper half of his mother's body.

I FEEL FINE, I INSIST; my sleep is just out of control. No matter how early I go to bed, I always wake exhausted, irritated, and in desperate need of more sleep. I sleep for ten, twelve, thirteen hours a night. My dreams are long, vivid, and often repetitive.

In one dream, I am sitting at a desk during an exam, filling a blank sheet of white paper with answers. Time is about to run out. I realize that my scribblings are only draft notes on scratch paper, not the test paper. I scramble to write more, only to find that I am writing on another draft page.

In another dream, I find myself walking toward a checkpoint. A few men in uniforms are standing there, their rifles strapped to their backs. How did I end up here? I have my blue Syrian passport in one hand. How did I go back? I didn't want to go back. Over and over, my mind sends me back to the checkpoint. And I am jolted awake when I reach it. I wake up shivering with anxiety, my heart pounding. I look around the room. I'm safe, I tell myself; I'm alive.

Some nights, I dream I am walking down my street in Jableh. It's so vivid I can feel the heavy, humid summer air sticking like glue to my skin and hair. I think to myself that this must be a dream—I have no way to return without being killed. I look up to our balcony. The lights are on. It is a signal. When we first moved to Jableh, and Alia and I would play at the nearby park, my mother had instructed us to come home when the lights on our balcony were turned on. I was always grateful for this gentle rule; other mothers just yelled at their kids. My mother trusted that, once the lights were on, we would come home.

In the dream, as I walk up the stairs, I think to myself that I should not tell my mother that she has died. (This was a common feature of these dreams—I feared that, if I told my mother about her death, she might die again.) I start taking the stairs two by two to go faster. I hear footsteps. I turn. My father is behind me, looking much taller than he is. I run faster up the stairs, screaming for my mother to open the door for me, only to realize that it is a trap, and my mother is already gone. Someone pushes me from behind, and only then do I open my eyes.

When I wake from this dream, I often feel pain throbbing in my back and neck, as if I had indeed fallen onto the floor. It takes me a few seconds in bed to remind myself of where I am. I am not trapped.

ONE MORNING BEFORE WORK, I wake with the usual jolt. The time on my phone reads 7:00 a.m. I get up to check that my door is locked and then sink back into bed to try to salvage some rest. When I open my eyes again, the time reads 1:30 p.m., and I have twenty-seven missed calls and messages from Laila.

"Are you okay? Answer me. If I don't hear from you we'll come to your house."

I call her and say, "I'm fine! Sorry, I overslept." I compose myself and rush to the office.

When I arrive and sense that everyone is tiptoeing around me, I become angry—angry that they assumed I was not doing well; that I should be looked after because I'm troubled. I spend most of the afternoon with my headphones on, in one of the individual rooms.

Later that day, Robbie, one of the Americans on the team, opens the door and asks if she can talk to me. I nod. She closes the door behind her, pulls up a chair, and sits next to me.

"I have a friend," she says calmly. "I told him about you. He can meet on Skype if you want to speak with someone."

"About what?" I ask.

"You've been through a lot. It's okay to seek help."

I feel the air being sucked out of my lungs when I realize she's suggesting mental health treatment. I'm so insulted I have the urge to physically push her away. I've never met or even heard of anyone who sought therapy.

When I was growing up, no one ever brought up mental health. Even when I saw my mother taking pills to sleep, I knew we could never inquire about that. Mental health and therapists were for crazy people who got locked up in Ibn Sina, the mental hospital, where custodians were known to rape female patients.

"I'm not crazy," I say, my voice much louder than I intended. "I just overslept."

"Loubna, I know you're not crazy. Grieving is a human and necessary thing. When you're ready, give him a call," she says.

I don't argue. I nod, open Skype, and type her friend's name. I promise to reach out to him. But I never do. Why should I? I am fine.

TWENTY-TWO

Here, in Istanbul, I may not know exactly who I am anymore, but I know I am not a refugee. Refugees are the Palestinians who, in Lebanon, Syria, and Jordan, lived in camps that became city neighborhoods. Refugees are the Iraqis who thought they would return to their beds as soon as the Iran-Iraq war ended, and the Iraqis who thought the same during the 2003 war. In both cases, those Iraqis who fled could never truly return, because their Iraq—their barefoot-in-the-dust childhood football Iraq, their sisters' dried lime tea Iraq, their sleeping on the roof of their own home Iraq, their cousins chattering with the fruit sellers Iraq—no longer existed.

We Syrians consider ourselves different. It's about time for us to go home. Perhaps before New Year's Day or even before Eid. It's only a matter of weeks. There is no way a government that has killed thousands of its own people, many of whose deaths are documented, can remain in power.

No such injustice can persist. We are going back. For now, we are "visitors." This is what the government of Turkey calls us.

Life here in Istanbul is temporary. So temporary that it's pointless to learn the names of the streets I walk each morning from my building door to the office. It is pointless to memorize my phone number and my street address. "German Hospital" is all I need say to any taxi driver to be dropped off a few blocks away from where I live. It is pointless to get too familiar with a world I am going to leave so soon. I am skimming the surface of surroundings without engaging with them. I am a visitor only and it feels like a betrayal to let myself settle into a life that my mother is no longer part of.

Our American project manager tells us that the organization is willing to pay for us, the members of the Syria team, to take Turkish language classes. Not one Syrian enrolls. Learning the language of our land of refuge would be an acknowledgment that our refuge is becoming a residence. I don't feel the need to learn Turkish. By now, I know enough words to order a crisp cheese and sausage toast smothered with butter and a glass of pomegranate juice from Laz Bakal, the tiny store at the end of my street. I know that "sharfsis" and "namosis" both mean "whore" because taxi drivers shout these words at me through their half-opened car windows when I jaywalk.

Not knowing Turkish has little impact on my life. At work, everyone speaks either Arabic or English. Laila and my other friends are Syrian. Most evenings after work, Laila and I go to the Grand Boulevard Café, located at the end of Hazzopulo Pasaji, which opens onto the famous Istiklal Street with its antique tram and buskers. The crowds move in waves; we navigate through them and make a left into a narrow passageway that smells of burning incense and leather, walls covered with silver necklaces and colorful prayer beads, rings and earrings and fake Russian gold that reflects the light from the bare bulbs dangling above.

At its far end, the passageway opens onto a small square hugged by worn brick buildings that give off the scent of burnt firewood. The square is strewn with small, low wooden chairs and tables where cubes of sugar are piled up in mounds in tiny, pounded-copper bowls. Spoons clink against tea glasses and men with broad silvery trays brush against people smoking and talking at crowded tables. Raise five fingers and five teas will magically appear. This is the "Syrians' café," as we call it, for there are so many Syrian patrons that the owner eventually had to hire an Arabic-speaking waiter.

I don't know why this place, of all places, becomes our café. Perhaps because we followed the pull of our collective Syrian gravity, for Syrians would often come without knowing anyone and be drawn by the Arabic words, the chatter in Syrian dialects, the Syrian faces hunched over laptops, watching videos of recent clashes, or reading the news. I like the Grand Boulevard because it's reminiscent of the coffee shop in old Damascus where I used to sit with Amer and listen to dice clattering on wooden game boards as old men played and others looked on, studying, playing along in their minds. Where the melodies of old songs mingled with bubbling hookahs.

Every time a Syrian friend shows up, someone must drag a chair across the flagstones and find an improbable opening in the ever-expanding circle of occupied seats. We don't need to know one another. We are bound together by the pain of being exiles in a city that is so beautiful and alive, a city where wealthier Arabs enjoy their honeymoons and celebrate their plastic surgeries and hair transplants. We see these people come and go while we bide our time.

The number of chairs increases each week. Many Syrians, young and old alike, fled the country down dirt roads and, once they'd crossed the border, took buses or flights to Istanbul to meet a friend or family member. There, they looked for any job—something to pay the rent until they could return to Syria and resume the lives they had put on pause.

Others flew in from Jordan and Lebanon. I didn't understand this at first: Why leave a city where you can decipher concert posters on buildings and bus stops, converse with taxi drivers and barbers and shopkeepers, read slogans and curses spray-painted on walls, and understand all the subtle gestures and quips that make a city home?

"Speaking the same language is the problem," a photographer friend coming from Beirut explains.

"The Syrian dialect reveals our origins. In Jordan and Lebanon, Syrians are not welcome. Neither of those countries give Syrians the freedom Turkey allows."

In Turkey, Syrians do not need work permits. In Jordan, most Syrians are not allowed to leave their refugee camps. Renting a place somewhere else is rare and requires a security clearance. In both countries, Syrians bring their class divisions with them. The Lebanon available to rich Syrians is not the same as the one experienced by the poor.

Turkey is different. The government turns a blind eye, allowing hundreds of people to cross its border daily. Locals do not hate us, and Syrians do not stand out as they do elsewhere. Here, we are lost in a sea of yabanji, foreigners. Istanbul is cosmopolitan; being a yabanji is nothing exceptional. Turkey welcomes international NGOs who open offices and fill them with highly paid employees.

This will later change: Syrians will get killed at the Turkish borders, and politicians seeking election will make promises to deport us. But in 2012, English is all one needs to land a job, whether at an NGO or as a fixer or translator for television crews or journalists. The Syrian government is still repressing any information; they continue to detain local journalists and rarely allow foreign journalists across the border. The only way for international media to report on the conflict firsthand is from Turkey, where they can interview exiled Syrians or cross into one of the rebel-held areas.

LOUBNA MRIE

. . .

A COUPLE OF MONTHS after my mother's death, I finally receive a message from Naji. He is now in Istanbul. I have mixed feelings about the news: a heavy agony, considering how intent he was on staying in Syria, but also a selfish happiness that we'll be reunited. It's reassuring to have him nearby. Beyond what I experienced in the presence of random Syrians, this brings the simple comfort of knowing I am not alone in my exile and that I am lucky to be alive. Naji is special; he belongs to a time in my life before displacement became the dominant reality, before my mother's death opened a great chasm in my existence. He knows another incarnation of me, a version that I lost when I lost my mother.

Naji and I meet at the "Syrians' café." I don't recognize him at first; he has lost so much weight that his face is gaunt. He tells me that right after he fled Syria, Assad's security forces raided and confiscated everything from his office in Jaramana, the place that smelled of paint and dust, where he gave me my first lessons in videography. He had traveled from Damascus through Daraa and southward through the desert to get into Jordan. He hid in caves near the Syria-Jordan border and filmed the rebels hunkering down inside. His wife will join him in Istanbul once he has settled down.

When the conversation turns to me and what happened to my mother, I deflect. "I don't want to talk about this now," I say, as calmly as I can. Naji tells me he's sorry he didn't call when he first heard the news. He didn't know what to say.

To change the subject, I bring up my falling-out with Amer. Naji is still stunned that Amer would raise a hand to a woman; then, to my surprise, he mentions that Amer is also here, in Istanbul, waiting for his visa to Germany.

My heart sinks. Despite my anger toward him, it is devastating to learn that even Amer, who was so adamant about remaining in Syria no matter the consequences, has ended up in exile like the rest of us. Naji suggests that Amer and I meet to talk.

"Over my dead body," I say.

I PUSH HARD TO GET Naji hired at Laila's organization and succeed in securing him a trial run. Naji is one of the instructors at our first workshop. He is offered a position after that. Soon, Naji joins our after-work routine, and things start to change. It was rare for Laila and me to stay out late after work because she had to go home to her daughter. She and I would walk out of the coffee shop and toward the main street, where she would grab a taxi, and I would take a short walk home. But now, Naji and I accompany Laila to the main street, then go with a few other people to cheap neighborhood bars where we yabanji and Turks clink glasses and sing along to their music, high and happy.

Alcohol, always a crutch, becomes my savior. I drink so much that when I wake up for work, I'm often still drunk. Every Syrian I know in Istanbul drinks. Some are trying alcohol for the first time as a rebellious act. Some drink to forget. Some, like Naji and me, drink to remember, to grieve, to mourn. Topics I refuse to discuss while sober become the central focus of our conversations.

I tell Naji that part of me wishes I had been killed by Abo Ammar and never filmed that video. If I had died, Alia and my mother would still have each other. I tell him how much I hate myself and that I know I will feel this way until I die. I tell him how alive my mother is in my dreams, her death just a dark, passing thought. I tell him how I've woken myself up shouting for her.

Though speaking about this is cathartic, it also embarrasses me that I can only talk about my mother with the help of alcohol. It pains me that, sober, I am not able to honor her by telling everyone how loving and devoted she was. I feel weak for burying her memory.

But our nights out are not all consumed by darkness. Often, on the weekends, our table is so big and crammed that our laughter and chatter drown out the Turkish songs blasting from the speakers. We spend hours joking and talking about everything but Syria. When one of us withdraws into silence—arms crossed, wiping away a tear before anyone notices—Naji blurts out, "This is our therapy!" and raises a glass of Turkish raki. "They'll need a hundred years to learn from us!"

Naji always makes fun of the organizations that have sprung up along the border to offer Syrians mental health consultations. "This," he laughs, "is our mental health workshop!" We all nod in agreement, raise our glasses, and down whatever is left in them before calling for another round. My recollection of these nights often stops at this point. The best-case scenario is waking up the next morning in my own bed and spending the day watching YouTube videos and drinking water to wash away my throbbing headache. I only leave the bed to use the toilet and get more water.

On Monday mornings, back at work, I am always amazed when the Westerners show us photos from their long walks and what they have seen and eaten in Istanbul. I have yet to visit a single tourist attraction. They gush about how lucky we all are to work in one of the most beautiful cities in the world, and I just nod.

The worst-case scenario after a night out is waking up in a bed or on a couch in an unfamiliar apartment. Sometimes, I roll over to realize I'm not alone. Perhaps it is someone from the table the night before or some random man from the bar. I head home and try to wash off the smell of alcohol, a stench so nauseating it makes me hate myself even more than usual.

At this point, hooking up, like everything else, feels like an act of revenge. I was always told that my body, my honor, my reputation are not my own—they are the property of the family, of the system, of my father, of his last name. And with the hatred that has nested inside me toward all of them, I find myself inflicting revenge on them, using my own body.

Casual sex becomes a weapon, something I wield to defy the control they have over me. No protection, no attachment—just a reckless attempt to reclaim something that has been stolen from me. But there is no liberation in it. I hate my body as much as I hate my father. It isn't an escape; it is a mirror of my rage. It is revenge—a revenge I can impose on them, on him, on his legacy.

Even as I act out, there is a part of me that wonders if I am also punishing myself. If my anger at them has become so entangled with my anger at myself that I can't distinguish between the two. It isn't about pleasure; it is about destruction—of their power, of their control, of myself. I try to sleep through the day, and when I wake up, I vow never to drink again, though I never honor the pledge.

One morning, I wake up in my own bed, but I know immediately that something is not right. The drilling in my head is different. The room is spinning with the same accelerating force that I experience when I go to sleep drunk. I close my eyes. I have never felt this way before.

When I finally push myself out of bed and into the shower, every step sends another wave of throbbing pain into my head. As I undress, I notice bruises on my thighs. When the hot water hits the back of my leg, I realize there is a burn there the size of a palm.

I don't even try to remember what happened. I fear that someone I know and trusted—someone I can't afford to lose—tried to hurt me. I pray that whatever happened remains forgotten. The bruises change colors over the week, shifting from the blue of a storm cloud to a sickly yellow-green before finally fading away. Each time I press on them, I swear that I will never drink again.

WINTER BRINGS RAIN, and though my sandals squish and squash along the pavement, I am reluctant to spend money on new clothes. Somehow, admitting changes in the seasons would be an acknowledgment that I have lived here longer than expected. A warm coat and a couple of sweaters are all I allow myself to buy. Everyone calls me cheap; our salary is more than enough for new outfits from Zara, H&M, and other brands that feel upscale and exclusive because we don't have them in Syria. Our office is minutes away from Istiklal Street, Istanbul's most famous promenade.

The first time I got paid, I counted my salary three times to confirm that I was truly earning $4,000 a month—about 200,000 Syrian liras. The web design company in Damascus and the money I got from Naji were somewhere just north of 15,000 liras. This new income makes me feel ashamed; I don't deserve it. I recall Amer's words: "They are being paid to remain outside of Syria, distant from us Syrians, our suffering, and our resistance." Foreigners support us so they can feel good about themselves. I pay my rent, send Alia some money, and save the rest.

"Loubna, what do you do with your salary if you don't buy anything new and you live with roommates? Do you stuff your cash into your mattress?" Laila jokes with me one day during our lunch break.

"How did you know?" I say, laughing.

"No, really, tell me," she says.

"No, it's true," I say, my laughter fading. "I put my money under my mattress."

The next morning, Laila comes by my house, still dumbfounded that it is where I am keeping my money, and demands I open a bank account. She walks me to the bank across the street from the office since it's apparently the only one that will open accounts for people with Syrian passports. I am reluctant until the Turkish banker, who is wearing a tie and exuding a heavy aroma of sandalwood cologne, assures me in irritated and broken English that yes, I can withdraw the money whenever I want.

◆◆

Technically I have everything I need to settle in Istanbul, and I hope that, with time, my dislike for the city will diminish. But it doesn't. The more I see of it, the more I hate it. It has everything I miss about Syria, readily available in a way I can't accept. It has Jableh's air: thick, laden with humidity. It has the same wafting sea breeze that invades the narrow alleys. It has Damascus's old city cobblestones, and shops with beautiful rugs and soaps, and sellers that call after you down the street. It has Jableh's promenade along the water, lined with small cafés, and people who occasionally stop and ask men wielding long fishing poles what they've hooked and netted.

But even if it had none of these, how could I—how could we—see the beauty in our place of refuge? I feel cursed to be exiled in one of the most beautiful cities on earth. A city where young Europeans take gap years to explore and learn Turkish and stay awake till the early hours of the morning drinking arak and eating small meze plates and singing along to songs whose lyrics they don't even understand. Istanbul is nowhere to mourn.

The worst for me are the shop owners and their friendly conversation. "Nerelisin?" they ask in Turkish—"Where are you from?" It is an opening, a trick they use to keep you in their shops longer. If I am lucky, my answer that I am from Syria will put an end to the conversation, establishing that I am not a tourist in Turkey buying gifts for family members back home. I am here because I've fled death. Images and videos from my country are being played constantly on the small TV sets in the corners of their shops, on mute. They know that they can't get much money out of me. They turn to the next person.

But when I am not lucky, more questions follow: "Where in Syria?" "Is there fighting in your city?" "Is your family still there?" Their curiosity stops when tears pool in my eyes. I know such questions are coming from a good place, but I can't help but wonder why people don't think twice before asking. It's easier to lie to them, so I often tell them I'm from Lebanon.

One day, I find myself stopping at a shop on Istiklal Street, drawn by a pile of pink soaps with dried rose petals. I close my eyes, cup my hand around one of the bars, and inhale deeply. The fragrance is hypnotic, bringing back the rosewater my mother would keep in the fridge, dab onto a cotton ball, and run over her face and neck at night, a habit she had inherited from her mother in Damascus to calm the skin and senses at bedtime. I am reminded of the smell of my bed after my mother slept in the room I shared with Alia, which only happened when thunderstorms raged through Jableh's skies. Alia and I would push our beds together and beg my mother to sleep between us. We would hug her, breathe in her familiar scent of rosewater, and finally drift off to sleep, safe and happy. I was so warm with my head upon my mother's chest, one leg wrapped over hers, squeezing tighter each time lightning flashed through the slats of the window shades, less afraid after each roll of thunder.

"You are almost my height now!" my mother would say. She would caution me to learn to face my fears since she wouldn't always be around to protect me. "I won't last," she often said. I knew she just wanted to sleep in her bed alone; back then, her death felt so far away.

The shopkeeper, a woman in her fifties, touches my shoulder and restores me to the present moment.

"Are you okay? Take one! Free!" she says.

I wipe my tears, embarrassed. I apologize. I assume she thinks I don't have enough money to pay because she rushes and slips a few soaps into a brown paper bag and hands it to me as I walk out the door. I feel pathetic, angry, and foolish for even trying to act normal and do some stupid, ordinary little thing any other girl my age would do here, like shop for soaps. I hate gestures that intend to make me feel better and loved. I hate feeling weak. I hate crying in public. I hate people feeling sorry for me.

Back in my apartment, I keep my soaps in their paper bag, and every time I see it, shame burns in my chest. But the scent of rosewater comforts me.

Soon after, my Italian roommate tells me she heard me crying in my sleep. She says she is worried for me. She says we can talk, and if I ever feel the need, I should not hesitate; I should just knock on her door. I nod. A few days later, I move out.

TWENTY-THREE

Our organization's first journalism workshop is scheduled for early December. Because most of the participants we have chosen do not have passports, we decide to hold it in Gaziantep—or Antep, as everyone calls it—a small city in south-central Turkey about forty miles from the Syrian border, which saves the participants the sixteen-hour bus ride to Istanbul. Over the past few months, broad stretches of land in the Aleppo and Idlib governorates have been liberated. In retaliation, the Syrian government has been firing missiles and dropping barrel bombs from helicopters over residential neighborhoods. When challenged about the jarring death toll of civilians, the Syrian diplomats speaking before the United Nations Security Council claim the images are fake. They deny the rocket attacks and the barrel bombings.

This is exactly what we are training local journalists to combat with their cell phone cameras and the internet. With the equipment and training we are going to provide—DSLR cameras, mics, laptops, and high-speed satellite internet—they will be able to capture and produce high-quality clips instead of shaky cell phone videos and send them via high-speed internet to international media outlets in no time. My role in the workshop is logistical—helping participants with their travel and accommodation and, most important, paying just as much attention as they are so I can improve my own skills.

Seventeen participants arrive at the hotel we've chosen. It smells of strong air freshener, and the air-conditioning system blows hot air that makes my face ache. One of the participants is Mezar, a law student from Raqqa I met once in Amer's studio back in Damascus. In the time since we last saw each other, Mezar has fled into the rebel-held countryside of the Aleppo governorate, where he has become one of the main providers of footage to the news networks from that area.

For five days, from early morning until after sunset, Naji and a Moroccan journalist who specializes in conflict resolution lead training sessions. They teach us how to interview sources and discuss sensitive topics, how to construct questions based on the source's previous answers, and how to use the equipment the organization is providing.

After each day's session, Laila, Naji, and I take everyone out for food and drinks. Because we know the organization will foot the bill, we order much more than we can eat, covering the tables with grilled meat that oozes fat and red spices and washing it down with tall glasses of ayran. After dinner, we walk through the covered, flagstone-paved alleys and narrow streets of Antep's old city. We stop to eat kunafeh that sizzles on copper plates smothered in orange blossom syrup. The nights only end when Naji warns that if we don't go to sleep, we won't be able to focus tomorrow.

SCHOOL HAD ALWAYS made me anxious. But when education connects with real life, motivation comes naturally. I wake up early, ready to absorb every word. It feels surreal being here, in safety, learning from someone who has risked his life to teach me and others these essential skills. In the final days of the workshop, the participants share their old work—clips they filmed in their local areas before coming here. This gives them the chance to self-assess and revisit their technique.

There is footage of young men and women debating slogans for protests. They take us behind the scenes of the newspapers and schools being run by locals. They show the Syria I hoped to see when I first met Abo Ammar in the rebel-held Syria. Naji is assigned to select the most promising students to film regularly for the organization. His main job will be to give assignments and provide feedback. Back in Istanbul, our job will be to edit their work and forward it to news channels. After watching the clips, however, I realize that I do not want to sit in an office in Istanbul anymore. I want to cross back into Syria and film with them. I want to be in the Syria embodied by the slogans we chanted, not the Syria that questions and kidnaps and kills activists based on their sect.

Our project manager doesn't like the idea. "Why risk your life?" he says. "We trained people from these areas to film. Your job is in Istanbul. We have enough people inside."

"If it is unsafe, why are we encouraging them to film for us?" I argue. For days, I insist that conditions are indeed safe enough for me to go back with Mezar. He knows everyone, after all.

When the organization eventually gives in, I feel hopeful for the first time in weeks. On a personal level, returning to Syria will allow me to prove to myself that the rebel-held areas of the country are not all ruled by men like Abo Ammar; that Istanbul is not definitive displacement, merely a temporary base; and that Syria is not lost. I want to prove to myself that I have been right not to settle for a life of exile in Turkey. Syria can still be home.

◆◆

On a wall across from the rusty gate that marks the border between Syria and Turkey, someone has written "Welcome to Free Syria." Three kids sit on the wall, and I lift my camera and snap a photo of them, their fingers stretched into victory signs.

It takes less than two minutes to walk between the two countries. Alongside Mezar, I enter Jarabulus. "Live free or die standing tall like the trees" is written in red paint on a school wall near the city center. On the same wall, there is a portrait of Bassel Shehadeh, the Christian filmmaker I had crossed paths with that afternoon in Damascus, who had left his Fulbright scholarship at Syracuse University in New York to return home and document the uprising before being killed by mortar shrapnel in Homs. "Freedom means reclaiming the simplest things," says another slogan. It's true, I think. Throughout our lives, walls have been dedicated to praising our president. It is time we reclaim them.

I wander through the school, filming. Nothing shades the steel-barred windows. Sunlight has bleached the green chalkboard. Wooden desks carved with graffiti have scraped the floors. It is like the school I went to as a child, but things are different now. On the classroom's walls, rectangles of bright white paint replace the portraits of the president and his father that once hung there. I am told that students no longer recite the words "Our eternal leader, the immortal Hafez al-Assad" three times a day. For the first time in forty years, students are just students—not pioneers of the Ba'ath Party, not little soldiers who are told that being a good Syrian means sacrificing their blood and soul for the president.

I sit by the playground to wait for Mezar as he finishes shooting and watch the kids running behind a ball, shouting. I feel a strange, heavy weight in my chest, and realize I am jealous: I never had the chance to learn in a classroom without a portrait of the president. I don't know what school would have been like without his presence, his smiling face hovering over me, his words painted in the hallways. I know I should be grateful that I am witnessing this moment. But I cannot help but feel bitter. I unzip my camera bag, take out my purple velvet notebook, and write a short note for myself on the last page: *Go to school.*

From Jarabulus, we drive south for almost an hour to Manbij, a small town that was once under the authority of the governorate's capital, Aleppo. Here we are greeted by a member of the local council who calls himself Sheikh Munzer. His hair is light brown, and his olive-colored scarf matches his eyes. He shakes my hand. "You don't look like a sheikh," I say, laughing. He hardly has a beard. Munzer says he was given the "sheikh" title after he obtained a master's degree in Islamic studies at Al-Azhar University in Cairo.

The next day, Mezar and I join Munzer to film the election of the city council. Despite the constant air strikes, a few dozen people are gathered in a warehouse. They've bundled up against the cold and drawn their scarves tight over their heads. The air inside smells of fresh paint and exhaust from the diesel heaters burning in each corner. The windows are sweating, and the revolutionary flag is nailed to the wall behind the four candidates for office.

They take turns addressing questions: What are your plans for the judicial system? How will you deal with trash collection now that we have no municipal services? Who will hold rebel commanders accountable if they abuse their power?

None of them can answer these questions. These are problems for a city government to solve, not a group of activists funded by international NGOs who are managing the community through trial and error.

"After 2011, Syrians realized that they had a voice, but learning how to speak is not easy"—so goes a common phrase almost every Syrian politician and intellectual in exile has repeated in the media. It never made sense to me until this moment, witnessing this election. The candidates keep interrupting each other. The crowd keeps interrupting the speaker. I realize that every adult in this room under fifty years old is voting today for the first time in a process where ballots have more than "yes" and "no" checkboxes. It is overwhelming.

DEFIANCE

One journalist I interview is the editor of a local newspaper, who tells me that democracy hit the region like a massive wave. Syrians like the concept, he says, but we don't yet know how to apply it. Journalists forced to hide behind pen names for forty years are now receiving support to write freely. "But it is not easy. We would be naive to think that, after forty years of dictatorship, democracy can be achieved smoothly," he says. Sometimes he wishes he could keep his pen name. "Having my real name on an article requires that I count to ten before criticizing a rebel commander. If he doesn't like it, who will protect me?"

He tells me that the main problem here in Manbij is tashweel—the local slang for looting. "Everyone condemns government soldiers for doing it. Why do we not talk about the rebels' vandalism? Are they immune because they drape themselves in the flag we display at our protests? It's like the immunity the government grants to pro-Assad thugs who parade the president's face on their cars."

I hadn't heard about the looting before, but as I talk to more locals, I realize it's a major problem. My interviewees tell me about people who fly the revolutionary flag on their cars but whose main mission is to steal and extort money. They install checkpoints, claiming it is for the locals' protection, but their only aim is to collect "tolls." Whenever a battle is taking place, they arrive after the fighting and loot the houses abandoned by those who fled. Later, they sell whatever they can: fridges, electronics, crates of cheese and olive oil. Some have even demanded ransom for family photo albums. I hear a few examples of people who have escaped clashes only to be forced to pay thousands of liras to have their memories restored to them.

"The Prince" and "Hassan Sex" are the nicknames of the two most famous mobsters in Manbij. I have no idea how the Prince got that moniker, but I hear different stories of how Hassan came to be known as Hassan Sex. One rumor says that he earned his name years before, in high school, when he would download porn from the internet, copy it onto compact discs, and sell them after class. Another claims that, before the war, he fought off efforts to close Manbij's three brothels.

In Aleppo, there is another man who calls himself Hassan Carrot. Before the war, the police detained him forty-nine times, mostly for looting and drugs. Now, he is in command of a brigade, and his men call themselves the Carrots. They even have an anthem: "We are the Carrots. We are the Carrots. Hassan the Carrot raised us. We don't fear death. Hassan, we are your men and your Carrots." I burst into laughter as I watch a "music video" of the song. Men sit in a circle and pass a joint from one person to the next. It is absurd.

A FEW NIGHTS BEFORE I'm scheduled to cross back to Turkey, a group of us gather around the heater in Munzer's living room. Big paintings of Quranic verses written in gold hang on the walls. I say I had never heard of Hassan Carrot and the Prince before now. What do they think of these men? Is it true they are looters? If so, why are they allowed to wreak havoc under the guise of the revolutionary flag?

"The Carrot has lost many of his men," one guy shouts. "He is brave. There is no part of his body that doesn't bear a scar. This is what matters. Yes, he loots. But he has to fund his brigade. So what if he's looted abandoned houses or sold ancient artifacts? What is more important, fighting the government and protecting our families, or preserving meaningless ancient ruins?"

Another guy insists that Hassan Sex and Hassan Carrot are secondary. "We should not focus on them. Their misdeeds are individual misdeeds. Highlighting these people's actions will only serve the government narrative that our uprising is made up of thieves and thugs. We should keep our eyes on the big picture and the great things that are taking place within the liberated areas."

I come away content with their answers. They are right; these are the actions of individuals. I bury the stories of thugs, hiding them not just from my consciousness but from my camera, too. I return to Turkey with hard drives that only reflect what I want to see: interviews and reports on local councils, rebel commanders who protect bread lines, classrooms where students are no longer forced to memorize the president's speeches and those of his long-dead father, police officers who defected from the government and are now volunteering to ensure the country does not devolve into chaos. My reporting shows a promising new version of Syria, one that can justify my staggering losses.

"Rampaging through houses and factories and extorting tolls at checkpoints isn't as bad as throwing barrel bombs from helicopters onto children or detaining and killing thousands under torture," I say to Naji when he asks if what he has been hearing about the anarchy in the rebel-held regions is true. "No revolution is perfect. Everything done in the name of defeating evil is acceptable."

Naji disagrees with me. "Replacing evil with another form of evil is not liberation. It is a failure."

THROUGHOUT WINTER, my Facebook inbox fills with messages from local councils around the rebel-controlled areas asking me to come and film what they have accomplished. I cross into Syria again countless times, always accompanied by Mezar. With him, I travel to Al Bab, Azaz, Marea, Saraqib, and other countryside towns in the vicinity of Aleppo and Idlib— parts of Syria I only knew existed because we chanted for them back in Damascus. When I return to Istanbul, Naji leans back in his chair, rests his feet on the table, and watches my interviews, eyebrows furrowed in concentration. Hours later, he removes his headphones, stands up, runs his hand through his hair, and asks if I remember how, almost a year ago, I came to his office in Damascus with footage of feet jumping. I should be proud of how fast I am learning. I give him the credit. He is the reason I picked up a camera in the first place.

The reports I shoot over the next few months are aired on some of the most watched news channels in the region, like Al Jazeera and Al Arabiya. People in Syria start to call me the Sahafyah, the Journalist. They know that if I film them, they will appear on TV, and everyone wants to be on TV. My mother's death becomes one of the examples dropped in debates and arguments to emphasize that not all Alawites support the government. Although I'm glad my work is being recognized, I often wish that people would know me as anything besides the Alawite journalist who lost her mother.

Sometimes when I am back in the office, reviewing film and reassuring Naji that, yes, it is safe for me as an Alawite to cross again, a dark thought washes over me. I wonder if speaking publicly about my mother is *why* I can cross back to Syria, film, and return to safety without encountering danger from men like Abo Ammar. I am not just any Alawite woman like I was last summer. Now, I am an Alawite woman who has lost and grieved; therefore, I deserve *their* trust. Did I have to lose my mother to prove that I am trustworthy? Why does this feel like it's *their* uprising, and anyone who has not grieved is not to be trusted? I push these questions aside the same way I leave the thugs and chaos out of the frame of my lens. I'm proud to capture a side of Syria worth suffering for.

One evening, the lights in the office go out. I assume it is a blackout, but the battery icon on my laptop screen still shows a little lightning bolt. I look up and see an orange light flickering across the room along the white wall covered in posters. Suddenly, voices erupt from the shadows.

"Happy birthday to you! Happy birthday to you! Happy birthday, dear Loubna . . ." the voices sing. I turn twenty-two tomorrow. I start to cry.

Laila walks toward me with a small round chocolate cake dotted with bright strawberries. I blow the candles out. The lights turn back on and Laila hands me a few bags. They are full of clothes and shoes and jackets. My tears drip onto bright pink and red scarves of soft wool. There are a couple of two-button blazers with shoulder pads, just like the one Laila wears whenever a donor visits the office. There are oatmeal-colored heels. And a strapless little black satin dress.

"If you don't want to buy yourself clothes, we will!" she says. "We must celebrate. Go home and change."

This is their attempt to pull me to the surface, to help me breathe, to impress upon me that I am turning twenty-two and must enjoy the simplicity of a birthday cake and new clothes and dancing. But I do not go out. All I can feel in this moment is the deep shame that prevents me from telling them that I cannot drink because I am preparing to have an abortion.

A COUPLE OF MONTHS before my birthday, I returned from Syria and felt the urge to have a drink. I convinced myself that, having maintained a period of sobriety following the workshop, I could have only one or two drinks. Just like that, I found myself slipping back into the routine I had promised to avoid.

With alcohol came blackouts, and with blacking out came more one-night stands; then came a day when I found myself suddenly craving tomato juice, which I had always found disgusting. Out of the blue, it became the only thing I wanted to drink with every meal, and I would drench whatever I was eating with ketchup.

I was in the office kitchen slapping the bottom of a ketchup bottle over a piece of toast when Laila asked if I had lost my mind. "Who eats a ketchup sandwich? You've got the craving of a pregnant woman!" she laughed.

In that moment, I felt the air being sucked out of my lungs. I realized that I felt different. My body even *smelled* different. I abruptly remembered how, in a car on my last trip to Syria, I got so nauseous that I had to ask the driver to pull over to vomit. I blamed it on the bumpy, bombed-out road. It was horrifying to measure how detached I had become from my own body—so much so that I hadn't noticed missing my period for over two months.

I threw the ketchup bread away, rushed to the pharmacy, bought a pregnancy test, and headed for the restroom. It was a stick, the kind I had often seen in the movies and Syrian TV shows. The scenes were almost always the same: The camera would zoom in on the stick, the two lines would appear, and then there would be a shot of the woman's face in the mirror, slapping herself, tears running from her eyes and snot from her nose as dramatic music played. One of three predictable scenarios would follow. The first and most frequent was a confrontation during which the woman begs the unborn child's father to marry her. (He refuses, of course, because no good man would ever take a woman who gave herself to him before marriage.) The second scenario unfolds in a dimly lit abortion clinic where the woman bleeds to death as her lover prays to God to forgive them for their sins. In the third, the woman either throws herself down a staircase—this was the most common method in the Egyptian soap operas—or beats her belly with a heavy stone until she vomits blood. The camera focuses on the rock hitting her flesh, and with each blow, a flashback recalls the sequence of events that led the woman to this dark place. The lesson was always the same: Unwanted pregnancy before marriage will be your demise.

Two lines appeared on the stick. I didn't slap my face. I stashed the stick as deep as I could in the metal trash bin and went back to my laptop, put on my headphones, and forced myself to take a deep breath. I stopped myself from doing anything that would lead anyone, including Laila, to suspect that I was pregnant. I feared I would be fired if this news got around. I would lose everything and everyone. What would people say? Loubna, a whore, a pregnant whore? I knew I couldn't cross back to Syria to film until I figured this out.

I reached out to a Turkish girl, a stranger I only knew by her first name. I had met her at a solidarity protest for Syria, and she'd later invited me to a talk given by bearded men who reeked of smoke and body odor and called themselves anarchists. They discussed Syria and looked at me as if they had only brought me there to nod and give them approval.

"I need your help," I messaged her.

Two hours later, we were in a room waiting for the results of my blood test. I didn't have to explain why I had called her and not any of my Syrian friends. As we waited, she tried to comfort me by talking about the agency women have over their bodies. On having this choice and how liberating that is. Being here, taking control, is empowering, not shameful. She went on and on about patriarchy and misogyny, and the more she spoke, the more nauseous I felt. I needed silence. My body was aching. I closed my eyes and promised God that if the stick was wrong, I would never sleep with anyone ever again; I had learned my lesson.

The nurse returned and informed me that I was indeed pregnant. I started crying. The girl tried to console me. She told me her sister had had an abortion and that the procedure was safe and that I shouldn't worry. She said I could speak with her sister, but I didn't want to talk to anyone. Why would I willingly bring disgrace and scandal upon myself? I just wanted this nightmare to end.

"It is seven weeks old," the doctor said as he handed me a black-and-white image of the fetus. I glanced at it and put it down. I refused to see; I feared it would make me change my mind. I knew I was doing the right thing, even if the doctor was trying to convince me otherwise. I confirmed that I did want an abortion and that I would sign the papers.

While inputting my information, the doctor noted that my birthday was approaching. I halfheartedly suggested a birthday discount, but no one laughed. The surgery cost about $1,100, while the average monthly salary in Turkey at the time was around $1,000. The appointment was scheduled for two days after my birthday.

IN THE OFFICE with my colleagues, my stomach churns from the smell of the chocolate birthday cake. I hold my breath and force myself to eat a few bites. I watch Laila, her sweet, loving excitement for my lonely birthday celebration. I feel the urge to tell her that I am having an abortion and ask her to come with me, but I can't make myself do it. I don't want a witness to yet another event I know I will shove into a deep corner of my memory and pretend never happened.

Alia's name flashes on my phone the next morning to wish me a happy birthday, and I feel a knot in my throat. It is a reminder that I have a sister, and I shouldn't feel so alone. But I know that I will burst into tears at the sound of her voice, and she won't let me go until I tell her what is wrong, and I cannot risk adding to her resentment toward me with another instance of my recklessness. I still don't have the ability to grasp that the shame I project onto her is mine alone. When, years later, I end up telling Alia what happened, she rolls her eyes and laughs, and tells me that I was out of my mind for assuming she wouldn't have been supportive of my choice. But in the moment, I don't have the emotional strength to gamble on her support. I reject her call.

Two days later, in a room bathed in fluorescent light, I lie on my back as a nurse with long curly hair asks me where I am from. We engage in awkward small talk, my legs parted under a cloth sheet. "Count to ten," she says. Then she fits a plastic mask over my mouth, and I close my eyes.

I wake up in a room that smells of bleach. Snow is falling so heavily outside that it seems as if a white blanket has been draped over the window. It takes me a few seconds to believe that it is all over. I feel a pang of loneliness. If my mother were alive and here, I know she would have been by my bedside, waiting to comfort me.

When I was a kid, I hurt myself often, coming home from playing outside with new injuries. My mother would carry me in her arms to the doctor's office for stitches. Along the way, I would feel her tears wetting my forehead. She would hold me so tightly that I would mistake her heartbeat for my own.

I try to imagine what my mother would have said if she had learned about the abortion. She would have been angry with me, probably, but she would have been by my side, nonetheless. I wonder if I would have even gotten an abortion if this had happened in Jableh. Maybe my father would have found out and killed me or forced me to marry a random man to conceal my mistake.

Despite the loneliness, I feel an overwhelming sense of relief that is so powerful and so warm it confuses me. This version of the story contradicts all the unwanted pregnancy scenarios I grew up watching and hearing about. Not once did I encounter an example, in real life or on TV, of a woman getting an abortion and waking up in a clean hospital bed before moving on to live her life. Becoming a mother was supposedly our one true purpose; otherwise, we were nothing. And yet every woman's life seemed upended at the sight of those two lines on the stick—and it always altered her destiny, never the man's. According to Syrian law, even in cases of rape, a woman could be sentenced to three to fifteen years in jail.

Lying here, safe in a hospital bed in Istanbul, the words of the Turkish girl begin making sense to me. I'm alive, I think to myself. I haven't thrown myself down a staircase or pounded my belly with a rock or lost my uterus after a traumatic procedure in a secret clinic. I have the right and the power to determine my own future. It occurs to me that, despite her fears, my mother might have supported me in making my own choice to defend my independence, and I wonder how different her life might have been if abortion had been legal and accessible to her. I close my eyes, take a deep breath, and realize, with a jolt of surprise that almost makes me laugh, how much I still want a glass of tomato juice. Right now. Perhaps with pepper.

TWENTY-FOUR

A few weeks later, I receive an update from Aleppo. The rebel-held eastern side of the city has become infested with sandflies that spread the disease leishmaniasis, which can produce ulcers of the skin, mouth, and nose. Hundreds of people, mainly children, have been affected. Residents have been burning trash; corpses are decaying under rubble; stray animals are everywhere. I quickly plan my next trip across the border. I want to film something that could help bring more awareness and solicit financial support.

The only problem is that this time, Mezar cannot accompany me. He is in Raqqa, his hometown, for the first time in two years, as it is being liberated from government forces. He suggests reaching out to a mutual Syrian friend in Istanbul whose younger brother is a well-known fixer, assisting foreign journalists with logistics, access, and safety during their reporting trips in eastern Aleppo. His name is Abdullah, he says, and I will be safe with him.

By the time I meet Abdullah at the border, it is late afternoon. The sun is dim in the cloudy, gray March sky. Abdullah is tall, with green eyes and sun-washed skin. He takes my bag without deigning to look at me. But rather than unnerving me, it gives me the impression that he has done this many times before, which is comforting. We stand in a line of people and, minutes later, we cross the border and climb into a white van. The driver is another fixer who works with Abdullah.

I ask Abdullah if he is happy with his job. Almost all the fixers I have met before are based in Turkey, and their role only requires some knowledge of English. Abdullah is different. To be a fixer inside Syria, one needs connections with the rebels for protection, transportation, and a safe house—a place where journalists can sleep and use satellite internet to submit their work.

"Everyone wants stories from Syria," he says. He is proud of what he does and appreciates the courage of the journalists he's met. Most outlets want to limit the risks their staff take, so the reporters stay in Turkey and interview Syrians there. It's often the desperate freelance writers and photographers—eager to place a pitch and jump-start their careers—who cross the border. Abdullah tells me he charges about $150 a day for his services.

When he notices me counting on my fingers how much $150 makes in Syrian liras, he laughs and tells me not to worry. "I won't charge you," he says. "At least we'll get to enjoy meals together! I can never understand these foreigners." He tells me about one French journalist who, for three straight days, only ate from a can of hummus he bought as soon as they crossed to Syria, and an American who only ate candy bars that looked like cardboard. "A Syrian will never turn down a meal! I think they assumed I'd charge them extra later for the food," he says. "These journalists have so much money but act so cheap." His driver nods in agreement.

I later realize that this belief that Western journalists are all rich and only pretending to be poor is what leads to dozens of kidnappings. It doesn't matter if they work for a TV network with unlimited spending power or freelance and live on a shoestring budget; every non-Arabic-speaking person with a notepad could be worth a king's ransom in dollars, which the rebel commanders desperately need to fund their brigades.

"It is good money, but it is not an easy job," Abdullah tells me. "The rebel-held areas are chaotic. Lawless. Everyone with a gun has power. We thought that, with the government gone, people could take care of their own cities. It is not the case. People are lost. Any small argument or misunderstanding between two armed men can lead to bloodshed." He shares my fear that exposing foreign journalists to this aspect of the conflict will confirm the government's narrative that we are all nothing but thugs.

"I am not only responsible for their protection," he says. "I am also responsible for what they see and film."

Abdullah asks what is keeping me in Istanbul. "If you fled because of the Syrian government, why don't you relocate to one of the rebel-held areas? There is so much work to be done, especially in eastern Aleppo. Syrians who speak English and know how to film and take photos are vital. Is it the money? How much do they pay you?"

"It is not the money!" I say. "I am doing my best to help."

"Are you really, or this is what they are telling you back in Istanbul? These NGOs claim they want to help Syria, but they emptied Syria of people like you when they were most needed. They offer jobs and money to secular activists and keep them in Istanbul. This revolution is like a child that is being born after forty years. The labor won't be easy. It will be long, grueling labor, and we should be patient and push through.

"It will take as many people as possible. People like you and me have to fight everyone—thugs, Islamists, foreigners, the government. Our battle is difficult."

A moment of silence follows. I bristle at his condescending tone, but I know that if I tell him my salary, his eyes will widen, and he will demand the fee he charges Westerners. I keep quiet, but his question haunts me. There is plenty to fear that keeps me away—between the government's bombardments, my father, men like Abo Ammar who doubt my loyalty as an Alawite, and the general carnage—and yet, whenever I am in Istanbul, I feel the urge to go back to Syria.

I try to change the subject and ask Abdullah what his plans are once the war is over. "I will get married and have children," he says. "Two of my brothers were killed by the government. My mother wants grandchildren before she passes away. I just want to make her happy." He smiles. I stay silent until we reach the rebel-held Aleppo.

A FEW DAYS BEFORE, when I had reached out to Mezar to see if he would accompany me to Aleppo, he had asked if I was sure I wanted to go there. "Aleppo is not like any of the places you have been to so far," he said.

I hadn't understood at the time, but driving along the city's buildings and cramped streets, I see what he meant. Aleppo is a city turned upside down. Refrigerators and washing machines hang from the ripped open sides of bombed-out buildings. Streets have become craters. There are flags of different colors: the green flag of the revolution; the black flag of the Islamists; the white flags printed with the words of the Shahada, the Islamic creed, "I bear witness that there is no deity but God, and I bear witness that Muhammad is the messenger of God"; and the yellow Kurdish flag.

And there are checkpoints—countless checkpoints where masked men gather around firepits. Maybe the cold is the reason no one gets up from their chair to search our van. But I notice they do not seem to be stopping anyone. Checkpoints here, Abdullah explains, are intended to mark which areas each brigade controls and which each brigade can loot.

Abdullah tells me I shouldn't walk alone. Death doesn't announce itself. It comes with the surprise sting of a sniper's bullet, fired from a rooftop or a room in a vacant building located in a government-controlled neighborhood. Sometimes the government forces and the rebels are so close to each other that they can talk across the same wall, tossing hand grenades when the conversation grows heated.

From the car window, I snap a picture of a detergent billboard, tinted orange from the sunset, that rises between two bombed-out buildings, promising a deep clean for both colors and whites. The car slows as we enter a crowded street. There's a juice shop with plastic bananas and pineapples hanging from the ceiling and a few sandbags on each side of the entrance. There's a falafel shop with a large vat of oil boiling next to trays of bright green pickles and tomatoes. Next to it, you can buy grilled liver and sujuk—Armenian sausage—and hamburgers with eggs and unlimited fries for an extra fifty liras. Men with AK-47s hanging from their shoulders stand in line for rotisserie chicken that turns in grease-covered glass ovens. How can a city be so destroyed yet remain so alive?

"I love watching people who are seeing Aleppo for the first time," Abdullah says. He has grown accustomed to the destruction; my shock makes it new again.

"Spend a few days here," he says, "and you will become blind to the ruin and deaf to the sound of fighting. Probably you will keep your camera down, feeling there is nothing here to film. Everything becomes normal."

The car stops beside a building that Abdullah identifies as his office, and we take the stairs to the third floor. Inside, we're met with a blast of scorching air. I'm reminded of Naji's office back in Damascus: The room is empty save for a few couches, a coffee table covered with cups and white scald rings, and a computer desk with a cushioned wooden chair from a dining table set. There are muddy footprints. The air smells of coffee, cigarette smoke, bleach, and exhaust fumes from a loud gasoline generator on the balcony. The corners are cluttered with tangled extension cords and computer cables. Two men and a woman sit together in silence. I am later told they are local journalists. Each of them is glued to their phone, scrolling. The younger man is Abdullah's brother, Dia.

Abdullah sets my backpack down, his face serious. He tells me something urgent has come up and that he needs to take care of it while there's still some daylight left, before darkness settles in. But before he leaves, he makes me promise not to eat until he returns with food for dinner. Once he's back, he says, we'll finally sit down to discuss what I came here to film.

Sandflies, I think to myself as Abdullah leaves the house. I am here because sandflies bite people and then ulcers consume their skin. It suddenly occurs to me that I am not immune. What if I get bitten? Why did this not cross my mind? I pull my laptop out of my bag, connect to the internet, and read about how to protect myself. Does vinegar really help? Would it be strange to ask Abdullah to bring a bottle of vinegar back with him?

Just then, someone begins pounding on the door, interrupting my thoughts. Before I can answer, a voice shouts Abdullah's name. I hear one forceful push followed by the sound of splintering wood. I can't recall if I catch the other journalists' eyes before instinct takes over—I shove the chair aside and slip under the desk. I hear the clang of a rifle being cocked. Footsteps. I see military boots walking toward the couch where Dia was just sitting.

"Where is he?" a man yells.

"Leave me," Dia cries in pain. "I am injured."

"Where is he? Don't lie to me."

Dia screams. The other journalists run out. A gunshot blasts so close to me that it sends a sharp, deafening ring through my ears. I shut my eyes. The sounds become muffled, as if I am underwater. "I am injured," Dia pleads, trying to free his arm as the men drag him away. Boots stomp outside. I open my eyes. White dust and shards of stucco speckle the black satin dining room chair. I see a hole in the ceiling. I crawl out, grab my laptop, and message Mezar. My hands are shaking uncontrollably. "I don't know what is happening. I need help. Men came into the office. They were fighting. They took Abdullah's brother away. Please help me."

"Was it an argument?" Mezar responds. "Or a real fight?"

"I know when it's an argument! This was a fight. They shot at the ceiling!"

Mezar tells me to remain online. He has a few friends in Aleppo who might be able to come help me, but it's hard to know which one might be in a place with satellite internet right now to receive his message. A few minutes later, he instructs me to wait for ten minutes and then move toward the entrance of the building. One of his friends is driving my way.

Before the ten minutes are up, I hear a car stop in the street below. I crawl to the balcony. In the dim glow of flickering car lights, I see Abdullah. Dia's silhouette stands next to him. Abdullah is in the middle of the street, his gun raised.

"Lower your gun, and I'll lower mine," a man shouts at him from a distance.

"I did not see him," Abdullah replies. "I swear on my dead brothers' souls that I did not see him; I did not take him."

I try to piece together what is going on. I hear the same words, over and over. The two men are screaming at each other. No one is listening. From what I can gather, Abdullah is being accused of kidnapping someone, a journalist, and the group that broke into the office has come to free him.

Abdullah gets into his car, revs the engine, and takes off; one of the men points his rifle at the car and fires multiple rounds into it. The vehicle crashes into a building and stops. Dia screams from inside the car, then steps out, shouting. "You've shot my brother! Help him! Do not let him die!"

I crawl back inside the office and type a message to Mezar.

"They just killed Abdullah! They killed him! He was shot inside the car. I am leaving. I cannot stay here."

"Are you insane? Where are you going? Stay where you are!" Mezar replies. "My guy is on his way. Do not leave now."

But I cannot stay; what if the men come back? I am terrified. I descend into the darkness of the staircase. It smells of food and burning trash, engine exhaust and charred tires. I hear the crunch of boots on the street outside. It takes all my strength not to collapse under the weight of my bag. My tripod is pressed under my arm. My phone is casting enough light for me to see where to step next.

"Loubna," a voice whispers out of the darkness. "Is it you? It's Hussain, Mezar's friend! Are you okay? What happened? Is Abdullah really dead?" He takes my bag from my trembling hand.

"I don't know," I say. Everything inside my brain has turned to black. Only one thought lingers: Abdullah's mother has now lost three of her sons. Two by the government forces, and one by the rebels. The stairs are cold and the air is stale. I wrap my arms around myself, trying to stop shaking. We get into a car.

Hussain navigates the dark streets. On some stretches of the road we drive with the headlights off to avoid snipers.

When we reach Hussain's house, it is as frigid as the air outside. There is no generator, no satellite internet, nothing. Just a cold iron fireplace with a pile of trash next to it.

Hussain lights a fire using wrappers from take-out sandwiches, spindly wooden branches, and plastic potato chip bags. A tall man walks through the door. The smell of grilled meat spreads through the room.

Long white candles stand in little round coffee cups and cast flickering shadows on the walls as white foam plates are extracted from a bag and placed on the carpet with containers of grilled meat, pink cabbage, cucumbers, and baba ghanouj. Hussain balances bread on my knee as I sit cross-legged. I dip my bread into the food. I had promised Abdullah I would not eat until he returned. Every bite is a struggle.

"Who was it?" Hussain asks. "Was it Al Nusra? I heard that the Islamists hate Abdullah because he brings in foreign journalists and protects them while the Islamists want to kidnap them for ransom. What did they look like? Did they speak Arabic? Do you remember the logo on their military jackets?"

I cannot recall any images. I just remember Dia's voice pleading as I hid underneath the desk, convinced he was going to be killed just a few inches from me.

MY ONLY GOAL in the morning is to find an internet connection so I can arrange my trip back to the border. The minute I connect to the internet, many emails and messages appear in my inbox and on Facebook. The news of Abdullah's death has gone viral. Some articles say that I have been taken hostage for witnessing the killing. Some claim that I have been killed, too: "Al Qaeda killed Abdullah Yassin and kidnapped an Alawite activist," one article reads.

My project manager orders me to return to the border immediately. I call him. "Rebel-held areas are not safe. We told you that. Come back immediately. Do not argue with me," he says.

I hang up and scroll back through my messages again. One is from Munzer in Manbij. He asks if I need help reaching the border. Manbij is less than an hour away, and he says he can pick me up. "You can spend the night in Manbij, and I will drive you to the border the next morning," he says. We agree on a time and place, then I pack my tripod and ask Hussain to take me to the leishmaniasis clinic. I will not leave Aleppo before finishing what I came all this way to do.

Over the next few hours, I watch screaming children squirm in their mothers' laps as their eyelids, cheeks, and toes are injected with long, thin silvery needles. Their faces will forever be scarred, a tragedy that could have been avoided if they had access to the right sprays. Many of the real doctors who could have been here are now in Turkey for their safety, hired by NGOs to draft grants and proposals for funding. This has resulted in Syria being emptied of those who are needed the most. As a result, the staff here is comprised of students, housewives, and teachers volunteering their time after completing basic first aid training.

THE NEXT MORNING, I open my eyes in Manbij. I slept in the living room, the only space in the house with a heater, the same house where I had spent hours listening to people talking and debating on prior trips—long evenings during which I had giggled and hidden my face behind Mezar's back as people said the names "Hassan Sex," "the Prince," and "Carrots" in all seriousness.

I open my laptop. Every website featuring news of Syria has written about Abdullah's murder. He is being hailed as a "Martyr of the Second Revolution."

"Thugs killed him because he was fighting them," some state. Others claim that "the Islamists killed him because he was opposing the black flags." A few others write that Abdullah's death could only benefit the government, so the government must be responsible for it. He was bringing Western journalists into eastern Aleppo to document their atrocities and other horrors, after all.

Abdullah is described as a hero, but he wasn't. He wasn't killed because he was an icon. He was killed because of chaos and misunderstanding. As I'd once heard, truth is the first casualty in war. It is disturbing to see how little truth matters. What matters is who aimed and shot first—the anarchy of armed groups Abdullah was telling me about and that I, until now, refused to see. The chaos that, in the moment we were unknowingly driving toward his death, seemed ancillary. I wish I had listened more closely and asked him what could be done.

I read that the person believed to have shot Abdullah has been detained. According to him, he and his comrades had come to ask Abdullah about a guy they believed he had kidnapped. But it doesn't matter what the shooter says or what Abdullah was accused of, I realize. Abdullah is dead. That is the only concrete truth.

I shut the laptop and gaze at the rusty heater. Orange flames flicker behind a tiny glass window fed by drips of gasoline. Beads of condensation cover the windows. Sunlight reflects off the painting, highlighting the verses from the Quran written in gold. In this very living room, I heard people justify the rebels' "individual misdeeds," having no idea that Abdullah would become one of their victims. We are supposed to tell ourselves that no revolution is perfect to justify the consequences of this lawlessness.

"This revolution is like a child that is being born after forty years. The labor won't be easy. It will be long, grueling labor, and we should be patient and push through"—the familiar words enter my mind. But what if this labor is so long and so damaging that the outcome we seek is as cold and dead as Abdullah is now? Tears well in my eyes. I feel alone and ashamed of how naive I have been, and of the creeping intuition that, perhaps, we are not doing enough.

Years later, I would look back at Abdullah's murder and wonder if my guilt and grief were blinding me. Somehow, I had to prove to myself that the uprising that inspired me to stand up for myself and defy the system I grew up in—the uprising that also cost me everything—was as pure and perfect as I had hoped or assumed it would be. I wonder if my agony over my mother's death prevented me from seeing the truth: that perhaps, at this point, even our side was too divided, and a house divided against itself cannot stand. We were losing. And we had been for a long time.

Something I cannot explain pushes me toward a gray telephone on a table in the corner of the room. I lift the receiver, place it to my ear, and hear the dial tone. I hold my breath for a few seconds before dialing my grandmother's number in Damascus. I can hear my heart pounding between the long rings that shudder through the line.

The tiny blue LED screen on the phone says the time is 8:30 a.m. I know my grandmother. She's already awake. She's boiled her coffee and taken it back to sip in bed. The wooden window—the one that overlooks her lemon tree—is now cracked open to let in the fresh morning breeze. She is inhaling the sharp, dry March air and probably cursing under her breath that she has to leave the warmth of her bed and walk to the phone. Who is this, calling so early? She hurries through the living room, passing the red velvet couch where she sits to watch TV. I remember sitting on the floor beside her as a child, leaning my head on her knees as her fingers combed and braided my hair.

A click, then her voice comes on the line. "Alo?"

I am silent. It has been almost a year and a half since we last spoke, since the protest in Damascus, since the day I made the decision to question everything I grew up believing. A year and a half since my grandmother told me I was going to hell because I dared to curse the president. Not being able to talk to her after my mother's death had been agonizing. I always wondered whether she was worried for Alia and me, but I could never bring myself to ask her.

"Alo?" she says again.

I whisper a reply: "It's me, Loubna." Then I hold my breath. I struggle not to cry. She is silent. I hear her breathing, long and deep. She finally exhales. Her voice shakes.

"May God curse your soul!"

"Tata, I miss you so much!"

"Why did you do this?" she whispers. "You killed your mother! Are you happy now?"

"I am sorry. I miss you so much. Are you okay?"

"Never call here again."

The line goes dead.

TWENTY-FIVE

Naji is tasked with delivering the news to me: I am no longer allowed to cross into Syria.

"Your job now is to film the political meetings taking place here," he says, the soft light of a gray Istanbul morning illuminating the two large, framed photographs that hang on the wall behind him. One is a map of Syria; the other is of three kids raising their fingers in a victory sign, with "Welcome to Free Syria" appearing behind them—the photo I took on my first crossing from Turkey to Jarabulus.

"I can't bring myself to film something I have no interest in. Don't let them do this to me," I beg him. The thought of being stuck in this room reviewing and editing footage from boring meetings is unbearable.

"The future of Syria is being written here, and it's just as important as what's happening inside the country," says Naji.

I roll my eyes and try not to scoff. I don't have to explain myself; Naji knows what I think of these political meetings. Six months into the uprising, Syrian politicians in exile formed the Syrian National Council. It later grew to include rebel commanders and representatives of local councils and field hospitals, and the aim was to unite the opposition, on the ground and abroad, and lay the foundation for a democratic Syria. Funding came from various sources globally. In Istanbul, these meetings, like the activist workshops, took place in hotels all over the city, and we—along with the government media—referred to these politicians as the "hotel opposition."

When I was in Damascus, I would catch glimpses of the Syrian National Council meetings and press conferences on the news. At the time, despite my awareness of the money being wasted on them, especially when every lira was needed, I couldn't help but feel sympathy for these individuals. They had left Syria with the hope of returning one day, only to realize that their perception of the country was hopelessly outdated. We were in the real Syria; they were outsiders. We were on the ground; they were in their hotel meetings. Now, the idea of spending the day with them, being an outsider just like them, is agonizing.

I try to convince Naji that the incident with Abdullah was not a big deal, it was just bad luck, and that Syria is safe. I even try to convince him that I don't have the political vocabulary to interview these high-level politicians and that I will embarrass the entire organization if I try; that I am only saying no for his sake, not mine. I fail.

I find myself living my worst nightmare, spending my days roaming carpeted hotel lobbies, following the same men and women I once saw on television arguing about Syria so passionately that these shows often ended with them throwing papers and chairs at the government pundits who sat on the opposite side of the table. I attend their meetings in silence and watch women in high heels with clouds of perfume around them shout and demand more female representation in the parliament.

They spend hours debating the appropriate structure for the constitution of a free Syria. It almost makes me believe that the government has been overthrown and that the percentage of women in a nonexistent parliament is of timely concern, not the fact that children and adults are burning their old clothes for heat and that sandflies are eating their faces.

On days when non-decision-makers like myself are not permitted to attend meetings, I waste my time pacing outside the conference room and filling my pockets with tea bags and round bite-size cakes that look better than they taste. At the end of my workday, I go to the office, drop off my empty hard drive, and leave.

Naji, who eagerly awaits my return only to find that I didn't film anything, chastises me for not caring more—as if these meetings hold the key to our future and I am a bad Syrian for not taking them seriously. Though I have the urge to argue with him, I resist. I need the job; I cannot afford to lose my income.

◆◆

As I spend more time in the office, I start to notice new faces. The umbrella organization that supports us has another office across the street, and some of their staff stop by to chat.

One frequent visitor is a twenty-something American named Peter. He walks into the office with a large notepad in hand and a pen tucked behind his ear and picks through the boxes of new lenses, cameras, and hard drives—equipment we are about to send to our photographers inside Syria. He jots down the serial numbers and leaves.

I first notice Peter because his sleeves are often rolled up to his elbows, revealing arms covered with tattoos—a combination of images and illegible text. "They didn't have notebooks in America, so he had to write on his arms," I whisper to Laila in Arabic, and we both giggle, hoping he doesn't understand.

Whenever he comes in after that, I watch him from the corner of my eye. Even though pale-skinned guys with light-colored eyes are not my type, I remember the exact moment I found Peter handsome. He was standing by the window, and his white shirt enhanced the grayish-blue of his eyes. I watched him a little longer, noticing how his straight nose, thin lips, and high cheekbones looked just perfect. When Peter glanced my way and smiled, I felt awkward and unsure of how to react. I ended up frowning at him and ducking behind my laptop—the kind of passive-aggressive gesture one makes when someone is being too loud while they're trying to concentrate.

In the days that follow, whenever Peter steps in, I try to hide in the bathroom. When I can't, I become so nervous that I pretend to concentrate hard on my screen, privately opening Photo Booth to fix my hair and make sure I look presentable.

Laila tells me that Peter recently moved to Turkey for this job; previously, he was working in Lebanon. I google him to see if I can find his Facebook page, and a CNN video pops up. I watch the same tattooed arms wrap gauze around the leg of a young Syrian refugee in a hospital in Tripoli. The reporter says that Peter is a United States Army Ranger who served in Iraq and comes from a state in America called Indiana. My heart flutters as I hear his deep voice in my earphones for the first time, talking about how he is neither a doctor nor a nurse, but someone who knows how to clean wounds, replace bandages, run IVs, and help out as best he can.

ONE FRIDAY NIGHT, the team from Peter's office asks me if I want to join them for a live music show. They often extend invitations to parties, birthdays, and gatherings, sending emails with subject lines like "Back to Skool!" that encourage us Syrians to dust off our school uniforms because we are going to "P . . . A . . . R . . . T . . . Y!" We never go, of course—these emails are just another reminder of how different we are. They fondly reminisce about their school days while we, almost a decade later, still collectively have nightmares about our educational system.

But that night, I've just come back from another hotel meeting, and I'm stewing in my feelings of betrayal and frustration with Laila and Naji for not allowing me to cross back into Syria. Figuring I have nothing to lose, I accept Peter's colleagues' invitation.

At home, I shower and put makeup on. From the closet, I grab the strapless black satin dress that I received as a birthday gift. I fasten a necklace of colorful stones around my neck and drape an oat-colored scarf over my shoulders that matches the color of my heels.

When I walk into the bar we agreed to gather at before the show, I recognize a few people at the table: Alice, the beautiful Brazilian photographer who has been living in Istanbul since the beginning of the uprising; Danny, the Lebanese guy who invites us out every week; and a few more journalists whose names I don't know. And there, at the far corner of the table, is Peter. His elbow rests casually on the back of his wooden chair, his sharp, deep voice rising above the hum of conversation and music.

It's as if a wave is crashing into my body, knocking me off-balance and making me awkwardly aware of my limbs. Here, there is no bathroom or laptop screen to help me hide, and I suddenly feel very exposed. I consider turning around and leaving, but Danny is already pulling a chair for me to sit and shouting that he can't believe I finally decided to join them. Peter reaches over to shake my hand.

"I'm sorry," I say, trying to keep my voice even. "What's your name again?"

"Peter," he replies. "You're Loubna, right? I've wondered why you always seem so suspicious of me when I walk into the office. You never say hello!"

I pretend to laugh and squint my eyes, acting as if I'm trying to recall his face.

When we arrive at the venue, it is packed. Muscled men in thongs, their bodies glistening with oil, dance onstage, the silver and blue flashing lights illuminating their chests and butts. This is a side of Istanbul I've never seen before; I am scandalized but try not to show it. I glance over at Peter. He is speaking with Alice, nodding intently and taking sips of his drink through a black straw. The deep lines on his forehead tell me they are discussing something serious.

I chug my drink and promptly order another. While I wait for it to arrive, I lean in close to Danny's ear. "This is really weird," I say, looking pointedly at the naked men.

"Why?" he replies. "They're beautiful!"

"Beautiful? They're gay!"

"You'll get yourself in trouble if you don't think before you speak," Danny says, laughing.

I don't understand what he means. I am twenty-two, and this is the first time I am seeing homosexuality celebrated. In Syria, being gay is considered a pathology and treated like an illness. Everyone assumes homosexuals are child-molesting monsters who roam the streets looking for kids to take to rooftops and deserted alleys. The only representation of gay people I have ever encountered on screen was in some melodramatic Egyptian movie where a wealthy gay businessman uses poor, straight men for his pleasure until, of course, he meets his untimely demise at the hands of one of his victims. A lesson for all the gays out there.

It would take me years to learn that I was misinformed, and that no one should be judged by their sexuality; but in this moment, it feels as if I am being forced to watch something that is simply wrong. I drink even faster to ease my discomfort. Perhaps part of me wants to prove to these people that, despite everything, we Syrians are as fun as they are. I can drink as much as they do, maybe more.

I find myself inching closer to Peter with every sip. By the end of the show, I'm standing so close to him that I can smell the laundry detergent on his clothes. Then, as often happens, the night becomes disjointed. Fragmented.

The stage empties and Turkish songs fill the room. Tall, empty glasses and spent wedges of bright lemon rest on sticky tabletops. My feet hurt. I slide off my shoes and push them under a leather couch in the corner of the bar. I see Peter dancing with a girl I've not seen before. I catch his eye, take off my scarf, wrap it around him and draw him in, away from her.

When we finally leave the club, the sharp cold of the flagstones under my feet wakes me up, as if reminding me to imprint this evening on my memory. On the way home, we stop at a café and eat mussels stuffed with rice and herbs from a cocktail table, our faces sore from smiling.

THE NEXT MORNING, as Peter closes the door to my room behind him, I tell myself that my crush will be short-lived. I know by now that, once the door clicks shut, I shouldn't expect to see the person again. But after Peter leaves, I can't stop thinking about him. Instead of the usual shame and emptiness I've come to associate with drunken nights, I feel a flutter of happiness that I at least found the courage to pursue someone I was previously too shy to even look in the eye.

Alone in my room, I watch the CNN report again just to see his face and hear his voice. And when I notice his smell on my hair, I bring it closer to my nose, and I do so over and over again, feeling a knot in my stomach each time. I try to stop myself by remembering what Naji once told me: "You are always looking for a distraction."

Later that day, at a café with a view of Istiklal Street with my friends, my phone vibrates on the glass table. "This is Peter," the message says. "I'm thinking of you." He asks if we can hang out when he returns from Lebanon in a few days, reminding me of a conversation we probably had but that I was too drunk to recall. "It's okay if not," he says. "No pressure." My legs carry me to the restroom, where I lock myself in a stall and reread his message.

When I return home, I clean my room for the first time since moving to Istanbul. Not only do I make my bed, I purchase matching sheets and pillowcases and a plug-in air freshener that I unplug shortly after my housemate notes that our house smells like a bakery. Then I allow myself to message him back.

WITHIN A FEW NIGHTS, we develop a routine. A routine that makes the meetings, my new assignments, and the fact that I'm not allowed to go to Syria more tolerable. I leave the window next to my bed open and wait for Peter, who often stays in the office past 10:00 p.m., to whisper to me from outside my ground-floor apartment. "Habibti! Open the door!"

Each night, I jump out of bed to greet him, and Peter hands me a bundle of tulips. Soon, flowers in jars, cups, and bottles cover every surface in the apartment. I knock on the door of my Turkish housemate, Hussain, to give him a bouquet. "Is there a man in your life?" Hussain asks.

"Yes, there is," I reply, unable to conceal my smile. But Peter is not just a man in my life; he has become my whole life.

With Peter around, I don't need anyone else. I wake up missing him. I see Naji and Laila less frequently, not only because I still resent them for letting me down when I needed them, but because, here in exile, friendships are not built on common interests but on the shared reality of pain and loss. Peter is the first person in my life who does not become close to me because he is Syrian—though we often talk about Syria.

I ask Peter about his time in Lebanon, and that is when I first hear about SERA, Special Emergency Response and Assistance, the small organization he founded to provide medical supplies to field hospitals. He wants to return to that work, he says. But first, he needs to make sure he has enough money to do it. We both agree that our work in Istanbul feels pointless. Temporary. I explain to Peter how, after Abdullah's death, I found myself trapped filming meaningless political meetings. I tell him about the unbearable pain of being stuck in Istanbul, so close to the war yet so far from the Syria I know—the Syria that needs real help.

Although we talk about the war for hours, Peter seems to keep the chaos of the conflict at bay. We are in our own happy bubble. I feel that we have become, in his words, "a team." "We will survive this together and take care of each other," he says. He sends me handwritten letters, and I'm too embarrassed to tell him I have difficulty deciphering his cursive. *I know that in you I have a teammate and a friend I can count on, and I hope that I can show you that you have the same in me, no matter what comes our way*, he writes.

As April arrives, Istanbul becomes a different city; there are no more gray skies, and the air is fresh and sharp and no longer smells of smoke and burnt plastic. Tulips, just like the ones Peter brings me, force their tiny pink and yellow heads up from under clumps of grass. Almond trees bloom and their petals swirl in the breeze. Peter picks them from the coils of my hair.

I no longer spend my weekends in bed, disgusted by the stench of alcohol seeping out of my pores and praying to God to erase my hangover. I no longer numb my brain with hours on YouTube, alternating between videos of recent battles and episodes of Syrian soap operas that I rewatched with my mother so many times I memorized the dialogue. Now, Peter forces me out of bed the moment we wake up and takes me to a nearby café serving weird American coffee drinks that taste like mud. Then we walk around the city together.

With Peter, I see Istanbul as if for the first time. We visit the spice shops in the bazaars, where corridors are lined with baskets of jasmine tea, dry rose petals, and bags of lavender seeds. I sneak dried apricots and figs filled with walnuts from the sellers and eat them until my throat burns with sugar. At sunset, we walk along the Bosporus and watch the fishermen as we take bites from massive loaves of bread stuffed with raw onions and fish grilled on a boat that sways with the waves of the Golden Horn at Eminönü.

One bright morning, Peter shows up carrying a brown paper bag filled with burek wrapped in white paper and tells me I am insane for living in Istanbul all this time without visiting the Princes' Islands, another one of the many adventures I have yet to experience in this city. There are no cars on the islands, only horses and bicycles. We take the ferry over and spend the day riding up and down the shady green hills. We laugh as we try to lift one hand from the handlebars to pinch our noses to avoid the smell of horse manure.

Some days, we walk down a steep street and end up in a different, larger world. A world lined with shelves overflowing with books, a world that smells musty and warm. The books are as cheap as a cup of tea. These trips began when I told Peter how jealous I was of those who were able to turn their thoughts and our interviews about Syria into lyrical paragraphs. I confessed to Peter my desire to learn writing as another form of documentation, of witness, though I didn't know where to start. I didn't tell him that I had studied English literature, because it was embarrassing to explain that the writing and composition assessments at my university in Latakia consisted of memorizing essays, which we would then transcribe onto the exam paper, word for word.

"The first step is to read," Peter said, and that marked the beginning of our bookstore adventures. The first stop was a used bookstore because, according to him, "Used books always smell better." The first book I grabbed was *Memoirs of a Geisha*, a title I recognized from the movie adaptation that was a hit on Arabic TV. We spent hours reading together, with me circling words I didn't know and asking Peter for definitions. For the first time in years, I remembered my old fondness for learning new vocabulary. Peter stopped me from using my Arabic dictionary as a crutch and insisted that I "train my brain to think in English if I want to write in English." The margins of the books we shared darkened with my scribbled notes.

At some point, Peter decided we should read a nonfiction book together. A book that could teach us both something. He chose *The Looming Tower* by the American journalist Lawrence Wright, a book about the origins of Al Qaeda and the events that led to the September 11 attacks. It had won a number of awards, including a Pulitzer Prize. On the title page, he wrote me a note that, even years later, I would reread:

Look for the small connections and pathways that both separate us and bring us together.

Love.

TWENTY-SIX

One evening near the end of April, Peter puts his arm around me as we stroll through the alleyways of Cihangir, their slick flagstones tinted orange by the shop lamps. We pass cloth merchants, carpet sellers, tea shops, and small restaurants with huge jars of pickles on display. I tell Peter it reminds me of old Damascus.

We descend a foot-worn stairway and join the flow of pedestrians walking down Istiklal Street. A Domino's pizza delivery scooter buzzes past and Peter jumps aside. "Jesus! One of them is going to kill me one of these days."

"It would be a worthy way to die. They make a good pizza," I say as we squeeze between two parked cars and step back onto the sidewalk.

"Are you serious? They put corn on pizza here!" Peter says. "I tell them to leave it off, but they put it on every slice."

"What's wrong with corn on pizza? In Syria, we always put corn and ketchup on pizza. It's good," I say.

"This is unacceptable," Peter says, slapping his forehead. "Let's go to my favorite pizza place. They make wood-fired pizza, and there's a glass floor you can look through into the wine cellar. I think they also have lasagna. Do you like lasagna?"

"I've never had it," I say.

"Paula, my mother, makes the best lasagna. I really miss her food. She's the best cook," Peter says. "I should call her more."

I remain quiet, searching my mind for a dish my mother perfected, something to share with Peter to prove she was also a great cook. But I draw a blank. I am horrified to realize that I have pushed my mother to the very edges of my memory, so much so that I can't recall a single dish to tell him about in the moment.

My eyes well up. Before I can stop myself, I wonder about what she was given to eat at the end of her life. Was she starved like all the other detainees in the government's dungeon cells? Those lucky enough to be released always emerge skeletal; their shoulders are bones, their thighs the size of arms. I regret not having had one last meal with my mother at home, a chance to tell her how much I loved her and how thankful I was, and would always be, for the meals she affectionately prepared for us over the years, for all the ways she showed us her love.

"I really want you to meet my parents. They'll love you." Peter's voice interrupts my reverie, bringing me back to Istanbul, to my exile, reminding me that it is too late. My mother is gone.

"We should go there this December, for Christmas." He lifts my hand to his lips and kisses it.

"I'd love to," I say. My voice trembles. I clear my throat and squeeze his hand.

I've known that Peter has been aware of my mother's death since he and I started dating. He knows what everyone else does from the few interviews I have given, but nothing more. I've appreciated the unspoken agreement we seem to have, in which he never brings up anything related to family that might make me sad.

Now, it feels like he's unwittingly broken that agreement. I resent that he can talk about his mother so freely while I must bury all remnants of mine just to endure her absence. It angers me that I can't even ask him to stop mentioning her because doing so would expose my fragility and pain and lead to conversations I'm not ready for. The strong facade I wear would crumble, revealing how tenuous my grip on sanity truly is. I cannot convey to Peter the unbearable weight of recalling my mother and being overwhelmed by sadness once more. He won't understand how grief has tainted every memory I have of her, and that the only way to escape her loss is to obliterate them all, happy and painful alike. As I've worked to erase my mother from my mind, I find myself wishing Peter would forget about his mother, too. But he doesn't.

He goes on about Paula, Christmas, and the harsh, cold winds of winters in Indiana. He says something about his father, Ed, and snow boots, and promises to buy me a warm jacket because I am wholly unprepared for the Midwestern weather. As he talks, I feel increasingly claustrophobic. I grip Peter's hand tightly, silently begging him to stop. He laughs, a warm two-beat laugh that articulates, without words, another pleasant memory. Spasms of pain rip across my chest.

"Will you stop?" I shout suddenly. This seems to be someone else's voice, not mine. The people walking ahead of us on the sidewalk turn around, their gaze lingering on us for a moment. I take a step back, feeling the weight of their stares, and draw in a deep breath, trying to calm myself. I glower at Peter. He stares back wide-eyed, confused.

"You keep talking about your mother and father and your home you can't wait to visit. It's really painful for me. Please stop," I say. Peter furrows his brow and presses my hands between his own. I look away.

"I'm sorry," he says quietly.

I hold my breath, trying to stop my tears from welling up. But I fail, and soon feel them hot on my cheeks. Embarrassed, I wipe them away. Peter and I stand there motionless, the stream of humanity moving around us on the sidewalk. The shops glow with light, and the shopkeepers' calls fill the air.

"I'm okay," I say, trying to regain my composure. "Let's walk." But Peter holds me back.

"Loubna, I was adopted. Paula and Ed aren't my real parents," he says. "But that doesn't matter. They're my family. You will have your own family one day."

I take a few seconds to fully process his words, then take another step away from him, feeling my anger boil over. "Are you really comparing being adopted to the way I lost my mother?"

"I didn't mean it that way," Peter says. "I know I can never compare what we've experienced, and I can never imagine what you've been through. I will never pretend to know. I'm really sorry, Loubna." He tries to hug me, but I flinch, still horrified by his insinuation that our experiences of absent parents are somehow similar or a wound we can bond over.

"A family?" I spit, my words spilling out before I can stop them. "Two months ago, I didn't even hesitate to have an abortion because I knew I couldn't bring a child into this chaos. I was seven weeks pregnant." I hear my voice growing louder. Since the procedure, I've pushed the memory of my abortion so far down that it feels like a distant nightmare. But hearing myself say the words aloud brings the reality rushing back.

"I'm sorry," he says again. "I had no idea about the abortion. I don't know what to say."

I feel dizzy and unsteady as the enormity of what I've done bears down on me. I lean against a parked car. Peter stands beside me, silent.

For years to come, I would wonder why I chose to share that with him then. Peter would later view it as a moment of openness for which he was grateful, but to me it was more of a desperate attempt to direct us both away from my mother's memory, to prove to him that I could take care of myself even though I had lost her.

He reaches for my hand. "I'm so sorry, Loubna. I didn't mean to upset you. I will never bring up my family again." I sense his hand closing on mine, but he hesitates. I can feel him looking at me, though I refuse to meet his eyes. "I will do everything I can to help you. But please, let's not ruin our night."

"I know you feel sorry for me," I snap. "That's why you're with me—so you can feel good about yourself."

"Is that really what you think of me?"

"I don't need your pity. Just leave me alone." I turn and walk quickly up a stairway, wiping my nose and cheeks with my shirtsleeve and tying my hair back. I keep walking until the anger subsides. When I finally turn around, part of me hopes that Peter might be there, following a short distance behind, but there is only the emptiness of the street and the orange light reflecting off the worn flagstones. I realize that I have never cried in front of him before.

THE NEXT DAY, Peter walks into the office, places a bunch of bright red tulips with tiny white flowers and a handwritten letter on my desk, and leaves without saying a word. I hesitate to open it. *You are insane*, I imagine it might say. I unfold the paper and skim the words, barely understanding what I am reading. Then I begin again. To my surprise, I can't help but laugh. The letter is an invitation to the wood-fired pizza place we were going to last night and a request to refrain from eating pizza with corn and ketchup.

That evening, when we meet up, I apologize to Peter. I tell him that I didn't mean what I said and try to explain how little control I had over my words, how they bypassed my brain and just spilled out. He apologizes, too, and thanks me for telling him about the abortion. He wants me to feel like I can talk to him about anything.

"Nothing you say could possibly make me love you less," he says. My guard is already down; I allow myself to believe him. I realize I don't have to act strong all the time to prove I'm not broken.

Peter asks me what I believe I should do to have a bright future. I tell him that I want to go back to school and study something I love, like photography, but in a different educational system that encourages my creativity. Leaving Syria allowed me to see that I never had the chance to truly learn, to understand rather than memorize. I confess that I worry I'm not smart enough to pursue a real degree, but I want to try.

"You're smart," Peter says. "Never give up on your education. Just promise me, no matter what happens between us, you'll apply to schools. Promise me." I promise, and something inside me unlocks.

Whether it's my attempt to make up for my outburst the night before, or simply the wine, I find myself telling Peter about my family for the first time. How Alia and I were raised to believe that finding the right husband was the key to a happy future. How my father threatened us and used our inheritance to control us. How my mother was the reason I learned to trust and listen to my inner voice; how she always encouraged us to study, because education was more important than any money or husband. How she believed in my independence long before I did. How I risked everything—my past, my future—for a cause I believed was worth losing it all. I know I am responsible for my own choices, I tell him, but I can't bear the consequences they had for Alia, who lost everything because of me. My mother always reminded us that if anything bad were to happen to her, Alia and I would have each other. But she never imagined we would have to try to survive her loss like this. I tell him I fear that Alia left Istanbul to escape me, the intolerable reminder of our shared past, and though I feel responsible for her agony, my guilt is the reason I can't confess any of this to her in a way that might bring us closer again.

At the end of the dinner, Peter asks me to put him in touch with Alia. Buzzed by alcohol, I agree. I let myself enjoy his request, taking it as a gauge of his seriousness about me and the progression of our relationship. As we leave the restaurant, I feel hopeful and sense a tiny flicker in my stomach, wondering if my rage was what I needed to tear down my walls and bring us closer.

The warm feeling doesn't last. In the weeks that follow, as Peter develops his own friendship with Alia, I feel a punch in my gut every time he mentions their Skype calls, updating me with the details of her life in Egypt. He talks about her cat, her job, and her recent move to a new apartment. How funny it is that we have the same voice and the same sense of humor. He always ends these recaps with the suggestion that I should give her a call.

I start to realize that Peter is operating as if this is a relationship in a normal world, where I should be thrilled that my partner is bonding with my sibling. He doesn't understand that, in forced exile and amid great loss, family connections are fraught with trauma and memories we are trying to escape. That maybe the best way to support me would be to let me navigate my complicated, damaged relationship with my sister on my own terms. I wish I could find the words to tell him that this feels like a well-meaning but misguided attempt to bridge a gap that cannot be overcome. Instead, I swallow my resentment and let it grow.

TWENTY-SEVEN

It is early May when I tell Peter that I plan to leave Istanbul. Laila's organization has announced a project to open an office in Antep, the city near the Syrian border where our first journalism workshop was held in November. The new branch will be large enough to host regular training sessions and become a hub for the organization and its reporters inside Syria. I have asked to be transferred to Antep with Naji—not only because I need a break from Istanbul, but because Naji and I both know that helping with workshops and setting up the new office will be more meaningful than covering political meetings and spending our days in hotel lobbies, even if he won't admit it.

Peter tells me he wants to move, too. He says it is also better for him to be closer to Syria. He has saved up enough money to expand SERA, the small nonprofit he started in Lebanon. He says that if I am not in Istanbul, there is no reason for him to stay and he plans to join me in Antep in a few weeks.

My escape from Istanbul mirrors my rapid departure from Damascus.

It takes me less than an hour to pack my belongings into three bags. Nothing feels extraordinary about it, as if packing has become second nature, done on autopilot. Once you've left home the first time, every departure after that feels normal.

I had left Damascus for my safety; now, I am running away from the broken, chaotic version of myself this city has witnessed and constantly reminds me of. I know Antep is less lively, and Istanbul will always be my first refuge, but I hope its proximity to the border can offer a respite from the sorrow that has overwhelmed me in a town that abounds with reminders of our collective misfortune. With Peter also heading to Antep, distance won't create a fracture between us. Instead, it feels like the beginning of something new and exciting for both of us.

To MY SURPRISE AND RELIEF, Antep feels more Syrian than Turkish. Unlike Istanbul, Antep doesn't have a smattering of cafés that have become haunts for exiled Syrians. Here, Syrians have done what the Iraqis did in Damascus: They opened their own businesses, naming them after the cities and towns they may never see again.

Aleppo-accented Arabic can be heard everywhere, and with its affordable rent, the city could even become a place to call home.

It takes me less than a day to find an apartment in a small building just a short walk from Antep's main university. The top floor of the building has been converted into a common space with pool tables, bookshelves, and free coffee and tea, where young men and women my age hang out and study.

Being exposed to what regular life should look like for a twenty-two-year-old doesn't bother me. There are enough Syrians my age in Antep to normalize our collective exile, including Mezar, his brothers, and some of the young men and women I met in Amer's studio. I am increasingly reminded of the previous summer, 2012, in Damascus. Once again, our shared experiences and camaraderie bring a sense of comfort and belonging—a reminder that, even in exile, we are never alone.

Toward the end of May, the United States and the United Nations announce an international conference in Geneva with the aim of bringing both sides of the Syrian conflict to the table and finding a political solution to the war. Sensing an opportunity, I propose to Naji that I film a short report in Manbij on what the people inside Syria hope to gain from the peace talks. I argue that I am familiar with Manbij—unlike eastern Aleppo—having visited multiple times without encountering any danger. Naji agrees; I am given three days to complete the assignment and return. I decide not to tell Peter about my plans. I'll be back before he even notices I'm gone—it's just going to be a quick trip.

Generator fumes thicken the hot, dry air as I wait for Munzer to pick me up from the border. My hair is drenched with perspiration under the heavy headscarf I'm wearing, and streams of sweat burn my eyes. When Munzer arrives, I tell him that I have to leave Manbij as soon as I have finished my assignment. This is my chance to prove to Naji that Syria is still safe and that the episode with Abdullah won't repeat itself. But, to my surprise, Munzer tells me that no one in Manbij is talking about the Geneva peace talks—no one cares, he says. There is something else capturing everyone's attention: the Islamic State.

I listen intently as he recounts how, earlier in the week, an Islamic armed group, composed mostly of foreign fighters from Arab and Western countries, seized the town's cultural center, which the local council had equipped with fridges and generators for the public, and appropriated everything inside. This group had apparently been capturing administrative buildings across many rebel-held areas. A protest against the Islamic State is scheduled to march toward the cultural center tomorrow.

DEFIANCE

I have trouble believing what Munzer is telling me at first. Perhaps it's because I've recently only seen Syria through the perfectly crafted images and videos the activists inside are broadcasting. Or maybe my longing for a return to Syria has blinded me to the escalating dangers.

But sure enough, the next day, the protest begins. I watch as Munzer takes the microphone and tells the crowd that every building is important and must be defended, that Syria should not be painted black. As they march toward the cultural center, another group of protesters blocks their way.

"Islamia! Islamia!" the opposing group chants, waving black flags and demanding that Syria become a Sunni theocracy, an "Islamic State."

"God, Syria, freedom, nothing else," Munzer's group responds.

"Our leader forever, the Prophet Muhammad," the Islamic protesters yell back.

I stand between the two groups, watching silently as they shout at each other. I keep my camera down.

Through the crowd, I see the words "Islamic State in Iraq and al-Sham" written in bold white on a black wall. Near the wall, at the gate leading to the cultural center, stands a man with a black scarf wrapped around his head and a rifle slung across his chest. I walk up to him.

"Is it true that refrigerators have been stolen?" I ask in the Syrian dialect, using the word "baradat" for fridges.

The man refuses to look at me. "Baradat yaane aeh?" he sneers. "What do you mean by baradat? The word is talagat." The man's voice drips with condescension and irritation. I recognize his accent as Egyptian.

I glare at him. "Why are you stealing the fridges?"

As I step closer, I smell his body odor radiating from his heavy black clothes. Droplets of sweat cling to the tip of his round red nose. His beard is a tangled mess.

"Move out of the way," he says, his voice low and menacing. "You don't want to be hit by a stray bullet."

I stand still, stunned. No one in Manbij has ever spoken to me this way before. Accompanied by Munzer, who had a grip on the city, I've entered every building and interviewed everyone freely, my questions always answered. People here know that I can turn their stories into news segments that might air on major news channels.

I wonder what the difference is between the oppressiveness of the government and the oppressiveness of the Islamic State. The government's tyranny is perpetrated under the guise of security and protection, while the Islamic State's oppression is cloaked in religious fanaticism. Same injustice, different flags.

I stand my ground and repeat my question. The man responds by adjusting his grip on the rifle and muttering something about how it's better if I get out of his way.

"Can you answer my question?" I insist. Part of me knows I'm being reckless, but if I step aside, I will have to face the truth that Naji was right not to let me cross back into Syria—that our country is indeed a mess. I refuse to let this Egyptian challenge everything I've held to be true about the revolution. Manbij is our city, not his.

In a split-second motion, the man grabs the black strap of my camera and snatches it away. He points the barrel of his rifle skyward and fires one round. I run into the crowd. Another gunshot rings out, and the protesters push toward the gate, shouting, "They are attacking our women! They are attacking our women!" My brain blacks out for a few seconds, and when I come back to my surroundings, I find myself shivering behind a tree, one thought on loop in my mind.

How could we have been so naive?

◆◆

I first heard about the foreign fighters in Syria only a few months after I had fled to Turkey. I was on my first trip to the Syria-Turkey border, near

DEFIANCE

Antakya, where thousands of Syrian families from Idlib had fled a brutal government bombardment and crossed the border with nothing but the clothes on their backs. Under the scorching sun, they sought refuge under makeshift shelters of blue and white tarps, bedsheets, towels, and anything else they could find to tie to the branches of olive trees.

Autumn had already set in, bringing with it the first rains of the season. Aid workers, nonprofit organizations, and political activists from both sides of the border expressed their fears about the dire challenges these displaced families would face come winter. I hoped that capturing their stories would bring more attention to their situation and help them in some way.

After landing in Hatay, I reached out to a Syrian fixer named Karam, who worked as a translator for journalists across the borders. He offered to accompany me to the refugee camp.

One early afternoon in October we found ourselves standing beside the flimsy, rusty barbed wire that separated Syria from Turkey. The air was thick with moisture and the scent of woodsmoke from the clusters of tents in the distance, where families burned olive branches to heat water for cooking and bathing.

A few yards away from us stood a dark-skinned man with a rucksack on his shoulder. He wore white sneakers. His phone rang, and he began to speak in a Saudi dialect. I didn't pay him much attention at first. The border was always crowded with aid workers and journalists. Within minutes, a motorcycle arrived. The rider, a gray rifle strapped to his back, greeted the Saudi man and made room for him on the motorcycle. A cloud of dust rose behind them as they disappeared into the trees on the Syrian side of the border.

Karam shook his head and muttered something I had only heard on government news channels: "mokatel ajnabi," a foreign fighter. He whispered the words so quietly that I knew this phrase was something I shouldn't repeat.

Karam told me how irritated he was with the Western journalists who kept asking him to connect them with these men. "Freelancers try to sell their pitches on new and different angles. Everyone in the West loves stories about foreign fighters and radicalization," he said.

"Do you help them?" I asked.

"Of course not! I tell them foreign fighters don't even exist," Karam replied.

He didn't need to explain why. In a country like Syria, loyalty to a cause, party, or political stance meant withholding critique. Promoting stories aligned with the Syrian government's narrative, even if there was some truth to them, would be betraying the uprising.

"Why do they focus on these minor, irrelevant details instead of all this?" Karam said, gesturing toward the green hills teeming with people seeking shelter under white and blue tarps. I nodded in agreement, but at that moment, my mind clouded with confusion.

I wanted to believe Karam, but it was difficult to ignore the threat of foreign fighters entirely. I felt the air stick in my throat as I remembered how Amer once stood in front of a crowd during a protest and shouted that the government wanted people to believe we were all foreign fighters and Salafists, when really we were just ordinary Syrians—Christians, Alawites, and others—who shared the hope for a better country. I felt the urge to call Amer, despite the long silence between us, and tell him I had just seen a foreign fighter with my own eyes. These men were real.

I spent the rest of the day speaking with one family after another in the camp, filling memory cards with their stories. They had fled their homes in the middle of the night when they heard the roar of approaching planes. They brought nothing with them, fleeing in their house slippers, which were now sinking in the mud.

My interviews ended abruptly when a young mother, around my age, pulled her son into their tent and shouted, "Go away! Nothing good has ever come from talking to people like you." I tried to explain that this was my first time here, but she shouted again, "Leave me alone before I come out there and break your camera over your head." Humiliated, I turned off my camera and went looking for Karam.

A driver we had arranged to pick us up greeted us at the barbed wire fence. We climbed in, relishing the warmth and the pungent scent of cigarette smoke. We drove through verdant green fields, a somber gray sky overhead, leaving the camp and everything in it behind. I tried to reassure myself that this hell was only temporary. Little did I know that this patch of land would soon become the largest permanent refugee camp in Syria.

In my hotel room, I plugged my memory cards into my laptop and reviewed my interviews and photographs. In one video, a woman's voice cried out as my camera was focused elsewhere. "We used to live a good life; we had dignity. This revolution was supposed to restore our dignity, but where is it now?"

I wondered what I would say if I were in her position, living in a cramped tent, my child unable to attend school, being photographed for a humanitarian crisis report as proof of catastrophe. Would my perspective on the Saudi fighter change? Would I feel grateful for the sacrifice he made, leaving his home country to fight and potentially die for me? I realized that I was perhaps too privileged to form an opinion about men like him. Though I had lost everything, I still had a roof over my head, a door to lock, and a sink to wash my face in before I went to sleep. I did not have to wait in line for my turn to use the bathroom in the middle of the night.

AFTER I SAW THE Saudi man, it was as if a curtain had been lifted from my eyes. I started noticing foreign fighters every time I flew from Istanbul to the border. Men with heavy beards, shaved mustaches, and bulky backpacks were everywhere in Istanbul's airports, standing in line to board domestic flights to cities like Antep and Hatay near the Syrian border. Some traveled alone; others brought their wives and children.

I was surprised by how careless they were about hiding. Once, while I was waiting at baggage claim in Hatay, I saw a man in his mid-twenties wearing a headband with white letters spelling "Allahu Akbar" (God is great). I stared ahead at the luggage belt, trying to come up with some way to start a conversation with him before he walked away.

Conversing with these men became an obsession. Whenever I had to fly, I would arrive early at the airport and follow bearded men around, attempting to overhear if they were Arabs or Westerners. "To Syria?" I would ask if we made eye contact, but many walked away without glancing at me. Still, I kept trying. I knew my best chance to interact with these men was at the airports, where they walked around without their rifles and explosive belts. I wanted to understand who they were and why they were coming to my country. In my circle of friends, no one knew how to discuss the topic. It was always dodged with dismissive arguments: The men wouldn't stay forever, we needed to focus on our own struggle.

When I asked one rebel commander why a Syrian would willingly give a Saudi man a ride inside the country, he tried to help me understand the surprising support for foreign fighters.

"I don't want to sacrifice myself. But these men are willing to do it in a heartbeat. My brigade are my childhood friends. When one of them is hurt, it feels like a part of my soul has been torn away," he said, like many young men who found themselves turning into soldiers they never envisioned they would become. After he witnessed his best friend get shot dead during a protest in 2011, he knew that peaceful demonstrations were illusory. He welcomed the foreign fighters as useful allies, despite their differing ideologies.

"You should see how they congratulate each other when one of them is selected for a suicide bombing at a checkpoint. That's something neither I nor my friends would ever do. These fighters are in this to die, but we are in it to live," he said.

When I asked him about the possibility of these Islamist fighters becoming too powerful and turning against men like himself, he replied, "They will eventually find another war. They want to die; let them die."

Jordan, Lebanon, and Iraq had all closed their borders; the only access to rebel-held areas was through Turkey. Closing the Turkish border to ward off foreign fighters would have meant cutting off desperately needed aid and supplies to everyone else. Closing the Turkish border would suffocate these rebel-held pockets of the country. In light of all the horror taking place, Karam's rationalizations made sense: The foreign fighters were ultimately irrelevant; they were only here temporarily.

But some people, like Naji, refused to accept their presence. "These men will eventually hijack the uprising," he often said, though he was usually met with swift retorts: "Why don't you go fight them then?" or "If they are a threat, why did you leave Syria, allowing them to take over a battle that you abandoned?" This was the point that always ended the conversation—the reminder that if people inside Syria, who were being bombarded and starved daily, were welcoming foreign fighters, then those of us living in Turkey should keep our mouths shut.

For the past ten months, I've lived in denial. But now, hiding behind this tree, hearing the Egyptian fighter fire round after round into the sky, I am painfully jolted awake. I fear that Naji was right—these men, superior in power, can and will eventually rule over us.

When I'm finally reunited with Munzer, we return to his house, where we're joined by some members of the local council. I listen as they try to make sense of what happened. I observe in real time how, when such things occur, we all race to create a narrative that protects us from acknowledging the truth: Something is wrong, and Syria is no longer the place we knew.

One man, ignoring me as if I weren't even there, concludes that the incident with the Egyptian is my fault. He argues that I started the fight by not politely stepping aside and wonders to what extent I am really helping. All I do is take photos and leave, while the Egyptian is at least willing to sacrifice his soul for what he believes. Munzer defends me. "She has been coming to Manbij and risking her life to film long before this Egyptian showed up. She is Syrian. He isn't."

As I watch Munzer grow angrier, veins bulging in his neck, I begin to think that, in defending me, he may very well be defending his power and position in the city. After all, I am his guest. If I am being censored, then he will eventually be censored, too. He doesn't have the influence he used to have.

I just nod. Trapped in my own head, I am reminded of the refugee camp and my camera's relative worthlessness compared to the sacrifices of those fighting on the ground. I think of the shame I felt next to the man at the baggage belt, knowing that I had fled the very same country he was traveling to and would die for.

DAYS LATER, WHEN I return to Antep, I don't tell Naji about the Egyptian. Instead, I tell him the protest was small and no one had an opinion regarding the Geneva peace talks. But at a table in a small, noisy bar in Antep, where Peter has traveled to see me, between long swigs of cold Efes beer, I find myself apologizing to Peter for crossing without telling him and trying to explain the divide between Turkey and Syria.

"Here, everyone is focused on the Geneva peace talks, assuming they will determine Syria's future," I say. "But the reality is, the void we have all left behind is being filled by a group calling itself a 'state' and seeking to impose Sharia law. They are the ones who are going to write the country's future. Whoever is fighting on the ground will have the final say." I tell Peter how distant I feel from the Syria for which I sacrificed everything.

"Are you afraid of them—these foreign fighters?" Peter asks when he finally has the chance to interject, placing his hand on mine.

I think for a moment.

"They're there to die," I say. "Let them die."

TWENTY-EIGHT

As it turns out, I do not have to tell Naji about the incident in Manbij for him to learn about the rise of the so-called Islamic State.

That summer, during Naji's trainings and around dinner tables, everyone is sharing that the green flags of the revolution are being replaced by black ones, and "Islamic State in Iraq and al-Sham" is being painted all over the walls in rebel-held areas. Even the wall in Jarabulus that once carried the face of Bassel Shehadeh and the quote from Mahmoud Darwish, "Live free or die standing tall like the trees," is now covered with black ink.

Young men are growing beards to avoid detention at checkpoints controlled by ISIS, who are detaining anyone who doesn't agree with their agenda. Rebel commanders, aid workers, local council members, and journalists start to disappear, and ISIS claims it is all in the name of "public safety."

Naji teaches reporters how to hide their memory cards and film human rights violations without being identified—the same tactics he used to teach us in Damascus to thwart the government. Debates and arguments erupt as we try to pinpoint what went wrong, how we reached this dark turn. Some blame the rebels and their leaders who are spending their time in Turkey begging for international support while the Islamic State and Al Qaeda–affiliated groups are filling the void on the ground, implementing order and structure in towns and villages. Thugs like Hassan Carrot are now being detained and punished for their crimes, something the rebels themselves should have done months ago but didn't—or couldn't.

Hussain, who came to pick me up after Abdullah's death, attends one of Naji's workshops. When the topic of ISIS comes up, he doesn't blame the rebels for allowing their rise; he says that "Antep activists"—a term used to mock those who left Syria, accepted NGO jobs in Turkey, and contributed to "the void" in Syria—are to blame. "They criticize the rebels for not doing the right thing, but why don't they join them on the ground? Why did they leave them behind to fend for themselves? If exiled activists don't relocate to rebel-held areas," he insists, "the foreign fighters and Islamists will continue to fill the void."

Hussain and a few others rent a big house in eastern Aleppo and offer it as a free residence to anyone who wants to live and work there. I'm impressed by his commitment to bringing activists back to Syria; this revives my shame at living in Turkey. But when I suggest creating an office across the border—perhaps inside Hussain's house—Naji refuses. It's not safe, he tells me; everyone is fleeing, and reports of the Islamic State's kidnappings are on the rise.

Peter also tells me I should stay in Turkey, not only for my safety, but because Alia is moving back, having accepted a job at another humanitarian organization in Hatay. In the last few weeks, the political situation in Egypt has rapidly deteriorated. A military coup seems inevitable, and Egypt, once a secure place for Syrians to organize and meet, is no longer safe.

The prospect of Alia's return terrifies me; I've been grateful for our time apart. Finally, almost a year after my mother's death, her memory feels somewhat distant, the loss more manageable, at least on a day-to-day basis—especially in light of what I've witnessed on my trips to rebel-held Syria over the past several months. I can often convince myself that I am fine, that I am among the very lucky ones despite my losses. In theory I want Alia to be closer to me, but my body tenses whenever she crosses my mind.

When we're finally reunited, my anxieties persist. Though Alia now lives much closer, the distance between us remains. We never talk about our mother. We both pretend that her death never happened and continue to focus on our work.

All of these factors—my desire to escape Alia, my frustration with Naji, my guilt and admiration for Hussain—contribute to my decision to resign from Laila's organization.

I give my notice at the beginning of the summer and email samples of my work to one of the editors responsible for Syria at Reuters.

As the country has become too dangerous for its staff reporters to enter, Reuters and other wire services rely on local freelancers for their coverage of the war. Syrian journalists, desperate to increase international awareness of the conflict, agree to work without contracts, health insurance, or safety gear. In Homs, the suburbs of Damascus, and other besieged areas, some are even working for free. The editor replies that I should send him photos whenever I next cross into eastern Aleppo. If he likes my work, he will provide me with Reuters gear the next time he is in Turkey.

Thanks to the cheap rent and proximity to the border, I decide to keep my apartment in Antep in case I need to cross back to Turkey for payment and rest. I don't know how long I will be in Syria, but for now, my plan is to stay with Hussain, take photos for Reuters, and help however I can.

When Peter sees how determined I am to go, he sends me three links for body armor to choose from and advises me to invest in a "ballistic helmet." On the morning I am scheduled to cross the border, I wake up to a long email he sent the night before.

"As you depart tomorrow for your home, to the country you love, to do the important work you are so very good at," he asks me to always remember that I am not alone, that he is proud of me, and that he is confident I will make the right choices to stay safe. He ends with a promise: He will be there for me no matter what happens, for as long as he lives.

As I settle in Aleppo, waking up to an email from Peter about life outside Syria becomes a morning routine—a lifeline reminding me that I have someone who loves me and is waiting for my return. His messages range from updates about moving apartments and considering adopting a cat to anxiety-fueled emails where he confesses he's been praying for me every five minutes, even though he isn't religious.

Sometimes, despite being discouraged from using Skype to conserve our limited bandwidth—Skype being the only form of communication between most rebel-held areas and the outside world—I can't help but call him. I whisper into the mic, watching Peter's pixelated smile glow through my screen as he fills me in on any details he didn't include in his emails.

He has been crossing into Syria himself as part of his work for SERA. He tells me about the new donations and equipment coming in, as well as the trainings happening all over the country and the many places still in need of supplies. He shares his frustrations with donors and explains how major organizations' money is wasted on office rent, salaries, and first-class domestic flights between Istanbul and airports near the Syrian border. According to Peter, humanitarians justify this lavish spending by claiming that it's too dangerous to stay in a hotel or eat in a restaurant a few miles away from the Syrian border. They seem to forget that this luxurious lifestyle is only possible because of a conflict in which every dollar can make a difference. The cost of one first-class flight could feed a family of five for a month.

As I hear the excitement in Peter's voice when he tells me how welcoming and trusting the Syrians he's met have been because they see how strongly believes in the future of our country, I feel the same admiration I felt the first time I heard him talk about his work in the hospitals of Lebanon. But I also fear for him. I can't bring myself to tell him that Syrians may be united against the government, but they may not see eye to eye when it comes to kidnapping. I think about Abo Ammar and how narrowly I avoided being killed because of my sect. It's difficult to explain the lesson I've learned the hard way: In a civil war, your sect and religion matter more than your political affiliation. A stubborn part of me still wants to believe—and wants Peter to believe—that the danger we all face is from government forces alone. I try to warn him gently that the situation is even more complicated and chaotic than it seems and suggest that perhaps he should stay in Turkey.

But, just like me, he refuses. He reminds me that his organization is making a direct impact on the ground. After months of meetings in conference rooms in Turkey, the immediate action is purposeful. His only regret, he says, is not crossing into Syria earlier.

"Are you safe?" he often asks, trying to change the subject. Perhaps he is emphasizing that he supported my decision and that I should be supportive of him in return. "Yes, of course, I am wearing the body armor you bought me," I whisper, lying.

I don't attempt to explain why a flak jacket would only slow me down. In rebel-held eastern Aleppo, we run and hide from threats we can't see: government snipers. They seem to be everywhere and nowhere at once, invisible but all around us like ghosts, watching and waiting. Residents install curtains to block the snipers' sight lines. Wide tarps of colorful plastic hang from balconies. But snipers often shoot at the curtains anyway—not to kill, but to instill fear and remind us that these tarps can only block their view, not their bullets. Two or three people must be killed before anyone can identify where the bullets are coming from and which crossroads to avoid. I learn that it is safest to be the first to run across the street because the sniper's eye will be pressed to his scope for the second runner. Despite knowing this, I always find myself the last to run, desperately willing my legs to move. It's like jumping from a cliff into deep water. I count down and keep my eyes on the person across from me, reassuring myself that they managed to cross safely. They are alive. I am not going to die.

I sprint. I know my life depends on being as fast as possible, and I pray that my shivering legs won't betray me. My pelvic bones eventually turn blue with bruises from the constant pounding of the two cameras hanging from my neck. Keep moving, I tell myself. My mind, so practiced in denial, can almost believe that the bullets are not, in fact, hot, hard metal. They are abstractions. My head, my limbs, my heart—these are real.

We all know by now that snipers first target the legs. They enjoy watching people crawl across the road, and then, right before they reach safety, they fire at the heads. There is an unspoken rule: If you get hit, you are on your own. Snipers will use your cries to lure others into their line of sight. Many people have died trying to drag their loved ones to safety. As a result, the injured are left behind, their bodies strewn across the streets of the city.

In the absence of moral logic, we trade rationalizations to stay sane, trying to reassure each other and ourselves that we can outwit and outrun the danger. We've even come to believe that bombardment is avoidable, though hawen, or mortar rounds, are common here and deadly, thrown over from the western side of the city without any specific target in mind. "It is far; we are safe," we repeat like an incantation whenever we hear one rip through the air overhead.

But nothing eases the fear of barrel bombs. They are different: cylindrical metal containers, like oil barrels, packed with gasoline, nails, and chunks of steel, typically dropped from above by helicopters. Barrel bombs have caused most of the deaths and destruction here and in other parts of Syria.

The panic starts when we hear the chopper blades. We turn on the satellite radio to learn where the helicopter is hovering. Different voices pant through the speaker: "Above Bustan al-Qasr. Above Tareq al-Bab. Heading southward," they shout. I haven't spent enough time in eastern Aleppo to know the locations of every neighborhood, so I keep my eyes on Hussain, waiting for his reaction. I know death is near when his breathing stops and his hands freeze on his laptop. As the helicopter thunders closer, I mentally prepare my escape route. I grab my laptop, move upstairs, lift the mattress, grab my most valuable possession—my passport—and run as fast as I can, away from where the barrel bomb could fall.

During wartime, obtaining legal government documents has become difficult. Without them, immigrating, studying abroad, or legally crossing borders is close to impossible. The government uses this leverage to entrap and detain activists.

I keep reminding myself not to try to pack everything in these situations, having heard stories of people who were caught under rubble because they assumed they had enough time to grab that one last item—money stashed in a drawer, photo albums of the life they used to have, a gold ring or bracelet received on a wedding night.

After a barrel bomb hits, government helicopters often linger over their targets, waiting for a crowd to rush toward the rubble so another bomb can be dropped or mortar rounds from the west side can be fired. Despite knowing this, everyone runs toward the explosion—family members, rescue workers, photographers, rebel soldiers, and ambulances. Then the digging begins. A split second can save the life of someone trapped under the wreckage.

I went once, but never again. It was after a barrel bomb had flattened a three-story building. I arrived on the scene with my camera and stood there, frozen. It felt disrespectful to use my hands to take photos rather than help dig through the debris. It was horrifying to hear muffled screams coming from underneath the collapsed building and the voices of dying people begging to be rescued before they suffocated. Rescue workers constantly shouted, "Can you hear me?" to locate the living victims below. Children and families gathered to watch the corpses being hauled out. One man sat on the ground and started laughing uncontrollably. Some people were silent in their shock; others were screaming, begging the rescue workers to dig faster.

A few were cursing us photographers, certain that government forces and intelligence officers examine our photos to locate their targets. It's easier to believe that there is some logical plan when, in truth, any part of rebel-held territory is, in the eyes of the government, a legitimate target.

Somehow, I discover I still prefer it here over Turkey. In Turkey, surrounded by normalcy and stability, my inner turmoil felt out of place. Here, my inner and outer lives are in alignment. The chaos forces me to stay in the moment. The constant struggle for survival and unrelenting vigilance leaves little room for the incapacitating grief over my mother or the guilt toward Alia that plagued me in Istanbul.

I don't tell Peter any of this, not only because our time to talk is limited but because I know he won't understand. Instead, I fill our nightly Skype calls with complaints about mosquitoes and how scared I am of the sandflies I know eastern Aleppo still suffers from. I try to convince him that this is what scares me the most; everything else is manageable. I sleep with the windows closed and wake up every morning soaked in sweat on the stinking bare mattress. I can handle it as long as I have access to water.

Peter asks me to remember that, even though we grow accustomed to it over time, war takes a subtle but damaging toll on the mind and body. He says it's okay to have short breaks and return to Turkey every so often to rest and take care of myself. But I don't want a break, I insist. I feel perfectly fine.

There is another side of Aleppo that only those of us here on the ground can see. It doesn't make it to the front pages of newspapers because it doesn't fit with headlines about death tolls and the latest statements from the security council. It is the side of Aleppo that is alive and vibrant despite everything, the side that keeps us all sane.

Most evenings, before going home, I visit the main market on the outskirts of eastern Aleppo. No matter how bad the bombardment gets in nearby neighborhoods, the market is always packed. The narrow street is lined with wooden carts selling everything from ice to cucumbers, grapes, cans of tuna, instant noodles, cherries, potatoes, husked green peas, and garlic. There are uncovered plastic containers filled with brine for pickles, turnips, and giant olives. White buckets of tomato paste and ground red pepper. Small clouds of red-eyed black flies hover above the goods, and shopkeepers wave their arms to shoo them away.

I take in the sights and smells for a few moments. Coming to the market is a reminder that no death toll can drain this city completely of life. Before I leave, I always buy the same thing: a watermelon to share with our nightly guests.

Most nights, visitors pour into the house and sit on plastic chairs arranged in a circle around a tea table. They range from rebel commanders to journalists and activists. A few cross from the government-controlled western side of the city, braving sniper fire from both sides, completely shrouded to hide their identities and avoid being detained upon their return. Some evenings, the courtyard gets so crowded that people bring sleeping pads from the bedrooms and use them as cushions while we drink tea, smoke hookah, and eat the watermelon. The air is filled with the scent of grape-flavored shisha tobacco, coals, and grilled food.

During these gatherings, I feel the same sense of camaraderie I once felt in Amer's studio. It's as if class, sect, background, last names, and the neighborhoods we grew up in all vanish. What matters is where you stand politically. This shared sense of purpose gives me a feeling of belonging I haven't experienced in a very long time. It reassures me that I am where I am supposed to be.

TWENTY-NINE

Each night, I review my camera roll and select the best images of the day, write captions to accompany them, and send them to Reuters so I can earn my $150 daily rate. After that, I type up the interviews I've conducted for two academics in the United States who recently asked for my help with their research on Syria. But if Abdulwahab al-Mulla is in the room, I can't focus on anyone or anything else. I close my laptop and set it aside, scoot my chair closer to the table, take drags from the hookah, and enjoy his presence.

Abdulwahab is a frequent visitor to the house. He is a comedian whose talk show airs on an opposition YouTube channel. He doesn't have a strict schedule; episodes are released whenever he and his team finish filming and editing. His show is called "The Three-Star Revolution," meaning that if he were to rate our revolution, he would give it three stars instead of five—a sentiment many people share but few are willing to admit. On the show, Abdulwahab perches behind a desk, a revolutionary flag hanging on the wall behind him. He criticizes rebel commanders for looting and the Islamist brigades for seeking to establish an Islamic State. He takes jabs at politicians in Istanbul, the ones I loathed filming, who are so distant from the current realities in Syria that when they make comments on other television broadcasts, it seems like they're describing a different country. Listening to him reassures me that coming to Aleppo was the right decision.

Before the war, Abdulwahab was a monsheed, a reciter of the Quran with a beautiful voice. Now, at night, he sings while Melhem, another journalist at the house, picks and strums the strings of an oud. For hours, Melhem and Abdulwahab compose lyrics and set them to music, and when the song is good, they record it and upload it on social media.

The songs satirize everyone and everything, from rebel commanders who walk around heavily armed but never venture up to the front lines, to those who fire mortar rounds into the western side of Aleppo at random, believing that everyone who lives on the government-controlled side of the city is a government supporter. Abdulwahab also makes fun of Islamists who show up to gatherings with their friends and families wearing explosive belts. Who also think it's okay to loot houses and abduct activists as long as they shout "Allahu Akbar" first.

Abdulwahab's songs are so popular that some of those same rebels even play them in their cars. But he's also made many enemies; his Facebook posts are flooded with comments calling him a son of a whore and a government supporter. Whenever Melhem announces that the new song has finally been uploaded to YouTube, Abdulwahab jokes about how if he doesn't show up tomorrow, it's because he's been disappeared.

ONE EVENING IN AUGUST, while refreshing the Reuters home page on my laptop, I notice something different about the images from Damascus.

Instead of the usual gory scenes of destruction and armed men, the images are of lifeless bodies, clean and well-preserved, as if they were asleep.

On social media, videos start pouring in of children being sprayed with what looks like water. The death tolls reported by field hospitals and doctors rise into the hundreds. Whole families have suffocated to death in their own homes. They were gassed by the government with a chemical weapon.

I'm not surprised. At this point, the government's depravity can no longer shock me. What is puzzling to me and so many other Syrians is how the world reacts. After two years, it's as if the rest of the planet has suddenly realized that Syrians are being slaughtered. We don't understand why everyone seems so horrified by the sarin gas but not by the Scud missiles that obliterate entire neighborhoods in seconds. Why gas and not the torture dungeons that have killed thousands of men and women?

I was not aware of the history of chemical attacks or that chemical weapons were prohibited under international law. In a time when I had to rush under the marble kitchen counter whenever I heard a helicopter thundering nearby, it felt strange that the world would draw the line at chemical attacks. It did not make sense to me how empathy could be so selective.

In the days following the chemical attack, I repeatedly hear people say that, with this weapon, parents can at least bury their children whole. Entire families are murdered together at once, and nobody has to witness their relatives' mutilated bodies being pulled from the rubble. Across Aleppo, everyone hopes that this tragedy might unite the world to end the relentless bloodshed. Some admit to resenting Damascus, questioning why their dead seem to matter more than those in other regions; in general, though, people allow themselves a sliver of hope.

Had I been outside eastern Aleppo at the time, I might have been against intervention and argued that it would only bring chaos and destruction. But we believed we had already seen the worst, and everyone was desperate for help, no matter who was offering it. At that point in time, at twenty-two years old, I lacked the political awareness to recognize that the government's actions were part of a larger design or that Obama's speeches, his "red line," and the subsequent chemical attacks would not result in Western intervention to stop the killing. Our deaths had become normalized.

The longer I stay in Aleppo, the more I find myself withdrawing from Peter. Our calls and emails, once a great comfort to me, have become burdensome.

I feel irritated when he brings up the visa application to visit his family. After that night in Cihangir, the night I cried in front of him for the first time, I agreed to the trip because I wanted to show Peter that I cared about him and where he grew up. At the time, December seemed so far away. But for Peter, with only five months left before Christmas, the urgency has set in, and I can't ignore the application any longer if I'm going to meet his family.

If it isn't trip planning, it's Alia: She and Peter are friendlier than ever, and I resent his inability to discern how upset I am that he can be close with the only family member I have left when I can't. I rush to end the call whenever he brings her up.

And there's another development that bothers me: his curiosity about and openness to Islam. He tells me faith has been on his mind, and he is experimenting with fasting and talking to a sheikh. I hate that he is intrigued by Islam while people I know are actively persecuted in its name: women detained for not covering their hair correctly, men disappearing for cursing God and speaking up against the black flags.

I fail to consider that Peter's interest is perhaps an earnest attempt to fit in and connect with the people he is trying to help, as well as an effort to comfort himself. Instead, I think to myself how naive he is, and keep pushing for him to stop crossing into Syria altogether and stay in Turkey.

ONE DAY, HE CROSSES without telling me—so as not to bother me, he says. I only find out because someone in Raqqa messages me that he is there. Furious, I blow up at him the next time we speak, and we hang up after he calls me controlling. Hours later, he emails me: "Everything is fine. We will be okay; everything will be okay. I will come back to you safe. And I will make you proud. I'm not going anywhere. I promise."

I don't respond. Instead, I continue arguing with him in my head. It's impossible to express my growing intuition: Whatever we do, I can't imagine it will bring us closer. I worry for him in Syria, knowing I can't protect him. But I also fear that the moment we step into a place that is not saturated with crisis, and Peter is reminded of the comforts of normal life, he will realize that I am nothing but a burden to him, someone who will never belong in his life.

Despite his reassurances, I've always been scared that Peter loves me only because I am Syrian, and only for now. I worry that he is conflating his genuine desire to help me with true love. I'm afraid to see everything he has—his mother, his father, and his home full of childhood memories—when I've lost everything. There, if I stop and stare at one of the photos on his wall, he'll feel excited to share another quaint story with me. I'll nod and force myself to smile, trying to hide how much I envy his ability to recall his past without breaking down.

Even if I could take Peter back to my old life, I realize, I would still be ashamed of it. I would love to show him Jableh, the seaside promenade, the air that sticks to the skin like melted sugar. But how could I explain the invisible borders between Alawites and Sunnis, and justify the fact that, for years, this was accepted as normal? How could I justify the posters of the president and those who died for him plastered all over the city? And how would I ever introduce him to my family?

I can clearly picture my father wrinkling his nose at Peter—not an Alawite with a well-known family name. He would claim that Peter is only interested in me because of our olive trees and my inheritance. How would I explain to Peter that, for my father and the rest of my family, women of eligible marriage age are considered stupid sheep for men to herd, our fathers' names and our wealth our only redeeming qualities?

If I were with a Syrian man, I wouldn't have to explain any of this. Syrians know not to ask about childhood memories and family dynamics. I wish I could find a way to tell Peter all of this without feeling pathetic and weak or embarrassed for resenting him when all he has done is love me. He says we are a team, but we are not. He'll know it the minute we land in his country, and he walks effortlessly through customs while I am escorted to a separate lane for questioning about my potential ties to a terrorist organization. And when I finally make it out, I will try to hide my anxiety and irritation by calling myself Osama and laughing, but the joke won't be funny.

When I am around other Syrians, I feel lucky—I have my life, my limbs, a job, and a bed in a real house. With Peter, I am reminded of what a real normal life is, a life with a family that is safe and a dinner table laden with food, where his parents eat together and talk. No matter how hard I try to picture us visiting his family together, I always end up imagining him going alone.

◆◆

In early September, I make the decision to return to Antep for a medical checkup. I've been experiencing abdominal pain, and I know I need to see a doctor, but the thought of going to a local ob-gyn terrifies me. I am afraid of others finding out that not only am I not a virgin, but I've had an abortion. It will be my first departure from Aleppo since I arrived at the beginning of the summer—and the first time Peter and I will be in the same city in months.

Once there, I find myself making up countless excuses to delay seeing him. I fabricate meetings with Reuters staff; I say I have to console a friend who just lost a relative. I make up translation assignments for a journalist working on a big story on orphans. I recognize the cruelty of making up stories related to Syria, knowing that he would never ask me to cancel or postpone to spend time with him. It's like I am using his love for my country to avoid seeing him. Instead, he tells me to take my time and that he is here whenever I am able to meet up.

When I finally see him, in a small coffee shop in Antep, I notice how my body tenses when he walks in. He looks soft, with his light blue shirt and recent haircut. I realize the effort he put into his appearance before seeing me, whereas I have thrown my hair in a bun and am wearing a stained shirt. I recoil when I feel the sweat from his neck on my cheek. He hands me a bundle of flowers, and when I see others looking at us, I place the flowers on the chair next to me, hidden under the table. As we talk, at one point, something upsets him, and he begins to cry. I try to comfort him, not out of love but out of shame for the way people are staring. Men don't cry in public. I cut our date short. I give another excuse I know Peter won't argue with. But my heart drops when, after I get out of the taxi and it drives off, I realize I left his flowers in the back seat.

Returning to Turkey means returning to binge drinking, and one morning, I wake up next to another Syrian photographer who is on a brief trip in Antep. I'm surprised to find I feel no shame about this—strangely,

I feel powerful. Yes, Peter has everything else, but I have the power to cheat on him, to prove I don't need him. Sleeping with someone else gives me a warped sense of security, a feeling I had lost ever since Peter's presence became a constant reminder of my inferiority.

I do my best to avoid Peter for the rest of my stay. When he asks if he's done something wrong, I tell him I am just busy. I find myself rushing back to eastern Aleppo to escape. Later, rereading the email I sent him before I crossed back to Syria, I am surprised to find that I seem to be addressing a stranger, not a lover.

Days later, Peter tells me over Skype that he is going back to Syria, too. I beg him not to go. The Islamic State is growing stronger every day and has already kidnapped two American journalists: James Foley and Steven Sotloff. Radical groups are taking any foreigners they can get their hands on to hold for ransom. Even as I'm putting distance between us to protect myself, the thought of losing Peter to what my home country has become—of him being betrayed by those he trusts and has tried so hard to help—is unbearable. I can't grieve anyone else.

But my protests are useless; Peter will not change his mind, and there's no point in arguing with him further. He is just as stubborn as I am. After we hang up, he emails me:

> Take care Loubna, despite what I say when we fight or stupid shit happens, I do mean it when I say I am proud of you and I know shit is not easy right now. Sorry to have added to your troubles yet again . . . I am good at pretty much nothing else.

The reply I rediscover in my drafts folder weeks later sits empty except for the letter *D*. Looking back and knowing my mental state at the time, I wonder if it was perhaps the opening for "Don't talk to me again."

A few days later, a friend in Raqqa messages me that a group of Syrians and one American medic riding together in an ambulance were stopped at an Islamic State checkpoint between Raqqa and Deir ez-Zur. As I connect the dots—foreigner, medic, ambulance, traveling from Raqqa to Deir ez-Zur—my heart plummets into my stomach. The world around me blurs. There is no doubt left. This is Peter.

"And then?" I ask.

"They disappeared," he says.

Deir ez-Zur's local government confirms that it is Peter's ambulance that is being held by the Islamic State, along with a few members of the Deir ez-Zur local council. For days, I feel no sadness, only anger. I am furious with the Syrians who convinced Peter that nothing could go wrong. I know the exact line they used when Peter asked about the safety of the road to Deir ez-Zur: "What happens to you happens to all of us! Trust us." People I have worked with have used this line with me before when I've climbed up a bombed-out building or run into a street exposed to sniper fire, all for the sake of a photograph.

Peter himself pleaded with me not to believe them. He was the one who told me that those who live so close to the front lines cannot accurately assess danger. He said that they become blind to it, and we should trust our own judgment. Now, I wonder if Peter also became blind to the risks, or if he didn't want to sound skeptical and ungrateful because of his immense gratitude for the Syrians who helped him cross the border.

I wonder if he was debating whether he should say something as he rode in the back of the ambulance, his hands tensely clutching the frames of the open windows, feeling the outside air rush in as shades of orange and yellow refracted from the hay fields on each side of the road. Or perhaps he was truly unaware of what was about to happen, and when he heard the driver say that they were approaching a checkpoint, he comforted himself with the knowledge that the general rule for all rebel groups is that ambulances are allowed through. But the masked men did stop the ambulance. Through the window, they shouted something about Ramadan and smoking cigarettes before sundown. The men inside were taken away.

I pack my belongings and cross back into Turkey. I fear that Peter's captors will force him to open his email and Skype account and see who he was recently in contact with, just like the Syrian government used to do.

From Turkey, I call every activist, rebel soldier, and fixer I know, along with every doctor I have ever met in rebel-held areas. I describe Peter's pale skin, green eyes, and tattooed arms. "He's an American," I say, immediately adding that the abducted ambulance is from Peter's organization. "He's a medic who has been risking his life to help others. Please help me find him."

Some promise to spread the word. Others find it bizarre that I am so concerned about an American while hundreds of Syrians sit forgotten in ISIS jails. They reply that if they could help anyone, which they can't, it would be the Syrian rebel leaders being held in Islamic State custody. They remind me that ISIS soldiers don't care about the uprising. They're fighting their own battle to establish the caliphate. They'll eliminate anyone who stands in their way.

One person I talk to even goes so far as to blame Peter for his own kidnapping. It's Peter's fault for crossing into a country full of foreign fighters; many of these Islamic State guys were fighting the American occupation of Iraq. Peter, carrying the passport of the country that executed their hero and whoever supported him, has been incredibly reckless, and only God can help him now.

"Others have promised to help. I don't need you," I tell him.

"You're a girl. Of course, everyone will make empty promises to help you." I feel devastated. I know he is right. There is nothing we can do. The masked men hold the power.

"Just pray for him," he says.

My heart aches. I stay silent. I refuse to pray for him—praying means he's beyond saving.

"Pray for him," he repeats, and I end the call.

THIRTY

From Antep, I watch the Islamic State advance and capture parts of eastern Aleppo. Some activists continue to justify their actions, professing gratitude for the enforcement of law and order. Every time the Islamic State detains a rebel commander, they claim he was a criminal thug.

Seeing the writing on the wall, many of the rebel leaders who pushed the Syrian government forces out in 2012 flee to Turkey. Most local citizen journalists have either been detained or have left the country by this point. The small percentage who remain are doing what we used to do in government-controlled areas: hiding hard drives and memory cards in their underwear and changing the screensavers on their laptops and phones to blend in, which now means embracing black, pro-ISIS imagery.

Abdulwahab records a segment of his show and says Syrians want a state that doesn't dictate or interfere with people's personal religious beliefs. He says people should be free to decide the type of state they want, whether it's secular or Islamic. Before we focus on what type of state we want, we first need to clean up and manage the country. At the end of the episode, Abdulwahab, knowing that what he said blatantly challenged the Islamic State, looks straight into the camera and says, "I hope I live to make the next episode." Not long after, Abdulwahab is at home with his wife when four masked men push their way in, blindfold him, drag him into a car, and drive off.

The next morning, Hussain and the other journalists sharing his house receive the news of Abdulwahab's abduction and go into hiding. A few days later, twenty masked men break into the house and loot everything: the musical instruments; the whiteboard where Hussain scrawled instructions such as *No downloads, to conserve bandwidth*; the chairs that had borne the weight of so many people freighted with heavy stories and memories. Within a few hours of the raid, the journalists flee to Turkey.

A sense of defeat hangs over us here. Nowhere in Syria feels safe enough for us to work; I am stuck, living off the money I've saved and assisting academics when I can. I still help Naji with his workshops, which are now completely focused on strategies to avoid ISIS. Otherwise, I spend my days on Mezar's couch. People come and go. The houses we rent, designed to be temporary homes for college kids, become the shared spaces of our extradition.

Although we all crowd into the same living rooms, we barely talk, each of us lost in our own worlds on our laptops. Mezar is constantly searching for news about his missing brother; others are on the lookout for signs that our exile is momentary, that the men with their black flags will not write the end, that we will be able to go back.

Someone forwards me an announcement about a six-week human rights and photography fellowship funded by the Magnum Foundation, to be held at New York University. I think of Peter and how, every time he brought up school applications, he insisted that if I was serious about continuing my education, I should start looking at programs. Back then, it felt impossible to convey to him why it seemed selfish to leave. Merely reading through the application process deepened my guilt about pursuing a future while my country burned.

IF I LEAVE, I WILL be just like the politicians I refused to film during their meetings in Istanbul. They've been away from Syria for so long that when they speak about it, it feels like they're describing a different place altogether—a country that has moved on without them, one that now exists only in their imaginations after years of exile. I cannot be like them. I am not them. But now, almost five months later, unable to cross into Syria and losing hope, leaving doesn't feel like giving up. Maybe it would be more useful for me to go, I think. I am not accomplishing anything here.

I scroll through the fellowship application: They require a résumé, a few shots from a photography project, and an interview over Skype. I rummage through my Reuters archive, choose some photographs from Aleppo, and draft some words about the impact of war on urban areas. I write about the first time I drove through Aleppo, how devastated it was yet so alive. I reach out to Danny, from Laila's organization, and on a Sunday, he sits next to me in a coffee shop for hours, editing my draft and helping me compose my résumé in exchange for carrot cake and coffee. In early December, my cursor hovers over the submit button. It is only six weeks, I tell myself. I will be back. I submit the application.

LATER THAT MONTH, the Islamic State captures a high-profile rebel commander, tortures him, and releases footage of his dead body, blue and bloated, as a warning to other rebels who do not support their caliphate. The video sparks a rage that tears across rebel-held areas. The dead commander's brigade launches an attack on the Islamic State, other brigades follow, and within a week, hundreds of ISIS soldiers and rebel commanders die in the clashes.

While the killing in Syria rages on, I remain hunched over my laptop for hours in Mezar's living room in Antep. We spend our days watching videos, following the news, waiting for Syria to become safe enough to allow us to return. Outside our den, Christmas arrives. I take the bus to Hatay to visit Alia.

The stretch between Christmas and New Year's was once our favorite time of year. Christmas in Jableh was about everything except gifts. At night, string lights and plastic trees glittered through the curtains of most homes. We had a small tree in our living room with lights so faulty that they often stopped working before New Year's Eve. A man donning a red suit and a big white beard would come into our building ringing a bell and shouting our names, and we would run out barefoot to catch a glimpse of him, at which point he would wave and leave, careful not to provoke any questions about why Santa and my uncle's driver looked similar.

When we were young enough to believe that Baba Noel was real, my mother and aunts would take me, Alia, and our cousins to Christmas celebrations similar to Eid. We kids would dress up and gather at my grandmother's house across the street before setting out for one of the many parties around Jableh and Latakia. There was music, lots of Baba Noels—real ones, not my uncle's driver—and, when the party ended, my mother would take whatever chocolates were left on the tables and melt them down to make sukseh—the Syrian version of lazy cake, a no-bake dessert made with tea biscuits and chocolate.

There was something elegant about Christmas that made us Alawites feel special. It was, in a way, a festivity designed for us specifically, as we had always felt closer to Christians than to Sunnis. It originated from the Alawites' strategy to survive in cities during the Ottoman Empire: Our ancestors pretended to be Christians, and over time, Christian holiday traditions became our own. When we grew older, Alia and I would attend parties organized by Mustafa—aka DJ Steve—where we were allowed to drink alcohol. But not all Alawites could afford the steep entry fees. Showing up to these parties not only made us feel special and Westernized but also marked our wealth.

Alia and I do not talk about any of this in Hatay. We both know by now that evoking the past will only remind us of all that we have lost, of a different lifetime in which we had a mother. Instead, we talk about Peter. Alia tears up as she tells me that while I was in eastern Aleppo, she and Peter spent a lot of time together when she visited Antep for work or when he was in Hatay. He taught her a silly game: beer pong. The white plastic ping-pong ball turned gray from all the dust it collected, but they would still dunk it in the beer and drink. "Americans," she says, shaking her head.

I hesitate to tell her about the Christmas trip Peter was planning, how he wanted me to meet his parents, how I couldn't face them. We both laugh when I tell her that, right before I left for Aleppo, he had bought me an Yves Saint Laurent perfume along with body armor, juxtaposing the absurdity of our time. And, at that moment, I realize that, even in his absence, Peter has somehow given me a common ground for my sister and I to talk, to reconnect outside of the burden of our shared pain. I reassure her that Peter will be freed soon. The rebels are winning. It's only a matter of time.

I AM NOT ALONE in my hope, because by now the rebel brigades have forced ISIS to retreat from most of its areas of control. "Syria Is Free" is being painted over the black walls. ISIS fighters, soldiers, and their families are forced into Jarabulus and Manbij. Munzer and his family will never be able to return to their home city. Mezar's city, Raqqa, becomes their new caliphate—the ISIS capital.

A few days after New Year's Eve, the last ISIS soldiers withdraw from eastern Aleppo. The hospital that had been converted into an infamous prison, where Abdulwahab's wife once begged the masked guards to deliver clothes to her husband, is now being liberated. When we hear the news, I begin refreshing web pages incessantly for updates about the detainees.

It is late afternoon before rumors start to trickle in that ISIS has taken the most important detainees, the ones potentially worth substantial amounts of money, with them to Raqqa. Horrific photos and videos shared on social media reveal the fates of the Syrian hostages, the less important hostages: I see more than fifty blindfolded corpses, each killed by a throat slash or a gunshot to the head. Bodies lie atop bodies. Women and men. Some of the dead have wet their pants. With every click of the mouse, I feel a burning lump rise in my throat. I dread seeing a familiar face.

IN LATE JANUARY, it appears safe enough for me to return to Syria, and I cross into the Idlib governorate bordering Hatay to resume my photojournalism work. The air in Idlib is heavy with the rich, tangy aroma of pomegranates. Large copper pots filled with ruby-red seeds simmer gently. Idlib, a city famous for its bountiful pomegranate trees, sees families gathering to pick, peel, and boil these vibrant fruits. They painstakingly reduce the seeds into thick, syrupy molasses—a seasonal labor that has become a source of income for many. The tense atmosphere of the city has softened. The Islamic State flags that once loomed over Idlib have vanished. My driver tells me how men once grew beards as a shield of conformity. Now, they have clean-shaven faces. On the streets, vendors display crates brimming with oranges, a seasonal staple in Idlib's winter markets—another source of seasonal income. I snap a photo of rows of fruit crates dominating the foreground, each one overflowing with glossy oranges. Behind them, men and women barter over vegetables and other produce. A child stands close to his father, curiously watching the transaction. It seems this part of Syria is reclaiming its normalcy—a normalcy I hadn't imagined would return when I applied for the fellowship weeks ago.

WHILE THERE, I RECEIVE an email notifying me that I've qualified to be interviewed for the Magnum Foundation Fellowship. In the museum for ancient artifacts and mosaics in the countryside, the only place where I can get a good satellite internet signal, I sit at my laptop and take the Skype call.

I try my best to remain focused and avoid making grammatical mistakes as I answer the interviewers' questions. Toward the end of the call, the woman on the screen informs me that they have received more than six hundred applications from all over the world.

A few days later, I receive another email: "Congratulations! See you in New York!" It is surreal. I think of Peter and how I always assumed that if I ever went to the United States, it would be with him, to meet his family. It feels like a cruel joke that I will be visiting his country alone while he is trapped somewhere in mine.

I only share the news with a few people: Laila, Naji, my former colleagues at the organization, and Reuters. I tell them all the same exact thing: "I will be back by July! It is only six weeks!" When I think about what others might say, fear and shame cloud my brain. Even after all this time, I still hear Amer's voice in my head—"Of course they admitted you!"—insisting my acceptance letter only proves what he has always said. I got in not because I deserve it: I am just another Syrian being offered a scholarship by the West as a consolation prize to numb their guilt for failing us.

But when I finally tell Alia and see how happy she is, all my conflicted feelings about what Amer and others might say vanish. For the first time since our mother died, it occurs to me that this may be a way of honoring my mother, fulfilling her dream for me to pursue my education. Buoyed by my acceptance, Alia starts looking into opportunities for her own education abroad.

Back in Istanbul, where I must wait for my visa application to be processed by the American consulate, I find myself stuck in a place I've come to hate and have already mentally left behind.

Surrounded by the thrum of normal life and walking the streets that I will forever associate with my grief, my nightmares return.

Every night as I lie in bed, I see my mother standing by the door, asking me to come home. She is angry that I haven't called to ask how she is doing. I cannot bring myself to tell her that she has died. I am scared that if I tell her what happened, she will somehow die again, and I will lose her a second time. The dream is so vivid and haunting that when I wake up in a sweat, it is several long seconds before I come back to reality and am reminded that she is gone and that I will never know if she died angry with me or not.

In the daytime, I am surrounded by reminders of Peter. We started dating exactly a year ago. The weather feels like tissue paper against my skin, not quite hot or cold. There are tulips, seagulls squawking and circling overhead, flagstones, and the silly pizza delivery scooters that he swore would kill him. Everything about Istanbul in the springtime reminds me of him. I walk by my old house, past the window of my room on the ground floor, with its dusty white bars Peter used to squeeze his hand through to knock on my window instead of ringing the bell and waking my housemates. I walk by the used bookstore we regularly went to and realize that I haven't read any books since we stopped reading together. In the void created by his absence, I find myself clinging to the only thing I have left of him: his words.

I start poring over his emails, and as I reread them more closely, I notice things I hadn't before: how he always used ellipses when sharing something heavy or hard, or how his replies would include the right spellings of words I wrote, like "stay save" or "informations"—a subtle way to correct me. I start to see how reckless some of my responses were. In one reply to a long email in which he confessed how scared he was that I would never return from Syria, I responded by asking if he knew any doctors who could provide a plastic leg for someone who had been injured. Another time, after he wrote to me about his excitement for what the future held for both of us, I replied with a logistical query about transporting my hard drive from Antep to Aleppo. I find other emails I had completely ignored; in one, he told me how much he missed sleeping next to me, even though I know my snoring kept him awake.

I am struck by how often he used phrases like "I will be there for you as long as I live," and how I took his support and reassurance for granted. And I feel the pressure building behind my eyes every time I reread his final email, in which he wrote that he was not good at anything except adding to my troubles. It is unbearable to perceive a parallel between my losses—how both Peter and my mother disappeared before I could say goodbye or tell them how grateful I was for them. I took both of them for granted.

More aggravating still, I feel privileged to grieve Peter. Everyone keeps reminding me how lucky I am to have a valid passport and an acceptance letter to study something I love. Meanwhile, half of my country's population is either dead or displaced, and thousands of Syrian women my age are living in tents, dreaming of a home with solid walls. Some work hard labor jobs in Turkey, Lebanon, and Jordan to put food on the table. Some have even been sold by their families to wealthy Turks to become second, secret wives. I survived. I should be grateful.

I know I am lucky, but my guilt over my mother troubles me. What if there was something I could have done to save her? What if I am making the same mistake now—what if something can still be done for Peter, and I've been too selfish to see it? I am haunted by the thought. I realize that if I don't try one last time to help him, I will live forever with the shame and regret, just as I do with my mother. In that moment, I make up my mind: One last time, I must go back to Syria.

THIRTY-ONE

The following days are a blur. I focus on one mission: finding any piece of information about Peter. I need to talk to anyone who might know something that could eventually help, which means finding a way to talk to ISIS fighters—and then finding a way back to safety.

I contact an activist I trust named Fadi and tell him that I have to speak to a few foreign fighters for a research project I must finish before leaving for the United States. I ask him if what I've been reading is true—that there are still some ISIS fighters in Latakia—and whether it might be possible for me to spend a few days in the mountains conducting interviews with them.

He says he can help, but on the condition that I strictly follow his instructions. We will be dealing with men who won't think twice before shooting us if they sense something is amiss, he reminds me. If anyone asks who I am, I must remain silent. He will refer to me as his cousin and explain that he is helping me cross from a government-held area into

Turkey. I will be covered head to toe in a long black robe and headscarf. "That Aleppo hijab I have seen you wearing in photos with your neck and the top of your hair showing won't work," he says. "One mistake will get us both killed." I tell him I understand.

A few days later, the American consulate releases my passport. I cancel my flight to Antep and instead fly to Antakya, the Turkish city north of the mountains of Latakia. I tell Alia that I have unfinished work in Syria but not to worry; I will only be gone a handful of days, and this will be my last trip. She tells me this is exactly what Peter said before he was abducted. I'm speaking to both of us when I insist I will be fine.

On my first morning in the mountains, fresh, misty air wafts in through my window, carrying the familiar scent of pine trees from our coastal area, the one I used to inhale on childhood visits to my father. Outside, I can see a graveyard overgrown with long, dead weeds. A diminutive cross of white marble peeks out from a cluster of bushes, a reminder that the Islamic State fighters have evicted hundreds of Christian and Armenian families from their homes. I breathe deeply to steady myself and try to concentrate on my plan. Fadi is expecting a foreign fighter at the house this evening. After sunset, I'll have my chance.

As night falls, I walk down into the living room, where Fadi is sitting with a man named Osman. The room smells like diesel fuel from the space heater. A two-day-old pile of sunflower seeds rests in a silver tray on the distressed wooden table in the middle of the room. Fadi is typing on the couch; Osman is listening to voice messages on WhatsApp.

Suddenly, there is a hard knock on the metal front door. The three of us freeze.

"Who is it?" Fadi shouts.

"Abo Mariam," a muffled voice answers.

"Cover yourself," Fadi whispers to me. He puts down his laptop and walks toward the door. I wrap my hijab around my head and pat its edges to make sure none of my hair has escaped. I lean toward Osman. "Should I leave?" I ask.

"No. This is our friend's brother-in-law," he says.

The door opens and I see the silhouette of a man on the threshold. Fadi gives Abo Mariam a hug and a kiss on each shoulder and invites him in, and as he steps into the orange light of the living room, I glimpse his face. His large nose and round cheeks almost make him look Arab, but his formal, stilted greeting gives him away as a foreigner. He is wearing a desert camouflage suit and a black beanie, and his dark brown hair, which is tied back, falls to his shoulders. When he notices me staring at him, he casts his eyes down, turns around, and takes a step toward the door, as if rethinking the invitation.

Fadi grabs his hand. "She's my cousin. It's okay. Come in."

Abo Mariam moves back into the room but keeps his eyes fixed on the floor. He sheds his chest rig, with its magazines of ammunition, and sets it on the chair next to the door. Then he leans his AK-47 on the empty TV stand and bends over to untie his black, ankle-high military boots. Blotches of dried mud stain his pants up to his knees. He lifts his eyes momentarily.

"I can come another time," he says in broken, French-accented Arabic. He is clearly uncomfortable in my presence, so I stand and retreat toward the kitchen. He takes a seat on the couch.

"How is the front?" Fadi asks.

"The Nusairi troops are closing in on the mountain," Abo Mariam says, using the derogatory term for Alawites. He wonders aloud about the true cause of the Islamic State's defeats. Is it the government's artillery or the fact that some of the soldiers neglect God and fail to pray? Is it because of the clashes with the rebel brigades?

"The Syrians have forgotten that the government is the enemy. Now they fight us—we, who, by the grace of God, left our homes and families to help their cause."

I wait to hear how Fadi and Osman will respond to this. I know that one of Fadi's close friends, a rebel leader who was among the first to fight the Syrian government out of this area, was killed by the Islamic State almost a year ago for "cursing God." They say nothing. Have they ever criticized ISIS to Abo Mariam's face or are they, like me, compelled to be entirely different people whenever he is around? Do they feel forced into this "friendship," this camaraderie, because it's the only way to ensure they can stay here and not flee to Turkey?

"I will make tea," Fadi announces, walking into the kitchen. Once we're alone, he turns to me. "Come sit with us," he whispers. "It's fine. He won't protest. He's shy."

"Who is he?" I ask.

"A friend's sister's husband. He's French and has been here since last year. He was originally only working with ISIS but now he fights with a few different brigades. You can probably ask him questions, if you want. He loves talking about himself." Fadi lights the stove, puts the lid on the copper kettle, and returns to the living room.

I close my eyes and try to slow my heartbeat. I am terrified. What if I say something stupid and he senses I am lying? What if he realizes I am a "Nusairi" just like some of the people he's killed? But this is what I came here to do—I can't falter now.

"The water is boiling," I announce. When Fadi stands, I take his seat. Next to me, Osman and Abo Mariam are laughing about something. I slowly look over at them. Abo Mariam is definitely younger than twenty-five, I realize. His camouflage uniform is at least two sizes too big, and his socks are worn out. He and Osman are hunched over the phone in his hand. I can hear the audio: a man cursing in an exaggerated Latakian accent. I recognize the voice. It's from a TV comedy that was filmed here, in this village, six years ago. I always thought the show was too stupid to watch, but they seem to find it hilarious. They burst into laughter again. Abo Mariam's laughter is disarming. For a moment, he seems genuinely lighthearted and nonthreatening.

When the clip ends, Abo Mariam straightens his back and looks at me. "Fadi tells me you are trying to cross into Turkey. Why don't you stay here?"

"I'm scared of the jets," I stutter. "The bombing. I—"

"If everyone runs away, who will defend this mountain?" he says sternly. "People are coming from all over the world to help Syrians, and Syrians are running off to Turkey."

"You're right," I say, nodding.

Osman tries to lessen the tension. "She knows journalists," he says. "She will help us from Turkey. She speaks English." Abo Mariam seems unimpressed.

Fadi walks in with a tray of tea. "Maybe we could interview you?" Fadi says, stirring sugar into a glass and placing it in front of Abo Mariam.

"Whatever you want," Abo Mariam says, suddenly energized. "Start the camera." His excitement is confusing. He doesn't ask any questions about the nature of the interview or where it will be published.

"I don't have my camera on me now," I say, stalling. I didn't expect him to agree so easily, and now that he has, my mind is blank with fear. I glance at his gun resting on the TV stand and try not to panic. One wrong comment is all that stands between his rifle and my head. Fadi moves to grab his camera.

"Hand me my weapon," Abo Mariam says. "I want to pose with it." He adjusts his black beanie. I turn on my phone recorder and place it in the center of the table. Fadi sets up a tripod beside it.

"We can just do audio if you want," I say, looking at the camera. Abo Mariam is in the center of the frame with the AK-47 in his lap. "Are you sure you want to show your face?"

"I am not a coward," he declares, gazing straight into the lens. His right index finger points skyward in the sign of Shahada, a symbolic gesture emphasizing the singularity and supremacy of God. "I do not hide behind a mask. Everyone knows me. French intelligence, Interpol. I am proud of what I do. Everyone knows Abo Mariam the French."

I nod.

As I guessed, he is twenty-four, just a year older than me. He was born in 1990 in southern France to a Christian family, whom he refers to as infidels. Following his father and older siblings, he started drinking alcohol and smoking weed when he was young. His childhood was marked by addiction and crime. "Our lives were so hard," he says. "Harder than the lives of animals." At seventeen, he converted to Islam.

"Muslims in France do not live in peace," he says. "Western countries claim to believe in religious freedom, but they intervene in people's affairs and prevent them from exercising their religious rights. Westerners, those nonbelievers, sin twenty-four hours a day, seven days a week, but they deprive me of a five-minute prayer. In France, women are not even allowed to wear the burqa in public. But if you go outside naked, that's 'freedom.' They are waging an invisible war against Islam."

He wanted to live in a Muslim country, so he moved to Morocco in 2010, where he studied Arabic and the Quran. He met his first wife there, and shortly after they married, his first daughter, Mariam, was born. He was twenty-one.

"During those years, I prayed and looked after my family, but I always wondered—is this all there is to life?" He lowers his eyes, adjusts his grip on his gun, and continues. "My life had no meaning. I wanted something more. Something real. That was when I concluded that humans were created to worship God, and that jihad is the highest form of worship that Allah and the Prophet promoted. In 2013, I decided to go to the Levant, the Holy Land, which Prophet Muhammad asked us Muslims to protect."

He and his wife decided it was better for her and their daughter to stay and follow him to Syria later.

He packed some clothes, 250 euros, and five photographs of his family and friends. He flew from Morocco to Istanbul and then to Hatay, where he passed through the same gates as other foreign fighters I had watched enter my country. Two hours after he landed, he was walking down an unpaved dirt road into Syria.

"Was it hard to cross?" I ask him. He looks at me, lifting his eyebrows in surprise.

"The *easiest* thing to do today is enter Syria. Of course, I didn't say I was coming for jihad. I said I was an aid worker, and they didn't suspect otherwise. I didn't have this back then," he says, grabbing the end of his beard.

"Were you in touch with anyone before your arrival? Did you trust them?"

"I cannot tell you that," Abo Mariam replies firmly. I realize immediately it was a stupid question.

"Do you miss your family in France?" I ask, trying to ease the tension.

"We talk every day," he says. "But they are still infidels. Now I have a new family. I married a Syrian woman here and she is pregnant. If it's a boy, Abdelrahman will be his name, and if it's a girl, she will also be named Mariam."

"Do you miss your first wife?" I ask cautiously. Abo Mariam pauses and sets down his tea. "She tried to get a passport, but she couldn't. The government knows that her man is Abo Mariam, the terrorist. We can't see each other."

He keeps a tight grasp on his gun, but his voice softens. "But we talk. She is out of sight but close to the heart."

"Do you Skype?"

"No," he says, suddenly slamming the bottom of his rifle on the floor. "I have a problem with Skype. What if someone hacks her and sees my wife without a cover? I am a very jealous man." He sighs. "I am so jealous that I don't even allow people to visit me here in my house. What if my

Syrian wife leaves a strand of hair on the floor? On the couch? I don't want visitors to know what kind of hair she has: black, blonde, long, short. I don't want anyone to know anything about her. She is *mine*. My wife. My habiba. Only mine."

"Do you sometimes think of going back to your first wife?"

"To leave this glorious holy life and return to the animal life? Of course not." He pauses before adding, "If I return to France, I will be sentenced to fifteen years in jail. In Morocco, thirty. They know that here I learned how to use weapons, to shoot and make bombs. They consider me a threat. I can't even go to Turkey—Turkish intelligence would deport me to France." He stares at the lens as if he is debating whether he's been too honest, if his answer might make other foreign fighters reluctant to join him. The goal of the interview for him, I realize, is to encourage other young people to move to Syria, the Islamic State, where everything is just perfect and holy.

"I have no regrets," Abo Mariam says, as if reading my mind. "I am not sad at all. I am actually extremely happy," he smiles. "This happiness will double once I am martyred and am reunited with my friends in heaven. Thirty-seven of us have been martyred in the last ten days, and I swear I did not see a single person die without a smile on his face." He is quiet for a few seconds. "I would never hesitate."

"You are not worried about what will happen to your wife here if you die?" I ask. "Your child?"

"God will take care of them. I place all my faith in God." He says he believes his wife should never have to work, even when he is gone.

"Why?"

"Because she is a Muslim woman. She is a queen. She is more precious than all the gold in the world. That's why I don't allow her to go out. I will give you an example: If you go to a shop, cheap products will be everywhere within reach. Anyone can touch them. But the more expensive stuff—like jewels, gold, and diamonds—is hidden away. Caged in a box. Protected. A Muslim woman is just like that. Only her man should see her."

He falls silent again. I cannot tell what is going through his mind.

"I ask God to take me to heaven," he says, finally. "Martyrdom is the shortest path to paradise. This is not just something I was told. This is something I have *witnessed*. My dead friends' corpses appear peaceful and smell like musk, unlike the bodies of the enemies of Allah, whose corpses are hideous and reek worse than pigs."

I try not to react. It dawns on me that, from the government's perspective, everyone in this house is on the same side. We all belong to the opposition. Even worse, Abo Mariam and foreign fighters like him wouldn't be here in the first place if not for our uprising.

"Are you married?" he asks, interrupting my thoughts. The question catches me off guard. I tell him I'm not.

He pauses, and for the first time since he walked through the door, we make eye contact. He holds my gaze for several seconds until I look away. I feel a rush of blood in my face and my hands start to shake. Maybe I should have lied. Did Fadi tell him I was married? Am I in trouble for being in a house with men without a mahram, a group of escorts? How had we not thought of this?

Abo Mariam slowly turns to Fadi. "Do you want to marry her?"

"Of course not!" Fadi laughs. "She is older than me."

Abo Mariam turns back to me. This time, he stares directly into my eyes, and he doesn't look away. "Do you want to marry me, then?"

My face burns and my hands start to shake. I pull at the edge of my hijab to cover myself further.

"Don't embarrass her," Fadi says. "If your Syrian wife knew about this, she would kill you."

He, Abo Mariam, and Osman all laugh. After a moment, I laugh nervously along with them, my eyes cast downward. I feel my lips tremble.

Just then, a strange thought passes through my mind—for a second, I forget everything that is wrong with this man. I forget that men like him are the reason I was forced out of eastern Aleppo. I forget that he is ignorant of the fact that I was born and raised by the people on the other side of this mountain, the Alawites, whom he left his wife and child to kill—and that, if he knew this, he would use the rifle in his lap to fire a bullet into my forehead, certain that he was doing the work of God. I forget about the camera on the table, the recorder, the presence of Fadi and Osman. I forget why I am here, the questions I should be asking. I forget about the anger and the agony and the longing for Peter. It all disappears.

For just a moment, I want him and the afterlife he is talking about, the eternal peace. I want the protection and love. When I lift my head, I find Abo Mariam still staring at me, smiling, waiting for me to answer his question. I look over at Fadi, who motions for me to leave.

Struggling to breathe, I go to my room and lock the door behind me, then remove my hijab. The space suddenly feels so messy and small. Despite the cold night, I am covered in sweat. I open the window. The sky is clear, the silence broken only by the hum of generators. I take deep breaths despite the heavy scent of gasoline and smoke. I resolve that if I have another chance with Abo Mariam in the coming days, I will find the courage to ask him about ISIS's hostages.

The next morning, I hear a car pull into the driveway and leave my room to find Fadi and Osman sipping coffee out on the balcony. We watch as Abo Mariam walks to the door, his rifle strapped across his chest. He is wearing the same camouflage outfit from the night before and carrying a bag of food.

"He will be visiting every day now," Osman says, laughing.

Abo Mariam tells us his wife is away visiting her family, and he doesn't want to eat alone. When Fadi goes to gather plates and glasses from the kitchen, Abo Mariam steps between Osman and me. The thought that he might be serious about pursuing me is terrifying, but I try to remain calm and smile. I remind myself that this may be my only other chance to ask about Peter; I can't waste the opportunity.

"I haven't spent much time out here," Abo Mariam says, scanning the landscape. Suddenly, he gasps and points the tip of his gun at a white cross on the hillside across the way.

Osman raises his eyebrows. "You can't hit it," he challenges.

Abo Mariam swings the door open. Osman follows him outside. I press the palms of my hands into my silk hijab to cover my ears and step back into the living room, fixing my eyes on the cross.

For a few seconds, Abo Mariam is completely still. Then the sound of the blast permeates my body. A puff of white dust rises over the stump that was the cross. I realize I am shaking. "First try!" he says, laughing.

He hands Osman the rifle. Osman fires at another cross in the distance and misses. Abo Mariam laughs and slaps his vanquished comrade on the shoulder. "Try again," he demands. I press my palm against the fabric covering my nose to block the burning smell of gunpowder. Osman fires again, but the cross remains standing. Then a third shot rings out as he tries in vain to repair his ego.

I feel disgusted and betrayed. Osman is just like Abo Mariam: He pulls the trigger like it means nothing, like it's just a game.

"I'm the real soldier," Abo Mariam says, laughing. "All right, enough. Let's eat. I'm hungry."

They file back inside and we sit down to lunch. As we eat, the conversation turns to the rebels who are continuing to battle both ISIS and the government forces.

"They should be grateful we're here," Abo Mariam spits.

"To be fair, some Islamic State members have done horrible things to Syrians," I hear myself say. I freeze, my eyes wide.

Abo Mariam stares at me. "What are you talking about?"

"Just that I know people who have been seized at checkpoints and tortured," I say, trying to keep my voice steady.

"This is a war. Interrogations are normal. If they aren't guilty, they're released."

"But there are people who never made it out."

"Who?"

"Obaida Batal, for one. Samar Saleh is another. Abdulwahab al-Mulla from eastern Aleppo. And Abdulrahman Kassig." I hold my breath. Abdulrahman is the Islamic name Peter chose for himself and used on his trips across the border.

Abo Mariam cocks his head. My heart pounds. I don't know if he recognizes the name or if he simply finds it odd that it sounds Western.

"Who is the last person you named?" he asks.

"He is a medic. He gives Syrians first aid training. I've heard he's saved many fighters' lives," I rush to add. I list all the reasons I can think of for Abo Mariam to sympathize with Peter. He shakes his head and sighs.

"I've heard of him," he says. My heart drops. He is silent for a few seconds. "He is the American soldier."

"American soldier?" I say, feigning surprise. "But he went to the front lines to help."

"He could still have been a spy," Abo Mariam says. "We had people fighting with us on the front lines who turned out to be spies."

"How did you know? Did you catch them?"

"Because they were afraid. If a soldier fears dying and meeting God, he is not sincere. We shoot such men in the head."

I nod slowly and decide to try a different approach. "There was a rumor that Kassig was recruited by ISIS as a medic and that he's working in Raqqa."

Abo Mariam laughs. "The Islamic State has a hospital in Raqqa where their surgeons perform open-heart surgery. They don't need some first aid medic."

"Of course not," I say. "So, do you think they will let him go? Do you think they might kill him?"

"That isn't my concern, but I hope so," he says. I fear my voice will betray me if I respond, so I hold my breath and wait for Fadi to change the subject, forcing myself to stay at the table as the conversation moves on so as not to arouse suspicion. After a few agonizing minutes, I tell the men I'm a bit tired and stand to clear my plate, then walk as casually as I can toward my bedroom. Before closing the door behind me, I take one final look back at Abo Mariam, who is already distracted again by his phone, chewing and texting as if nothing has happened.

It was a mistake to have come back here. I'm so disappointed. I risked my life and have nothing to show for it—Abo Mariam will never give me any useful information, only confirm the Islamic State's brutality. It's part of a larger pattern, I realize—whenever I'm in pain, I find myself running toward the next burning building, toward more chaos. Danger distracts me from my grief. I cheated on Peter because I wanted to numb the vulnerable feelings he provoked; I crossed back to Syria after losing my mother to hide from Alia and my memories; and I keep finding more reasons and justifications to cross, even now.

But I cannot keep running. I need to face my grief and accept that there is nothing I can achieve here. I shove my camera and clothes into my backpack and zip it shut. It's one o'clock. The border closes in three hours. I sit beside the window and wait for Abo Mariam to leave. Unlike him, I want to live.

A FEW MONTHS LATER, Abo Mariam drives a truck loaded with three tons of TNT into an Iraqi military base in Haditha, a city in the Al Anbar governorate. He detonates the truck, killing himself and a dozen Shi'a soldiers. The Islamic State media congratulate him for securing a place in heaven for himself and his family. They share a photo of him captioned "A true Islamic State French knight." His wife and children will live in a refugee camp, surviving on handouts.

PART IV

THIRTY-TWO

After a ten-hour flight and a few small bottles of Turkish wine, I arrive at JFK Airport on the evening of May 24, 2014. A Syrian American I once helped in Turkey offers to drive me to the dorm in the East Village where I will be staying for the next six weeks.

The first thing I notice about New York is its smell. As we wait outside Joe's Pizza on Fourteenth Street and Third Avenue for my first meal in this country, I notice the air is filled with a mix of dough from the pizzeria and burnt chicken fat from the bright halal cart nearby, along with the fumes from cars, which, despite it being close to midnight, abound.

I can't stop myself from calculating how much the fifteen dollars we paid for our slices and drinks would equal in Turkish lira and what it would buy me there. It's a habit that will stay with me.

The next day, I meet the other photography fellows: a Brazilian, an Iranian, a Chinese, a Bosnian, and an Egyptian named Muhammad, who is two years younger than me and began photographing the Egyptian uprising when he was only eighteen. Since the protests I first watched on television at home in Jableh almost three years earlier, Islamists have hijacked Egypt's uprising just as they have Syria's. Young people find themselves faced with an impossible choice: Join the religious radicals or an equally brutal secular army.

The last photos Muhammad captured in Egypt were taken in Rabaa Square in Cairo, where thousands had gathered to protest the new president, Abdel Fattah al-Sisi, who had assumed power after a coup. The protest turned into one of the most horrifying days in recent Egyptian history when the government opened fire on the crowd, killing hundreds of civilians. Egypt's state media reported that the protesters were armed Salafists. Muhammad's older brother, Abdullah, was detained for covering the events for Al Jazeera. By the time we landed in New York, he had already been incarcerated for nine months. Now, he is on a hunger strike, and Muhammad is trying to free him by bringing media attention to his plight.

There are many reasons why I feel an instant connection to Muhammad. For both of us, unlike the other fellows, photography is not something we chose because we had an affinity for it; it is what we had to do to support our people. We both know not to ask questions about the bloody images we show the other students. When the fellowship ends, we will both return to our countries of refuge, not our countries of birth. Finally, and most important, we both know the pain of having a loved one in detention.

We avoid the subject with one another. Instead, we try to make each other laugh. We have our shared language, Arabic, and we use it to joke about New Yorkers' pride in bagels and their ignorance of what is happening on our side of the world. We don't join our classmates' tourist trips to Times Square or walks across the Brooklyn Bridge. Instead, we seek out hookah bars or Middle Eastern restaurants and have lengthy conversations with the Arab men our age who run the halal carts. I never need to explain to Muhammad why I am not interested in seeing more of New York. We both prefer to stay fixated on our phones, obsessively following the news.

As the weeks progress, my time is divided between attending lectures, looking up new English words, taking photos for assignments, and stopping people on subway platforms to ask for directions. The lessons all aim at teaching us to slow down. Long-term photography projects are about building trust and returning to the same subject repeatedly. Photography for me has always been click and run. Slowing down to compose a shot feels impossible. Anytime I click the shutter, I feel the urge to flee. What kept me alive and sane in Syria is working against me here.

From the US, I am finally able to appreciate everything I took for granted in Turkey: the hookah smoke flavoring the streets, the Arabic chatter in the background, the food, and the vegetables and fruits sold by the kilo, not individually. I even miss how, in Turkey, I couldn't escape the news from Syria because Syrians were everywhere. Here, the dismissive "Ah, nice" I get when I mention Syria reminds me that my country is too distant to be relevant. "It is near Iraq," I say, attempting to explain where I come from. When Laila calls to ask if I love New York and if I've made any friends yet, I tell her about Muhammad and how glad I am that there is at least "one of us" here, because otherwise, by now, I would have lost my mind.

A WEEK BEFORE the fellowship ends, Muhammad's brother is released from jail. He arranges a Skype call between his brother and our classmates and teachers. He wants us and the directors of the program to hear about the horrifying incarceration conditions in Egypt. When Abdullah's image appears on the whiteboard, his face is pale and sunken between two slouching shoulders. He tells us he has lost more than fifty pounds.

"Trust me," Muhammad says, "our mother will make sure you gain back everything you have lost within a week."

The whole class bursts into laughter. I force a laugh, too, trying to conceal how much it upsets me to see Muhammad glow with happiness in the projector light. I mimic the rest of the class by asking questions about Abdullah's health and the events that led to his arrest. I nod during his answers, fearing that everyone else will notice how bitter I am.

I barely talk to Muhammad after that Skype call, though I am furious with myself for not being able to be happy for him. How can I feel that his brother's release is somehow, in my warped frame of mind, a betrayal of our bond? But I can't help it. I can't suppress burning resentment when I see him laughing and talking on the phone, walking up and down the hallway chatting with friends, celebrating the release. I despise his happiness, how it forces me to remember that detention doesn't always mean death. He will be reunited with his brother, but I will never be reunited with my mother, and Peter is still missing. Muhammad and I are not the same; he is not one of us.

One morning, I walk into the library and see the front page of *The New York Times*. The Islamic State has overtaken Mosul in northern Iraq, and they are growing stronger every day. Raqqa, Mezar's city, their capital, has become world-famous for the number of foreign fighters it is hosting. From the university library, where the world ostensibly revolves around photography and art and scoring a coffee appointment with a photo editor, I scroll through social media for updates. My feeds are filled with ISIS members posting photos of their food and joking that in Raqqa, you can find anything you want, even Pringles. The world seems to have agreed that Syria is fit to host these people. I find it jarring. Twitter has become ISIS's main recruiting platform. It is suffocating to think that these men can cross into my country whenever they want, whereas I may never be able to return.

When I ask them about ISIS, my friends who are still in Idlib and

DEFIANCE

Aleppo tell me coming back isn't impossible and everything is fine, and I imagine that I would say the same if I were there, consumed as I can be by my own denial and wishful thinking. But at a distance, I can see the situation more clearly; I know it's not safe, and if I can't cross into Syria, I increasingly feel that there's no reason for me to go back to Turkey.

I start researching ways to stay in the US. The money I saved under my mattress in Turkey will support me for the next two months—the length of my visa—until I find another program or fellowship. My only other option is to apply for asylum, though that would mean admitting that Syria will never be an option again with a finality I'm not quite ready to accept.

The cheapest room I can find is in Bushwick, a neighborhood of Brooklyn. The building reeks of cigarette smoke, and my room has no walls, only sheets hanging from water pipes. The stairs are always littered with piles marked "free stuff," which clothe me for the rest of the summer. Most of my neighbors are artists and quite friendly, often inviting me to spend time with them and their friends. Every day, I climb the stairs to the rooftop, where I am offered beer and joints. I spend evenings listening to them take turns playing music, singing, and gazing at the skyline, reminding each other how fortunate they are to be living in this city. The fascination with New York never makes much sense to me. I never consider myself lucky to be here. Despite being surrounded by people, I feel lonely and isolated. Everything is so alive, but I am stuck in my own mind, trapped in a fog of sadness. I miss my Syrian friends and the collective pain and exile that brought us together. We shared a past and looked forward to the same future.

"At least you speak English!" Naji tells me when I call him one day and start crying as I try to convey how lonely I am and wonder if I could get my job back at Laila's organization. It's true that I speak English, but not my neighbors' English. I often sit silently as they make jokes, having no clue what they're laughing about. Language doesn't suffice to ease the sense of alienation—sometimes it can even deepen it, revealing just enough for me to grasp how different our lives really are and how excluded I am from the collective memories they share. Toward the end of every night, when I am often so drunk that I have to ask one of my neighbors to help me down the stairs, I get into bed and spend hours on Skype or a messenger service, chatting and laughing with Mezar and other friends in Turkey until I fall asleep.

AT THE END OF the summer, I am awarded a full scholarship to a year-long photojournalism program at the International Center of Photography. It is a relief to have been afforded more time, but I am sure they regret offering me a spot since I find I can barely pay attention. While other students take notes and ask questions, I keep my head down, my attention locked on the news on my phone. Al Qaeda–affiliated groups are now targeting brigades that have received support from the West and are taking over their bases, money, and arms. The areas that were recently rid of ISIS are now being occupied by other Islamist groups. Rebel commanders and activists who returned to Syria, believing the threat of ISIS was gone, are now fleeing to Turkey once again.

Due to the seven-hour time difference, by the time I wake up, a whole new cycle of news is there for me to absorb. Some teachers start placing a box in the room to stow our phones during class. Although they don't explicitly mention my name, I know the effort is directed at me. By the middle of the first semester, whenever I see an email from the program director asking me to stop by her office, I know it's to talk about my phone usage and how I've been given a massive opportunity, a scholarship no other student received, and that I shouldn't waste it.

I promise her I will focus, but privately, I give myself permission to bend the rules. It's easier to lie than try to explain the uncontrollable trembling of my hands when my phone buzzes. It is my only connection to the country I left behind.

For years, we collectively deluded ourselves by insisting that our losses were a tragic but necessary part of the struggle. This was the price we were paying for a better future for ourselves and our children. But now, as our losses continue to accrue while our confidence wanes, any notification might bring either renewed hope or the final blow to our dreams.

THIRTY-THREE

One weekend afternoon, as I'm riding the Brooklyn-bound M train back to my room in Bushwick, my body swaying with the movement of the train, I feel my phone vibrate. I glance down to read the notification immediately, as always. It is a message from a Syrian friend in Turkey.

"Have you seen the video?" the message reads.

"What video?" I respond.

My friend forwards a hyperlink. I click on it, expecting it to be another report of a conflict or battle.

But as the video starts to play, I realize this is something entirely different. It's an execution video released by ISIS, issued as a challenge to the United States and as retaliation for Western military interventions in the Middle East. These gruesome videos follow a similar pattern: A single hostage kneels, a masked man wields a knife and makes threats, then slices the hostage's neck and watches them bleed out. Toward the end of the video, ISIS introduces the next victim they are threatening to slaughter. This time, to my horror, that person is Peter.

The text "Peter Edward Kassig" appears in one corner of the screen, leaving no room for doubt. There he is, wearing an orange jumpsuit, kneeling while the masked man clutches his collar with one hand and brandishes a knife with the other. I raise the volume, but the subway roars and shakes, making it difficult to hear what is being said. I pause the video and stare at Peter's face. It can't be him. This is the first time I've seen him since that evening in Antep when I rushed to leave our date with sweat gathering between my palms, gripping the plastic-wrapped flowers he had given me—the flowers I left behind in the taxi. He has lost weight, and his golden hair and wide smile, the features that drew me to him, are gone. I cling to the train's cold hanger pole with one hand and my phone with the other. My stomach churns when I realize that the only reason I'm seeing him again now is because he is next to be killed.

I turn away and close my eyes. This is not happening. This cannot be real. The train stops and the station is announced. I open my eyes as people step out and the mix of smells unique to Myrtle-Broadway seeps in: the comforting whiffs of fried chicken from Popeyes, the sharp tang of urine, heavy exhaust fumes, and the lingering odor of trash.

"Stand clear . . . closing doors." The wheels below begin to turn and screech. The cars lurch forward. Nothing ceases. Life flows on. Commuters read or rest, eyes on their phones or closed or staring off into the distance, headphones on their ears. Normality glides forward, slowly, rapidly, ineluctably, perpetually. It is horrifying how life can go on uninterrupted despite all the agony taking place elsewhere on the same earth. How is it that the whole world does not pause and come together to do something, anything, to stop this—or at least to mourn?

Thoughts race through my mind the rest of the day as I try to stay calm. I tell myself that Peter and I were not that serious, that I cheated on him, that I had urged him not to go, and that I had done my best to warn him. I remind myself that it was his decision, in the end. He decided to cross. I should grieve him as a friend, and he is not the only friend I have lost in this war. I try to recall all the people I have grieved and how my sadness did not kill me. This is a dark period that will eventually pass. Life flows on.

Later that night, as I lie in bed, Alia calls me. She asks if I have seen the video. I try my best to collect myself and convince her that she shouldn't worry for me. Alia tells me I can call her if I need anything, but I assure her I am fine and change the subject to my coursework. I mention that I have a locker like the ones in the shows and movies we used to watch, and I struggle with the combination. But as the call winds down, she asks if she can forward me an email.

It's a message that Peter sent her over a year ago. When I open it, I see that he cc'd his lawyer and a colleague. It begins with an apology for any stress the note may cause, then continues:

> This is simply a necessary step that needs to be taken to ensure the proper arrangements are made in the highly unlikely event that something happens to me. I have added Loubna's sister Alia to this email as I deeply trust her and need for her to be a part of handling affairs if something does happen. However, in the unlikely event that something does/has . . . occurred, these are my last wishes as I would like to see them carried out. Please respect them for what they are. I am sure it is not a legally binding document, but I would trust my friends and family to honor them as I would for any of you should I be in your position. Simply put, find a way to make it work. Turns out I can still be a pain in the ass! Basically, I will probably have some exorbitant amount of Student Loan debt . . . I don't know what they do with that when you die. I think they should forget it but I am sure the

Federal Government will do anything but. As I understand it, I will have some amount of money that has accumulated over time from stocks, bonds, and mutual funds. I have no idea how much it will be but it should be a good enough sum to do something with. Here is what I would like to see it used for. My mother and father should have whatever is needed for them to account for what expenses they have incurred on my behalf. Plus, their choice of whatever personal effects there are of mine. They have an exclusive right to these things at their discretion. Loubna Mrie is to receive the remainder of my assets to be used for her education and whatever else she needs in order to build a life and a future for herself. I understand from my father that there should be enough for a down payment on a house or something to that effect. Loubna is to have this money in order to have what she needs for a future wherever she wants it to be. Though I do not pretend to know exactly what the future holds for the two of us right now, I know that I have never loved a woman like I love her, and she is the strongest most resilient person that I have ever met, short of my mother, and Loubna deserves whatever I can give her in order to have the life that she deserves. The remainder of my financial resources are to be given to the Syrian people, in a direct and efficient manner of material aid to immediately affect suffering, poverty, sickness, and injury. I urge those of you who will read this email to come to an educated and informed consensus on how to do that in the most effective way. I am really sorry for doing whatever somewhat stupid thing I did to land you in front of a computer reading this email but please remember that whatever it was, it was a part of a larger attempt to bring about some positive change in dark places. With Love and Utmost Respect, Peter.

The email breaks me. I wish I hadn't seen it. It strips me of the lies I've put together to move on, to dull the pain. I can no longer deny that Peter was a major part of my life. Though he knew his work was dangerous, he could never have predicted that he would be on the precipice of such a brutal death. I feel so much rage inside I want to burn Raqqa, the so-called capital of their so-called state, and everyone there to the ground. I will torch every last one of them, one at a time, into oblivion.

My Facebook feed fills with conspiracy theories about Peter. People who only briefly crossed paths with him offer their opinions. They are convinced that Americans don't care about Syrians, so any American on the ground must be a spy. Some are angry about the disproportionate attention given to videos of white hostages, questioning why the West only seems to care when one of their own dies in our land, treating our deaths and losses as inevitable collateral. It is sickening to see this level of fury and skepticism directed toward the victim, not the oppressor. It is a continuation and an echo of the justifications we've made throughout the war, blaming ourselves in order to cope, to stay sane, to pretend we still had control.

Now, I see more clearly than ever how the conflict has deranged us all. I feel an intense, overwhelming hatred for my country—the nation I loved and gave everything for, but which gave me nothing in return but pain. I hate it for all the agony and sorrow it causes. It feels like being a Syrian is somehow a punishment from God, the reasons for which I'll never understand.

The following day, a pixelated screenshot from the video of Peter wearing an orange jumpsuit is splashed across the front page of the *New York Daily News*. The headline, in bold white font, reads "U.S. Vet Is Next" beside Peter's face, as if his execution is a teaser for readers to buy the paper's next issue. Seeing his murder sensationalized is nauseating in its disregard for Peter's friends and family who haven't stopped praying for his safety.

How cruel that his entire being—his love, his courage, the smell of him, his laugh, his eyeroll-inducing jokes, his warmth and kindness, all the life that radiated from him—is now reduced to his most recent identification as another American hostage about to be slaughtered by ISIS. How unfair for Peter that most people will only ever know him this way.

I worry that, eventually, I will become one of them—that, years later, his public execution is all I will recall of the man who, two springs ago, when I was convinced that my life had ended, took my hand and made me see colors again. In his presence I came to believe that the tulips and cherry trees of April in Istanbul had bloomed thanks to him and not the rotation of the earth. He told me that all the loss and pain I went through were just a chapter that would not define who I am but would make me stronger. I miss him so intensely I have trouble breathing. In my inner eye, I see him in his buttoned-up white shirt, his sleeves rolled up to his elbows, walking through the office door, his eyes large and green and focused on me, forcing me to duck behind my laptop to hide my embarrassment. I see him outside my front door in Istanbul after a long day of work, holding a bunch of tulips, their plastic wrapping crackling between us as he wraps his arms around me. I feel the dry skin around his nails as he brushes a finger under my eyes to wipe my tears, and the warmth of his palms encasing mine, promising everything will be okay.

It was Peter who told me I would have my own family one day, that there would be joy and beauty in my future. I always believed that the force that would inevitably separate us would be his desire to escape the chaos and suffering my country and I brought into his life. Never did I imagine that I would be here, in his country without him and alone, forcing myself to keep going, trying not to collapse under the weight of his impending death in order to pursue my education, something he believed I was capable of long before I even had the courage to try.

I walk fast, looking down, refusing to glance at the papers stacked outside newsstands, refusing to allow that image of him to sink in and replace all my other mental images of Peter, those I must cherish and protect. All our fights seem so stupid now. I hate myself every time I reread his last email, remembering how cold I was to him, walking away when he cried. Now he is captive, helpless, fatigued, kneeling, and bound. Though I want to believe that he may still be rescued somehow, the situation seems hopeless; I know the kind of brutality ISIS is capable of.

As the days pass, I think of Peter's mother, Paula. I know I should find a way to contact her, but I can't bring myself to do it. What is the right thing to say to a mother whose son's imminent execution is being broadcast on every news channel? My brain is in a constant argument with itself. One side tells me that Paula has every reason to hate me, Syria, Syrians, and anyone who has ever crossed paths with her son. All of us who painted a glowing, heroic, optimistic image of the uprising are responsible for her pain. I feel personally responsible. I feel that my decision to leave the organization and Istanbul resulted, in one way or another, in Peter's decision to put himself in harm's way. The other side assures me that it is egotistical to imagine that I lured Peter down that path. It wasn't me. It was his clear-eyed sense of morality that fueled his desire to do more to help, something that predated our relationship. Yet blaming myself and the others who encouraged him to go to Syria is easier than admitting that we lost control over the uprising long ago. The future of Syria and whatever happens within its borders is not up to us and hasn't been for a very long time.

This dispute lives in my head alone. I cannot talk with anyone. Who in Bushwick could I turn to? My only friends are photography students who are anxious about landing internships or moving apartments. Syria, Peter, and my mother are alien in this landscape of exile. How aware are those around me that ISIS is kidnapping and killing hostages whose only mistake was to care too much, in a country where barrel bombs bury entire sleeping families under their homes, and where the government has imprisoned thousands of people who will never again see the light of day?

DEFIANCE

. . .

Though getting out of bed each morning seems almost impossible, I have to keep moving forward. If I stop, I will lose my scholarship. Each day, I force myself onto the train and go to class. Once there, I put my phone away. Finally, I do not want to know what is happening outside the walls of our classrooms with their glossy prints of our assignments. The demanding workload saves me, leaving next to no time to think of anything else. I spend hours on the subway from the Bronx to Brooklyn, taking portraits and sidewalk shots of small businesses. I buy a 35mm film camera from my roommate for ten dollars, which has a shoelace in lieu of a strap, and set my digital camera aside.

Using an analog camera demands that I spend hours each evening in a dimly lit darkroom where the air is heavy and moist and smells of vinegar. I wear yellow gloves and immerse them in chemical solutions. My world here shrinks down to the seconds I need to get the right exposure. Every tick of the clock develops a new layer. And each mistake and bad frame can be tossed away and replaced with a new, blank paper. I am in control. And here, in the darkroom, phones are not allowed; the light of incoming notifications will blur the printing images. For the first time ever, I avoid my phone. It can only inform me that Peter is being executed, slaughtered. Any newsfeed might show me his bloodied body. Here, in the darkroom, I am protected.

Most nights, I leave the darkroom after nine o'clock, take the train home, climb the stairs to my room, and lie down without taking my jacket off. Sometimes, a few of the lingering students and I go for drinks and dollar-a-slice pizza a few blocks away from school. Drinking, as always, reveals the version of me I don't want others to see—weak, silent, often on the verge of tears. Alcohol scares me. I do not want to lose control over my thoughts and grief, but I also cannot stop drinking. I often leave the bar without saying goodbye and wake up in my apartment, pain pounding in my head. I hate how poor, isolated, and lonely I am. I want to do what I know how to do best—leave. I want to go back to Turkey. There, at least, I am surrounded by people who understand my pain.

Because my room does not have walls, every sound travels easily to the other side of the loft where my roommate, Molly, lives. One fall morning, Molly's voice comes through the white sheets to ask if I'm okay—she heard me crying the night before. I assure her I am fine.

"It's probably seasonal depression. It's common in New York in October," she informs me, and I agree with her. I want to be seen as normal. I want to blame the gray clouds, persistent drizzle, and soggy yellow and brown leaves lining our block for my sadness.

Molly makes her living by working at a "witch shop" a few blocks away. She charges money for reading cards with weird images of swords and owls that are supposed to predict the future and tell us what lessons we can learn from the past. She is allegedly so good at interpreting these cards that in the first three minutes of meeting anyone, she tells them that she once did so for Justin Bieber.

That morning, she offers me a free "Reiki healing session" because my sad energy might contaminate our shared home. I sit on the yellow love seat in our common space as she lights a small sprig of sage on a copper plate. The rising smoke curls into the still air. "Close your eyes," Molly says. For a few minutes, her hands hover over my eyelids. She breathes heavily. I tighten my lips, struggling not to laugh, when it dawns on me how, even in a place like New York, much like Jableh with its mountains and shrines, people believe there is some mystic power out there that can heal and cleanse you. For some reason, these rituals must include a copper plate with something burning, whether it's incense or sage.

A few minutes pass. Molly announces that I have not been an easy case: I had a weighty sadness. But now she has lifted it from my soul. She tells me that I should feel happy within a few hours.

DEFIANCE

Throughout the next few weeks, I allow myself quick glimpses into news reports about efforts to save Peter. His parents release a video pleading with his captors for mercy. I don't watch it. I refuse to nurture any hope that Peter might be saved. The main lesson this war has taught me is that clinging to hope only prolongs our pain and agony. It is always better to take a shortcut, grieve the loss, and move on. I know Peter is gone. It is only a matter of time before they kill him.

On November 16, my phone buzzes in my pocket as I'm doing the dishes in the kitchen. I quickly wipe one hand and open a message from Naji: "May his soul rest in peace." He doesn't need to say anything else; I know it means that Peter is dead, and now the internet holds a video of his execution.

I have been terrified of my reaction upon the video's release, wondering if it would be the final blow to my sanity. But when Peter's death is finally confirmed, I am stunned to find that I am almost completely numb. I sense a tiny flicker of relief in my heart. People released from ISIS jails often said the same thing that always stayed with me: "ISIS's guards made us wish for death." Peter is now at peace, and he is no longer suffering. That is a small, sickening comfort. I turn off my phone and finish rinsing my plates.

I fear myself in the days that follow. I know that the minute I drink again, I will watch the video. When it happens, as I knew it would, I regret it. Peter was not slaughtered like the other kidnapped victims who were bound and helpless. No, his video is different. All I see is Peter's bloodied head lying on the dusty ground. Just his head on the ground, no body, while the fighter talks in a thick British accent about how Peter killed people in Iraq—something he told me he never did.

I take a screenshot and zoom in. In Peter's face, I see marks of a struggle.

I know he did everything he could to resist as they recorded the video to broadcast to the world. I can imagine him spitting on the executioner's mask and punching back until the very end. He would have refused to sit quietly and obediently as they took his life away. In the end, I know why ISIS could not release the full recording: Showing his resistance would have revealed too much of the weakness, ineptitude, and pathetic cowardice of these men pretending to be "God's Warriors"—imposters too afraid to show their faces as they murder another innocent man.

THIRTY-FOUR

A year later, in the summer of 2015, the days leading up to my graduation from ICP are as uncomfortable for me as witnessing that Skype call between Muhammad and his newly freed brother. I hand out my extra ceremony tickets to other students whose family members in town outnumber their allotment. I try to stay calm, telling myself it's not a big deal that none of my friends and family can be here to see me graduate. Although I don't share the details with anyone, I can't help but feel pathetic and judged when I give all my white envelopes away.

At the ceremony itself, the suffocating loneliness I feel as I watch other students being embraced and celebrated is just another reminder that this place is not my home. I comfort myself with the thought that, now that I have graduated, I can visit Turkey—both to see my friends who remain there and to put my newly improved journalism skills to use.

Like many people around the world at the time, I'm haunted by the story of a two-year-old boy, Alan Kurdi, whose family was attempting to cross into Europe via the Mediterranean Sea when the overloaded inflatable raft carrying them and other Syrian refugees capsized after leaving Bodrum, a city on the western coast of Turkey. The harrowing image of his small, drowned body lying face down in the sand has made global headlines, calling attention to the increasingly dire refugee crisis. Alan's hometown had been mercilessly besieged by ISIS that spring. After being denied asylum in Canada, his family was forced to make the desperate choice that would result in Alan's death.

Watching the coverage from afar, it seems that the media wants us Syrians to be as apolitical as possible, and that the nuances in the story of the uprising are being lost. The men who operate the cheap rafts, charging thousands of dollars in exchange for seats, are criminals to many, but for those who have no other options, they are the only hands offering a chance at a new life. They are not entirely to blame for the drownings and deaths. Assad is to blame. ISIS is to blame. And so is the entire rest of the world, which does not have a functional system to process and deal with the needs of refugees. I decide I want to attempt to cover the refugee crisis more deeply than the mainstream press.

Two weeks after seeing the picture of Alan, I land in Istanbul with a Colombian photographer named Miguel who was in my class at ICP. It doesn't take long to see that Turkey has become foreign to me. Since I've been gone, Alia has moved to France, and soon plans to travel to the UK to continue her education. Laila has just left for Berlin, where she swears the Syrian food is better than it is at home. Mezar is still in Turkey, but he's in a new relationship with a Lebanese woman and, just like I was when I met Peter, is taking shelter in his happy bubble, which leaves him no time to hang out like we used to.

"Anyone who can afford it is leaving" is a phrase I hear repeatedly throughout my trip. Some are fleeing the war, its relentlessness, the mortar rounds being fired back and forth between the many sides of the conflict. Some are fleeing poverty and insecurity, seeing no future in either Syria or the "visitor" status they've been assigned in Turkey. Others are escaping mandatory military service in government-controlled areas. Everyone has one thing in common—they would rather face the risks of the journey than die without trying to reach a life of safety and opportunity.

On the beach at Bodrum, the shoreline is littered with clothing, shoes, suitcases, notebooks, and life vests. I find myself wondering about the fate of each item's original owner. I leave Miguel and walk alone down the beach to sit on a wet rock. As my feet sink into the sand, I feel a hard object and dig up a photo album with "Studio Bassam" printed on its leatherette folder. The salt water has turned its pages greenish. It hurts to know that someone recently held this album, one of the few items they had chosen to take on their journey, while standing in line to board a raft. In the best-case scenario, there was no space on the raft for the extra baggage, leaving them no choice but to cast off their memories of a past life for the chance to start a new one.

The seawater laps at my legs as I wade in, watching the sun sink behind the horizon. Kos, the Greek island that is the destination for the migrants' boats, emerges in the middle of the sea. I go deeper into the water, holding my camera over my head. I realize that this is the last thing someone drowning would see as they battle for their life.

In that moment, I feel a strange hatred toward the water itself. It is hard to believe that the Aegean Sea is part of the same Mediterranean whose aroma could instantly transport me back to my balcony in Jableh. It used to excite me when the first thick wave of humidity arrived, signaling the start of summer with its corniche walks and beach trips. But now, just like everything related to home, the Mediterranean is tainted with pain and agony. With hundreds and soon to be thousands of deaths in its waters, it has become a mass grave.

LOUBNA MRIE

. . .

I MAKE A VISIT TO NAJI, who is still training journalists in Antep, now mainly coordinating with a group of activists inside Raqqa who are documenting life under the rule of the Islamic State. On the couch in his living room, I sip my tea as we talk about Russia's involvement in the conflict, its bombs and planes supporting the Syrian government in its battle to stay in power. We talk about the bodies floating upon the sea and the siege of the Damascus suburbs, where people are boiling and eating tree leaves for sustenance. He brings up Peter's death and asks if I went to his funeral. I am embarrassed to admit that I couldn't face it; that even calling Peter's mother felt like a huge burden, and I struggled for so long to make it happen.

I tell him how, when I finally worked up the courage to reach out to her—around Thanksgiving—I had had a few drinks, so I cannot recall much of what was said. But I do remember that her voice was surprisingly deep, soft, and calm. I was solely focused on not crying. What I do remember clearly is the throbbing pain in my chest as I stood looking at myself in the mirror, picking away the wine-stained chapped skin on my lower lip. And I remember that, after we hung up, when I finally let myself cry, an unexpected wave of peace came over me—the first I'd felt since the first video of Peter was released.

As usual, when the conversation grows heavy, Naji finds a way to divert it. He shows me his electronic cigarette and jokes that it's healthier than normal cigarettes and allows him to work without incurring complaints from neighbors and colleagues about the incessant smell. So much has changed, but Naji has managed to retain the same spirit since we first met in Amer's studio.

When it's time for me to leave, he gives me a warm hug. My heart sinks. I have a dreadful sense that I won't see him again. This is our final goodbye.

"I can leave the US whenever I want," I tell him. "I haven't applied for asylum, so I can still travel. I want to come back and work here."

"No!" Naji says. "Everyone is trying to leave. Forget about Turkey; go where your future is. There's nothing left for us here."

"How can I feel at home in a city where I've barely known anyone for more than a year?"

"I'm thirty-six and have two kids, and I still believe I can start over. You're twenty-four. You have no excuse not to push through and build a new life. It's not safe here, trust me," he says.

Miraculously, Naji and his family are among the lucky few who are approved for political asylum in France—the only European country that has been granting Syrians asylum through its consulates in Turkey. He tells me that he has been receiving death threats from ISIS, and recounts one particularly terrifying story about discovering a small bomb under his car. I feel myself leaning toward denial. If the Islamic State has the power to reach into Turkey and kill people, wouldn't they murder rebel leaders instead? Why target such a minor figure? I decide not to take the threats too seriously, but I'm glad Naji was able to use them as a way out.

We hug one more time before I go, and I promise to visit him and his family in their new home. Their flight is scheduled to depart a day before New Year's Eve.

That winter, after returning from Turkey, I concentrate on my graduate school and asylum applications in addition to working full time. I move to the third floor of my apartment building where, through my room's windows, I can see the Empire State Building's spire with its Christmas colors glowing through the cold fog.

I am covering the glass with taped-up sheets of plastic wrap—a way to prevent the freezing air from seeping through the cracks around the windowpanes—when my phone buzzes. I can't take it out of my pocket right away; my hands are wrestling with strips of tape and tangled plastic. It buzzes again. And again. When I finally manage to unlock the phone and open the Facebook message, I crumple onto the floor, my back against the window, the plastic sheet sagging from the frigid glass behind me. Naji has been shot in the head in Antep.

I learn that Naji's wife and daughters had been at home packing while Naji went to pick up lunch from one of their favorite Syrian restaurants. He was walking to his car, food in hand, when someone pressed a gun against his head, fired, and fled. He died before the ambulance arrived. Later that night, ISIS announces they orchestrated his assassination.

The next day, I watch videos of Naji's funeral from *The Atlantic*'s media offices, where I am completing another yearlong journalism fellowship. The rows of desks are empty. Everyone else has left for the Christmas break, but I have nowhere to go, and the office has snacks and is much warmer than my apartment. I drink leftover vodka from the staff Christmas party as I watch hundreds of people follow Naji's casket in the procession. Although Naji was not a public figure, the news of his murder in Turkey pains even those who did not know him. Turkey was supposed to be our refuge; Naji's assassination proves that nowhere is safe.

In the videos, I see his wife leaning on the shoulders of two of her friends, her long black hair falling over the green revolutionary flag that covers her shoulders. She tilts her head backward, mouth open, sobbing. She slides her palms along the casket's dark brown wood.

It is devastating not be there to say goodbye, to grieve alongside his wife and our friends. I hate myself for assuming the danger he told me about wasn't real and for being half a world away, safe in a city decorated in twinkling lights, basking in the scents of cinnamon and apple cider.

Perhaps because the killer is affiliated with ISIS, or perhaps because it happened in Antep, where many Western journalists are living, major publications cover Naji's assassination. Journalists write about Naji the reporter, Naji the Syrian who wanted his country free of all dictatorship—in the form of both the bearded fundamentalist extremists and the clean-shaven secular men. I knew these Najis, of course, but I also knew Naji the husband, Naji the father, Naji the mentor who first empowered me to pick up a camera. Naji died before he was able to do what he wanted to do the most—start over. Meanwhile, I am here, safe, alive, and still shattered.

The following day, I write an article about Naji and what he has meant to me. By the time I finish, night has fallen. I forward the piece to one of the editors I work with at the office, tighten my wool scarf around my ears, and head out onto the street, setting off toward the subway station at Union Square. As a cold wind blows into my face, something lifts from my chest, and I feel a strange sense of relief. It is the first time I realize the comfort writing can bring, and I wonder if it's true—that pain and trauma are like vampires walking the earth in the dark, and that exposing them to light can diminish their power over us.

Though I've always told myself and others that I would eventually return to Syria, I've finally come to terms with the fact that I have nothing left to return to. My naive belief that my losses would not be in vain, and that my mother's death was not in vain, vanishes. It is time for me to let go of Syria and consider New York my new home.

This revelation gradually helps me settle. I first notice that my mindset has changed when someone asks for my phone number, and I realize that I have it memorized. When people stop me for directions on the subway platform, I no longer avoid them and keep walking like I used to; now, I can give them an answer without a map.

Unlike when I was in Turkey, I have allowed myself to learn many of the street names and addresses in my new city. There is none of the sense of urgency I once felt. My apartment in Brooklyn has become my most permanent address since I left my mother's home in Jableh. I know my neighbors by name, and some of them are now real friends. On Sundays, my whole building gathers for a weekly family dinner. We talk and drink together, and I find myself understanding and laughing at their jokes unselfconsciously. I no longer have to make up names and phone numbers to fill out the empty emergency contact fields on my applications; I have people I know will show up for me when I need them. Later, I begin a master's program in Near Eastern studies at NYU on a full scholarship. My classes range from history and politics to art and literature.

DESPITE THESE FOOTHOLDS, my future remains uncertain. That fall, I sit in a bar with my close friends, eyes locked on the TV, and watch the states turn red, one by one, as Donald Trump is elected president. I find it hard to swallow that millions have voted for a man who has promised to send me back to my death. For the next few weeks, I wake up anxious every day. I wonder if my asylum case is going to be rejected. I wonder if I made a huge mistake by coming here.

As time passes, I fear school may also have been a mistake. Compared to the other students, I seem to move in slow motion. It takes me two hours to read what native English speakers can absorb in twenty minutes. The margins of my books and papers are covered with translations and definitions of words I have never encountered before. I sit silently in class discussions on genocides and democracy.

At the library, I follow the news on Syria. By now, the government forces have seized most of the rebel-held territories through mass destruction and starvation. The world watches, releases statements, signs petitions, approves insufficient aid measures, and does everything but save lives.

A few weeks before Christmas, I open an email from one of my professors giving me feedback on a paper. I click on the Word document and am horrified to see that the first half is all red. I close my laptop, step outside the room, and sit on the floor, sobbing and shaking uncontrollably.

My friend Rohan follows me and puts his hand on my shoulder. "Loubna, it's just a paper. It's not even a final paper!" he says. He reassures me that when a professor spends this much time giving detailed feedback, it means they care. "It is a positive thing! This is how you learn!" he adds.

I know it's just one goddamn paper—why am I so devastated? The air seems to have been sucked out of the room. Rohan's confusion embarrasses me, but I can't stop crying. He stares at me helplessly, suggesting we go for pizza or tacos or fries, whatever I want. "Just please calm down!" he says. It takes me almost twenty minutes to regain control of myself. I make Rohan promise never to tell anyone about my meltdown.

But it happens again—and again and again—all for the seemingly silliest reasons, like losing my keys or not finding enough quarters for the laundromat. It's as if someone else inside me is taking hold. Friends suggest finding a therapist, but I don't see the point. Why waste time and money speaking to someone who will never understand what I've been through? Therapy is for privileged Americans. I don't need it.

In March 2018, news emerges from the rebel-held Damascus suburbs that government forces have cut off all roads, placing the area under siege. Although most of the rebel-held areas have either been decimated or restored to government control by now, for me, the siege of the uprising's last stronghold in Damascus marks the end of another dream. It is where I attended my first protest, witnessed my first killing. The buildings that echoed my first chants, the first time I heard my voice. The first time I had enough courage to see what standing up against injustice could mean.

The place that gave me the bravery I needed to later oppose my father and his abuse and to choose my own path instead of the future he wanted for me. Those whose courage inspired me to speak up are now pleading with Islamic clerics to issue fatwas that will allow them to eat stray cats and dogs.

I try to help by writing. I reach out to people inside Ghouta and ask about the siege and starvation. Through WhatsApp, I interview a relief worker. Their words and a few more end up in a cover story for *Time* magazine.

LATER THAT MONTH, I am in a grocery store near Death Valley on a spring break trip. As I wait in the checkout line, I see a woman, probably in her mid-forties, gazing at the magazine on the stand, which features a cover photo of three rescue workers. The light from their headlamps shines on the dust clouding their feet. I feel the urge to step closer and tell her that one of the men on the cover died a few days ago while trying to rescue a toddler trapped under the roof of his own house.

I want to flip through the pages and force her to read about children dying of hunger because a brutal government is imposing collective punishment on a population that simply asked for change. I want to tell her how painful it is that their stories, and many more, are competing for attention next to covers that feature YouTube influencers, keto diet insights, and twenty-four must-try tofu recipes, as if they all have the same level of importance. My heart aches, but I force myself to look away as the woman extends her arm, picks up a copy of *Bon Appétit*, and proceeds to pay.

How can we compel people to care? It's not like 2011 when we naively thought the world wasn't helping because they simply didn't know about our suffering. Now, everyone knows. How is it possible that the Syrian government, after all the atrocities and injustices they have committed, is still in power? To me, this sends one clear message to future generations in the Arab world, and to every repressed nation across the globe: If people want change and speak up, they will be starved and slaughtered; if journalists cover their stories, in the hope of enabling this change, it will make no difference.

I leave the market and do what I know how to do best: push my feelings aside and pretend that nothing major just happened. I focus on the moment and remind myself how lucky I am to be alive, to breathe, and to have a second chance in life.

ON THE SAME TRIP, I try psychedelics for the first time, and a surprising sense of warmth embraces me. It allows my mind to wander through my childhood with such vivid detail that when I close my eyes, I can smell the burnt oranges on the heater in my living room in Jableh and my mother's rosewater.

The rest of the day, I hike up and down boulders in Joshua Tree. I find myself crying, and for the first time in years, I let myself remember my mother and feel her presence without the overwhelming sense of guilt—the guilt that, for years, made me believe my pain was my fault. I blamed myself for what my father did, allowing him to tarnish her memory as he tried to convince me that her death was my fault, not his.

I allow myself to grieve her, to feel grateful for being raised and shaped by her. I feel intense gratitude that she shielded my sister and me from what my father was trying to instill in us. In a society and family structured to convince us that our lives should revolve around proving ourselves worthy of our father's wealth or finding the right husband, she encouraged us to look beyond those expectations. Rather than conforming to societal norms, she urged us to question and determine what we truly needed for ourselves. I wonder if I never allowed myself to grieve because, somehow, if I didn't allow myself to mourn her, I could deny her death. But now, I know being at peace with her absence will allow me to cherish her memory the way it deserves to be. She is the compass I press to my heart, the one I look to whenever I doubt myself or my path.

EPILOGUE

Between 2019 and November 2024, I tried to minimize my relationship with Syria. I spent less time on social media. I pulled away from old contacts. I cut ties—slowly, deliberately—until the country felt like something I could observe rather than inhabit.

Assad had triumphed militarily, and it was agonizing to watch the man we believed the international community would never forgive being welcomed back into diplomatic circles. The same governments that once called him a murderer were now rehabilitating his image with nods and cautious handshakes. The world hadn't just moved on—it had surrendered. Behind the scenes, cracks began to form within the inner circle. The old guard of Alawite businessmen—long untouchable—found themselves under pressure. I heard stories in fragments. My uncles had some of their assets confiscated. The fortress that once seemed impenetrable was starting to cannibalize itself.

Sanctions that were supposed to punish Assad, as always, only hurt those without a foreign bank account. The Syrian lira collapsed, and living conditions in the country led everyone to wonder about the point of a revolution if the end result is both tyranny and poverty.

But even after I left Syria behind, there were parts of my family's history I couldn't make sense of—silences I felt compelled to break. I had long suspected that my father's story was more complicated than the version we were told. One day, I found a thread. Bernard Bajolet, a French diplomat who had served as France's ambassador to Syria in the early 2000s and later headed the DGSE, France's foreign intelligence service, had published a memoir about his time in the Middle East: *Le soleil ne se lève plus à l'est—The Sun No Longer Rises in the East*—detailing French foreign policy from 1975 to 2013. In one passage, he described meeting my father in Damascus, where Jawdat worked for Rifaat al-Assad, the president's brother. According to Bernard, my father was a suspect in the assassination of Salah al-Din al-Bitar, who cofounded the Ba'ath Party with Michel Aflaq in the early 1940s and later fled to France, where he criticized the government of Hafez al-Assad. I wrote Bernard an email, almost certain he wouldn't remember my father—especially given that his book spanned decades of conflict zones. But Bernard replied immediately. "I congratulate you for your courage and endeavors for the sake of the truth," he wrote. Then he told me, in detail, about the first time he met my father—at the Sahnaya riding club, just south of Damascus on the road to Daraa. My father, he said, was leading Bassel al-Assad's security team. "He gave me the impression of someone a little mad," Bernard said. "Brutal, nervous, and therefore dangerous. All the Syrians present seemed afraid of him."

It was clear to Bernard that my father held a high position in Assad's security apparatus. Cautious but intrigued, he invited him for tea and asked a few questions. They spoke in Arabic—until my father suddenly switched to flawless French, claiming he had studied in Tours. Later that day, back at the French embassy, Bernard relayed the conversation to the

French intelligence station. They quickly identified my father. He hadn't gone to France to study, as he always claimed. He had gone to kill.

The intelligence officers told Bernard the rest. In 1980, Hafez al-Assad had ordered the assassination of Salah al-Din al-Bitar. The first team sent by Syria was discovered by France's domestic intelligence agency, the DST. French authorities demanded the agents be withdrawn. Assad complied. A few weeks later, he sent my father alone to finish the job. Traveling under the name François Najjar, my father carried out the assassination in July 1980.

Bernard also recounted another memory. Not long after their first meeting, my father casually remarked that he'd heard Bernard's groom, who cared for his horse, was excellent. He asked if the groom could be sent to Qurdaha to look after Bassel al-Assad's horses instead. Bernard declined, saying, "My men are not to be loaned out like that—but I'll ask him if he's willing." The groom—terrified of my father's reputation—refused. Soon after, he disappeared. My father had abducted and forcibly taken him to Qurdaha. A few days later, the man turned up in Damascus, shaken and desperate. He had been tied up in the sun and feared for his life. Bernard hid him in his home for several days, then went directly to Bassel al-Assad, who intervened. "After that," Bernard told me, "I never spoke to your father again."

When I asked him what made those memories stick after all those years, he said: "Your father was memorable—but not for good reasons. He was emblematic of the regime itself. Even someone as smart and relatively open-minded as Bassel al-Assad chose a killer to lead his security team. That says everything about the family."

THAT EXCHANGE WAS the affirmation I didn't know I needed. For years, I had carried questions I couldn't answer, guilt I couldn't name. But in that moment, the pieces came together. My father was never a student in France—he was a government operative. A killer. And in return for his loyalty, he and my uncles were given control over the port of Tartus and the steel trade. Knowing how violent, how remorseless he truly was, I finally understood: My mother's death was not my fault. My father was someone capable of killing, regardless of what I did or didn't do. It was who he was.

Then, in 2022, I received a message from a man I had met years ago in Jableh. His friend, he told me, had recently been imprisoned and had shared a cell with my father. Some claimed he had been arrested for the murder of a doctor close to the president. Others said it was related to tax evasion. Whatever the charge, I saw a sliver of karma in this: My father was locked up by the same regime he had spent his life defending. I ignored the message. But privately, I clung to it—selfishly—as a form of justice. Not the justice we dreamed of in 2011. But something humbler. A flicker of closure.

Over time, as the sharpness of grief for my mother dulled and my memory of her was no longer merely stained with sadness, I started to understand that she had not been an ordinary mother. She had challenged me and my sister in ways I couldn't fully comprehend as a child. Gradually, I recognized that she had offered us an escape—a quiet, subtle liberation that I never acknowledged when my father's shadow loomed so large over our lives.

THROUGH THOSE YEARS, alcohol remained an anchor I reached for whenever my world began unraveling. When COVID struck, and as I struggled through the often painful process of writing this book, the problem deepened. I spiraled again and again, slipping back into destructive patterns, torching everything I had worked so hard to build. Once more, I found myself running straight toward the burning building, toward oblivion. After many dark episodes of depression—and just as I had met a guy I knew I wanted to spend my life with—I finally surrendered. Alcohol was the last thread I needed to sever.

I knew, deep down, that I was capable of processing my grief without numbing it. So, after many failed attempts, I gave up on getting sober alone. In the fall of 2024, I checked myself into a rehab facility. With minimal access to my phone or the internet, I spent my days in group therapy, revising the final pages of this book, journaling, and reading about alcoholism. It felt like a long, extended goodbye to an old friend whose comfort I had desperately needed—but whose hold I now desperately needed to break.

Then, one day, an email appeared in my inbox with the following subject line: "You following? You might be getting an early Christmas present this year."

The Syrian opposition—then mostly confined to Idlib and its surrounding towns—had launched a coordinated assault on government forces. I blocked out the details. I refused to follow the news. I was too fragile, too exhausted from my battle of recovery, to allow myself even a glimmer of hope about the country that had brought me so much pain. Each update that seeped into my consciousness caused me panic, for I knew what could follow the government's withdrawal: barrel bombs falling again, people trapped beneath collapsed buildings. Some nights, I woke up gasping for air.

"Any using dreams?" they asked each morning in group therapy. It occurred to me then that perhaps Syria itself had become my addiction—one I had spent years struggling to rid from my mental landscape. And now, without warning, I was relapsing.

On December 8, two days before I was set to leave rehab, a fleeting thought crossed my mind: *What if Assad falls?* The notion felt so absurd; it vanished as quickly as it had appeared.

That night, as they took my vitals before bed, I asked if I could check my phone. The screen lit up with notifications, dozens stacked on top of each other. I unlocked the screen, and my legs gave out beneath me.

"Bashar al-Assad has stepped down as Syria's president and fled to Russia, bringing a sudden and stunning end to his twenty-four-year rule."

Assad has fallen. I whispered the words, too scared to let them sink in—I feared this might be just another hopeful moment that would be ripped away from me. I turned to the technician, who barely looked up from typing in my blood pressure results. He smiled politely, oblivious. How could he understand? There was no way to explain what those words meant to someone who hadn't experienced the horrors that gave them weight. How they were freighted with so much death, exile, and rage, so much silence and grief. How the waiting for this moment had shaped my entire life and the person I had become.

That night, I was grateful that phones were prohibited. I needed the isolation. I cried for hours—not out of joy, because joy was impossible. I felt physical pain for my mother, for all the years stolen from us. How cruel this president was, fleeing the country overnight, without even addressing those whose family members had died fighting for him. If stepping down was so easy, why hadn't it happened sooner? Why not when I was still in Damascus with Amer? When my mother was alive? Before my entire life was decimated by grief and loss and exile?

I watched the YouTube video on the smart TV in my room. The statue in Arnous Square—the one I'd hugged as a child, the one I'd feared might stand forever—was being torn down. For the first time during my stay, I asked for sleeping pills. Maybe my body feared that if I slept, I'd wake up and discover none of this had happened.

Alia tried reaching out. I knew what she wanted to ask, but I couldn't answer, couldn't talk, couldn't even begin to think about her questions until I was out of rehab. The fragile days that followed were painfully reminiscent of my first months in New York: sleepless nights, consumed by the news cycle, my body once again syncing to Damascus time. Facebook became my lifeline. What do we do with exile once a return becomes possible again?

When we spoke, Alia was fixated on my mother. She persisted in believing she might still be alive—or, at the very least, that we could find out where she was buried. If anyone knew anything, it ought to be our father. We'd learned that the jail where he'd last been seen had been liberated by the rebels, and everyone had been freed.

Alia and I reached out to anyone who might have information about his whereabouts. I admit now that I took advantage of the fear spreading among my relatives; after all, I was more aligned with the new authorities they feared. I was outside the country. I could offer them something in exchange for a lead.

Uncle Jamal—the same uncle who had thrown me out of his home—now swore on his children's lives that he'd never kicked me out, that he'd always loved me, and that he would never speak to my father again. Aunt Fadia said the same. Suddenly, everyone was cursing my father, trying to convince me they'd always been on my side, not his. Yet no one seemed to know where he was. We assumed he was hiding in the village, somewhere the new authorities couldn't yet reach.

This search was taking a toll on my relationship. It was impossible to explain to my partner why the mere sound of Uncle Jamal's voice triggered mental breakdowns and panic attacks. I was exhausted and overwhelmed by the work of caring for myself and a boyfriend who had only a vague idea of what was happening. I grew frustrated, tired of explaining why I was crying or whom I was yelling at in Arabic. Determined not to sabotage another relationship, determined not to let my past poison something good, I booked a one-way ticket to San Juan and told my boyfriend I needed some time away to process.

LOUBNA MRIE

. . .

A FEW DAYS AFTER I ARRIVED, Alia announced that she'd found him. A neighbor—eager to prove loyalty to our side—had revealed his whereabouts. He was living in a house that had once belonged to Grandmother Tamra with his new, twenty-four-year-old wife. I felt a twinge of something—pity, maybe, or shame. Not just because our father was now married to someone ten years younger than me, but because he was living in one of the houses my grandmother Tamra used to rent out. I knew those houses well—they were more like basements: damp, musty, starved of sunlight. I strained to picture him there.

Cursing the time difference, I contacted someone in the leadership of Hay'at Tahrir al-Sham—the Islamist militant group behind the rebel offensive that had overthrown Assad—in Jableh, a man who vaguely knew my story and that of my mother. I opened Google Maps and for the first time allowed myself to examine satellite images of my building, my neighborhood, Tamra's old house, and even the loquat tree. The buildings and streets that haunted my nightmares appeared right there on my screen. Carefully, I drew red circles and arrows marking the house. A few hours later, I received a message back from the commander. He was about to enter my father's house, he said, promising to call back as soon as possible.

I didn't even try to stop myself as I walked into a bar and ordered a double shot of mezcal, then another and another, hoping it might slow my racing pulse. Alia flooded my phone with anxious messages: What if my father killed him? An hour passed, and Alia convinced herself that my father had either bribed, lied to, or murdered the commander.

When the call finally came, I was passed out in bed. His voice reached me in fragments: "When the jails opened and the rebels checked if anyone was left behind, your father was there, paralyzed, sitting in a puddle of his own waste. He couldn't speak. The rebels went through his clothes, found some phone numbers, and called them. His wife's family came to pick him up."

I asked him to repeat this for me a few times. I couldn't believe that my father was weak. To me, the man I had feared and loathed my entire life would never break.

"I saw him. Trust me. He is half dead."

I CONTACTED THE MAN who had messaged me nearly a year before about his friend having shared a cell with my father. He confirmed the story. My father was indeed paralyzed; he had been tortured so severely that he had been urinating blood. While he was imprisoned, no one in our family inquired about him or attempted to help. It was too risky to aid my father once he'd officially been declared a criminal. To this day, we are left without the closure we need to lay our mother's memory to rest.

In the weeks and months that followed Assad's fall, Alia and I were far from alone in our search for answers. Tens of thousands had vanished into Assad's prison network, and his fall had created a long-awaited opportunity to confront Syria's darkest chapter. Thousands of families were determined to learn the fates of their children, husbands, and brothers. Prisons were opened, yet the light that relatives hoped for would not be shed overnight.

Families pleaded with the new authorities for transparency. They demanded to know what was being done to preserve evidence from these cells, these torture chambers—places so saturated with violence they became crime scenes. What would become of the countless documents found there, documents holding perhaps the only clues to the fates of their loved ones? No answers came—not for us, not for them. I made the decision to try to let go and make peace with whatever measure of justice I'd already received.

I once read that those of us who lose our homes at a young age spend the rest of our lives trying to find them. Today, I have redefined the concept of home and come to accept that it is not bound by the borders of any country.

Since moving to the United States, I've encountered and befriended so many Americans who are also living in a kind of exile, whether for political, sexual, or religious reasons. I've realized that the justification of oppression under the banner of protection and safety is not unique to my culture or to Syria. I find it comforting to know that I am not alone in seeking a sense of belonging away from the place I once called home, a place that turned out to be nothing but a jail, a cage. And I am not the only person battling feelings of isolation, exclusion, and estrangement. Even when we succeed in finding our new homes, we will always bear the scars of our displacement.

Today, I am still trying to break my old patterns and learn how to find a sense of home within myself. I feel it in little unpredictable moments of joy, like when I tear into freshly baked pita bread in an extremely overpriced Lebanese restaurant in Manhattan and inhale an aroma that transports me to my school trips in the mountains of Jableh. There was a time when I couldn't tolerate any reminder of the place I came from; now, I can allow my memory to wander there.

I joke with my therapist about how, despite the trauma of my uprooting, if I had never dared to look beyond the green cloth—if I had kissed it and averted my gaze—I would have become a person who, today, I wouldn't even want to know. Someone whose life and principles are controlled by the fear of losing her father's and society's approval. Someone who may live at home but is fundamentally estranged from herself. While many argue that the Arab Spring failed politically, with new dictators replacing the old ones, it succeeded in instilling in many of us a belief in the power of change and the conviction that we can never let our oppressors silence us in the name of order and protection. Today, I know so many men and women whose lives have been transformed by this revelation. Some came out. Some left their husbands. Some changed careers and pursued their passions, not the futures their families wanted for them. So many women I know rebelled against their fathers, as I did, firm in their belief in their own power and freedom.

When I told Amer, on one of the long video calls that became a feature of our renewed friendship, that I was planning to write about the time he hit me, his reply was simple: "You own your own story." He's right. I find solace in knowing that I have been able to write this story about us and for all of us, to honor the collective memories that we have kept buried for so long to protect ourselves from the agony of acknowledging the magnitude of our losses. Later, Amer read every single word I wrote about Damascus and asked if I thought we would ever have that kind of courage again, that pure belief in the possibility of a better future. We both agreed that if we could go back in time, we would still choose to be twenty and twenty-four all over again, whispering in his studio, feeling so courageous, so inspired, so right.

Maybe my mother was wrong about one thing, after all. Uprooted flowers don't have to die. They can regrow anywhere they are given the time, conditions, and resources to flourish. Within each of us is the possibility of a new spring.

ACKNOWLEDGMENTS

To Alia, I can't imagine what reading this book must have been like for you. Thank you for trusting me to tell it as it is. I love you.

To Bill Clegg, the best agent and reader I could have hoped for—thank you for your faith in me from the very beginning.

To Lindsey Schwoeri, Allie Merola, Marion Duvert, Andrea Schulz, Ibrahim Ahmad, and the incredible team behind this book: thank you for handling me and my words with such care and precision—for reminding me how transformative it is to work with editors who not only improve the work but protect its soul. I genuinely don't know if I could have written this without your guidance.

To Chuck Sudetic, who saw that I had a book in me before I could see it myself—thank you for pushing me to put words on the page, and for your criticism when you sensed I was holding back.

To my early readers: Rohan Advani, Mustafa Ajalyakin, Omar Andron, Anand Giridharadas, Shane Bauer, Anand Gopal, Michael Page, and Miguel Winograd—thank you for taking the time to read and for believing in my craft when I doubted myself.

ACKNOWLEDGMENTS

To those whose love and support made my exile less lonely: Paula and Ed Kassig, David and Katherine Bradley, April Goble, and to Timofey, I am blessed to share my life with you.

To Yaddo, MacDowell, Ucross, and the Hambidge Center for the Arts—thank you for the precious time, space, and solitude to write.

To those whose lives and voices shaped these pages and my life—thank you for your courage.